Judith Butler

For
Andrew and Daniel

Judith Butler

From Norms to Politics

Moya Lloyd

polity

First published in 2007 by Polity Press

Polity Press
65 Bridge Street
Cambridge CB2 1UR, UK

Polity Press
350 Main Street
Malden, MA 02148, USA

ISBN-13: 978-07456-2611-6
ISBN-13: 978-07456-2612-3 (pb)

A catalogue record for this book is available from the British Library.

Typeset in 10.5 on 12 pt Palatino
by SNP Best-set Typesetter Ltd., Hong Kong
Printed and bound in India by Replika Press PVT Ltd

For further information on Polity, visit our website: www.polity.co.uk

Key Contemporary Thinkers

Jeremy Ahearne, *Michel de Certeau: Interpretation and its Other*
Peter Burke, *The French Historical Revolution: The Annales School, 1929–1989*
Michael Caesar, *Umberto Eco: Philosophy, Semiotics and the Work of Fiction*
M. J. Cain, *Fodor: Language, Mind and Philosophy*
Rosemary Cowan, *Cornel West: The Politics of Redemption*
Colin Davis, *Levinas: An Introduction*
Andreas Due, *Deleuze*
Maximilian de Gaynesford, *John McDowell*
Matthew Elton, *Daniel Dennett: Reconciling Science and our Self-Conception*
Simon Evnine, *Donald Davidson*
Chris Fleming, *René Girard: Violence and Mimesis*
Edward Fullbrook and Kate Fullbrook, *Simone de Beauvoir: A Critical Introduction*
Andrew Gamble, *Hayek: The Iron Cage of Liberty*
Nigel Gibson, *Fanon: The Postcolonial Imagination*
Graeme Gilloch, *Walter Benjamin: Critical Constellations*
Karen Green, *Dummett: Philosophy of Language*
Espen Hammer, *Stanley Cavell: Skepticism, Subjectivity, and the Ordinary*
Phillip Hansen, *Hannah Arendt: Politics, History and Citizenship*
Sean Homer, *Fredric Jameson: Marxism, Hermeneutics, Postmodernism*
Christopher Hookway, *Quine: Language, Experience and Reality*
Christina Howells, *Derrida: Deconstruction from Phenomenology to Ethics*
Fred Inglis, *Clifford Geertz: Culture, Custom and Ethics*
Simon Jarvis, *Adorno: A Critical Introduction*
Sarah Kay, *Žižek: A Critical Introduction*
Douglas Kellner, *Jean Baudrillard: From Marxism to Post-Modernism and Beyond*
Valerie Kennedy, *Edward Said: A Critical Introduction*
Chandran Kukathas and Philip Pettit, *Rawls: A Theory of Justice and its Critics*
Moya Lloyd, *Judith Butler: From Norms to Politics*
James McGilvray, *Chomsky: Language, Mind, and Politics*
Lois McNay, *Foucault: A Critical Introduction*
Philip Manning, *Erving Goffman and Modern Sociology*

Michael Moriarty, *Roland Barthes*
Stephen Morton, *Gayatri Spivak*
Dermot Moran, *Edmund Husserl*
Harold W. Noonan, *Frege: A Critical Introduction*
James R. O'Shea, *Wilfrid Sellars: Naturalism with a Normative Turn*
William Outhwaite, *Habermas: A Critical Introduction*
Kari Palonen, *Quentin Skinner: History, Politics, Rhetoric*
John Preston, *Feyerabend: Philosophy, Science and Society*
Chris Rojek, *Stuart Hall*
Susan Sellers, *Hélène Cixous: Authorship, Autobiography and Love*
Wes Sharrock and Rupert Read, *Kuhn: Philosopher of Scientific Revolutions*
David Silverman, *Harvey Sacks: Social Science and Conversation Analysis*
Dennis Smith, *Zygmunt Bauman: Prophet of Postmodernity*
Nicholas H. Smith, *Charles Taylor: Meaning, Morals and Modernity*
Felix Stalder, *Manuel Castells: The Theory of the Network Society*
Geoffrey Stokes, *Popper: Philosophy, Politics and Scientific Method*
Georgia Warnke, *Gadamer: Hermeneutics, Tradition and Reason*
James Williams, *Lyotard: Towards a Postmodern Philosophy*
Jonathan Wolff, *Robert Nozick: Property, Justice and the Minimal State*

Contents

Abbreviations

AC	*Antigone's Claim: Kinship between Life and Death*
BTM	*Bodies that Matter: On the Discursive Limits of 'Sex'*
'CF'	'Contingent Foundations: Feminism and the Question of "Postmodernism"'
CHU	*Contingency, Hegemony, Universality: Contemporary Dialogues on the Left* (with Ernesto Laclau and Slavoj Žižek)
'CR'	'For a Careful Reading'
'CS'	'Changing the Subject: Judith Butler's Politics of Radical Resignification'
'End'	'The End of Sexual Difference?'
ES	*Excitable Speech: A Politics of the Performative*
GAO	*Giving an Account of Oneself*
'GB'	'Gendering the Body: Beauvoir's Philosophical Contribution'
'GP'	'Gender as Performance: An Interview with Judith Butler'
GT	*Gender Trouble: Feminism and the Subversion of Identity* (Tenth Anniversary Edition)
'GTFT'	'Gender Trouble, Feminist Theory, and Psychoanalytic Discourse'

'HB'	'How Bodies Come to Matter: An Interview with Judith Butler'
'Imitation'	'Imitation and Gender Insubordination'
'Kinship'	'Is Kinship Always Already Heterosexual?'
'OSRM'	'On Speech, Race and Melancholia: An Interview with Judith Butler'
'PA'	'Performative Acts and Gender Constitution'
PL	*Precarious Life: The Powers of Mourning and Violence*
PLP	*The Psychic Life of Power: Theories in Subjection*
SD	*Subjects of Desire: Hegelian Reflections in Twentieth-Century France*
'SG'	'Sex and Gender in Simone de Beauvoir's *Second Sex*'
'UC'	'Universality in Culture'
UG	*Undoing Gender*
'VSG'	'Variations on Sex and Gender: Beauvoir, Wittig and Foucault'
'WC'	'What is Critique? An Essay on Foucault's Virtue'

Acknowledgements

Writing a book about any living author is difficult, and particularly one as prolific as Judith Butler. Indeed, twice, the submission of this manuscript was held up because Butler published new volumes that I wanted to examine. It needs to be remembered when reading this book, therefore, that what I am evaluating is not a completed body of work but one that is on-going. It also means that it has been impossible to judge the full significance of Butler's work, particularly since, given the slowness of the publication process, responses to *Precarious Life* and *Undoing Gender* are only just beginning to appear while, as yet, there has been nothing published on *Giving an Account of Oneself* that I am aware of. The readings I present of these later books are, therefore, very much my own provisional readings. I hope, however, that they convey something of the excitement and intellectual stimulation that I feel when I encounter Butler's always challenging, always provocative, if not always convincing, theoretical offerings.

Numerous people have contributed to the development of this book. First, I would like to thank the two anonymous readers at Polity for their reports on the draft. I hope I have managed to respond to your criticisms adequately, though, of course, any remaining errors or omissions are mine. Conversations with Laura Brace, Terrell Carver, Samuel Chambers, Diana Coole, Mark Hoffman, Kimberly Hutchings, Birgit Schippers and Andrew Thacker on different aspects of Butler's work, as well as on the factors shaping it, helped me clarify my argument. These discussions also gave me immense enjoyment, not least when accompanied by good food and wine! Thanks also to John Thompson and the editorial staff at Polity for their assistance over the course of this book's production, and to Dave Allen, my head of department at Loughborough, for clearing time for me to make some final adjustments to the text. Finally, and as always, my biggest thanks go to my partner, Andrew Thacker, for listening to me talk endlessly about Butler, learning just how long it takes me to 'finish a sentence', and giving so generously of his time as this book neared completion, and to our son Daniel for distracting me when I needed it and for making each day so much fun. This book is dedicated to them.

Parts of Chapter 4 are drawn from 'Politics and Melancholia', *Women's Philosophy Review*, 20 (1998–9), pp. 25–43. Reproduced with the permission of the Society of Women in Philosophy.

1

Introduction

In 1990 one of the most influential books of the coming decade was published: *Gender Trouble*. Routinely cited in disciplines from literary theory to cultural studies, sociology to political theory, philosophy to performance studies, *Gender Trouble* has also been translated into twenty languages, while in 1999 a special tenth anniversary edition was published, complete with comprehensive new preface.[1] These twin publications of *Gender Trouble* book-ended a decade in which its author, Judith Butler, received the rare accolade (for an academic, at least) of being cited in *The Face* – a British style magazine – as one of fifty people who had the greatest influence on popular culture in the 1990s. It is not often that a scholar, a professional philosopher (she is the Maxine Elliot Professor in Rhetoric and Comparative Literature at the University of California, Berkeley), achieves iconic status. So, why did Butler? *Gender Trouble* wasn't her first book. That place is reserved for *Subjects of Desire: Hegelian Reflections in Twentieth-Century France*, published in 1987 and then also reprinted in 1999 (with a new preface). It wasn't her last. At the time of writing, there have been seven single-authored monographs since then, two co-edited books, as well as three co-authored texts.[2] Yet *Gender Trouble* is the text most closely associated with the name of Judith Butler: so what precisely is the basis of its appeal?

Slavoj Žižek suggests one answer when he argues that *Gender Trouble* was not only a timely piece of theoretical work. More significantly, it both inspired and legitimized 'a specific *political* practice', namely, the 'anti-identarian turn of queer politics'.[3] Although the influence of *Gender Trouble* on queer theory and politics cannot be overestimated, what Žižek misses is the enormous impact the book had on feminism. Butler, one critic notes, is 'the single most cited feminist theorist of the 1990s', while another points out that *Gender Trouble* 'rocked the foundations of feminist theory'.[4] *Gender Trouble* has been credited not only with defining the way that the relation between feminism and postmodernism has played out but also with setting the terms of the feminist debate about identity, both in the US and elsewhere.[5] Whatever the merits of these competing interpretations, in order to understand the significance of Butler's work it is necessary to understand something of the context in which it was written and of the kinds of debates that were taking place then.

The 1970s saw the emergence of the 'new social movements'. These movements, including the women's, civil rights, and gay and lesbian liberation movements as well as the anti-nuclear and environmental movements, brought about a change in the political landscape. Class politics began to recede as identity and lifestyle politics came to the fore. It is identity politics that is of particular interest to us. Identity politics operates with the assumption that one's identity – as a woman, or gay man, or African American – furnishes the grounds for a collective politics. This politics typically has a dual purpose: to overcome the forms of oppression and marginalization that group members experience (both collectively and individually), which limit their participation in democratic society, and to create greater opportunities for group self-determination. Identity politics can thus be seen in developments as diverse as anti-discrimination legislation, demands for group quotas, and in the challenging of group stereotypes. Undoubtedly, these new social movements had significant political impact. During the 1980s, however, those based on identity (particularly the women's movement and the gay and lesbian movement) soon began to experience certain difficulties in speaking of and for their constituencies. It is here that *Gender Trouble* is pertinent, for it is a central text in the debates on identity that took place in both movements.

It would be misleading, however, to assume that the critique of identity within either the women's or gay and lesbian movements began with Butler. Two years prior to the publication of *Gender Trouble*, for instance, Denise Riley had already published *Am I That Name?*, a highly significant book exploring the ambiguity and indeterminacy of the category of women, a book moreover that Butler herself cites as instrumental to the development of her own work on gender.[6] Similarly, throughout the 1980s, questions had been raised in gay and lesbian circles about the notion of homosexuality as an identity category. Here the work of Michel Foucault (himself frequently identified as the initiator of queer politics) was central. More generally, the work of Butler (and, indeed, of many other contributors to the debates about identity in both feminism and gay and lesbian theory/politics) owes much to the discourses on the 'crisis of the subject' that punctuated French theory from the mid-1960s onwards. In Butler's case, this includes writings by Louis Althusser and Jacques Lacan, as well as the work of poststructuralists such as Foucault, Julia Kristeva and Jacques Derrida.[7] In order to situate Butler's work more clearly, the next three sections will focus, respectively, on the debates immanent to feminism concerning identity and difference; the political developments within gay and lesbian movements that fostered identity critique and that led to the emergence of queer theory; and the broad terms of poststructuralism.

Although *Gender Trouble* is best located in terms of the above debates, since they explain the context of its composition and reception, both this text and Butler's writings more broadly engage with and are influenced by a range of other work, including the existentialist phenomenology of Simone de Beauvoir and the materialist feminism of Monique Wittig (both discussed in the next chapter), the feminist anthropology of Gayle Rubin and the psychoanalytic writings of Sigmund Freud (both discussed in Chapter 4), and the philosophical writings of Friedrich Nietzsche and G. W. F. Hegel. Although I touch briefly on Nietzsche's work in the next chapter, I devote more attention to Butler's debt to Hegel since, as she herself declares in the 1999 preface to *Subjects of Desire*, '[i]n a sense, all of my work remains within the orbit of a certain set of Hegelian questions' (*SD*: xiv). This engagement with Butler's Hegelianism – and, more specifically, with her interest in the relation between desire and recognition bequeathed by Hegel – begins in the final part of this chapter, where I examine *Subjects of Desire*, the revised version of Butler's doctoral thesis. I should make clear, however, that my aim in this book is *not* to provide an exhaustive and detailed account of all the theories that have impacted on the development of Butler's ideas. Such an enterprise would, I fear, be impossible. Nor is it to trace the influence of any one thinker on her work. Instead, my focus is threefold: first, I concentrate on elucidating and evaluating the arguments that Butler herself advances; second, I situate those arguments, as far as possible, in terms of the critical responses from *feminists* that they have elicited, though inevitably I have had to be selective here; and, finally, I pay particular attention to Butler's *political* theory, that is, to the ways in which she understands political activity and transformation. Before we turn to the substance of her ideas, as I indicated above, it is first vital to have a sense of the intellectual and political background of her writings. I begin, therefore, with feminist debates on identity and difference.

Feminism, identity and difference

Feminism is a political movement organized around transforming the lives of women. To begin with, therefore, one of the primary aims of feminist scholarship was to contest the male-stream definitions of woman circulating in culture and society at the time of writing. Simone de Beauvoir's *The Second Sex*, a text that was highly influential on Butler, exemplifies this aim perfectly. Here Beauvoir set out to demonstrate that humanity in a number of fields tended to be conceived of in terms of men and the male prerogative while woman was, quite simply, the 'second sex': weaker and essentially other to man. There was (and is) of course plenty of empirical evidence to back up women's inferior position in society at large: women's disqualification from many walks of life on the basis of suspect, masculinist conceptions of their nature, psychology, behaviour, and so forth. Important as it was to subject such misogynistic characterizations to radical critique, a later generation of feminists went a stage further. They articulated a feminism that was not parasitic on male-stream theorizing, as Marxist feminism or liberal feminism purportedly were, but was specifically woman-centred. Feminists such as Ti-Grace Atkinson, Robin Morgan and Mary Daly thus began to develop a gynocentric political theory and practice of, by and about women. It aimed to analyse women's oppression from women's distinct perspective, to revalue femaleness and femininity, and to forge a political movement that foregrounded women as women. This feminism, 'feminism unmodified' as Catharine MacKinnon famously called it, or 'radical feminism' as it was otherwise known, had a huge impact.[8] As Judith Grant suggests, its gynocentric focus radically altered the feminist agenda of the day, by politicizing ideas such as the body, sexuality and housework, and developing practices (such as consciousness-raising) that enabled the production of woman-centred knowledge.[9] Furthermore, as Robyn Rowland and Renate Klein note, it also created 'a new political and social theory of women's oppression'.[10] Indeed, radical feminism, it has been suggested, represents the first full articulation of feminist ideas *per se*.[11]

Generating woman-centred theory and politics was not, however, without its now very well-documented problems. These centred on the difficulty of trying to develop an account of women that could fit *all* women. Critics argued that rather than being universally applicable, such theories were, in fact, solipsistic (that is, based on the experiences of particular women), essentialist, ahistorical, over-generalized and partial.[12] Such was the effect of these debates that, for some time, feminism appeared to be characterized more by factionalism amongst competing groups than by the sisterhood and unity envisaged by its earliest exponents. Although there was some attempt to redress these difficulties by articulating feminist political theories more attuned to the specific experiences of different groups of women – for instance, lesbians or women with disabilities or Black women – even these accounts were accused of excluding certain women from their analyses, of silencing others and of failing to recognize the inter-connected nature of ethnic, class and gender identity.[13]

When radical feminists attempted to develop woman-centred theory, they were, of course, responding to one of the key intellectual problems faced by all forms of feminism: 'Who or what is a woman?'[14] Is it Woman, the singular noun with a capitalized 'W', a shorthand term for the idea that all women share an essential connection with one another through the fact of being female? Or it is it women, the plural noun with a lower-case 'w', a descriptive sociological category referring to real historical women in all their variety? When they wrote about Woman in the singular, many feminists certainly assumed that their writings were relevant to living, breathing women in the plural. Their priority was simply to identify what it was that women shared – what identity – that could form the grounds upon which to build a collective emancipatory politics. As a result of the ensuing criticisms of this project, noted earlier, some feminists turned their attention to the pressing issue of how to deal with the differences between women, and in such a way as to keep alive the possibilities of a united political movement.[15] These were the diversity feminists. By contrast, another group turned their attention to French theory, broadly understood, and began to focus on what might be called the indeterminacy of woman: that is, the idea that Woman as such does not exist. These were the *différance* feminists.

Diversity feminism, as the name suggests, concentrated on understanding the variety of experiences of being female. The question its proponents pondered was not just how to understand differences amongst women but, more importantly, how to understand the nature of the relation between different aspects of a woman's identity – her race, sexual orientation and class – and how these fitted with her femaleness. Was, for instance, a Black lesbian oppressed as a woman *and* as a Black person *and* as a lesbian, or was she oppressed as a Black lesbian woman? Could, that is, the different elements of her identity be separated out or were they inextricably entwined? Some feminists argued for the former: that it was possible to identify the different forms of oppression to which a woman was subject, and thus to deal with them separately.[16] Others contested this view and argued that sexism, racism, and homophobia, for example, worked through each other; that the relation between them was an interlocking or 'intersectional' relation.[17]

The other strand of feminism that is pertinent to the discussion at hand is what I have referred to as *différance* feminism, or what is sometimes called deconstruction feminism.[18] As I am using these terms here, it refers to the work *within the Anglo-American context* of those feminists who drew on the writings of thinkers such as Kristeva, Luce Irigaray, Hélène Cixous, as well as on Lacan, Foucault and Derrida. Despite significant differences between these French theorists, what most share is the idea that the subject is always in process (that is, is always incomplete in some sense) and that language, discourse and/or power (depending on the thinker) are central to its constitution. Taken up by *différance* feminists, these insights have been used to contest or 'deconstruct' the very category of Woman upon which radical feminism was predicated. Although Butler acknowledges some of the concerns of diversity feminism in her writing, her own work might reasonably be characterized as a form of *différance* feminism.

The impact of diversity and *différance* feminism both on the women's movement and on feminist political thinking was profound. Deconstructing the idea of a unified feminist subject seemed to put at risk the very politics of feminism. If women do not exist, who is feminism supposed to liberate? Diversity and *différance* feminism raised difficult questions for political representation, for justice and for an understanding of political agency. Just who is supposed to be represented if, because of their diversity, women are not representable *as women*? How can the claims of universal justice be squared with the need to recognize not just particularity and difference but also the fluidity and instability of any identity (group or individual)? If the subject is an effect (of power, discourse, language, etc.), then how can it act to alter the conditions of its own subordination? As I will show in the following chapters, not only did Butler's work respond to some of these debates within feminism, it was pivotal in shifting the terms of that debate away from a unified conception of women towards an alternative understanding of subjectivity, centred on performativity, and contributed to a reorientation in thinking about the nature of feminist (and, in fact, radical) politics. Before I do this, however, it is necessary to turn to the second contextual factor that locates Butler's work: the shifts that took place in gay and lesbian politics from the 1960s onwards.

From homosexual to gay and lesbian to queer

In many respects, the trajectory followed by feminism – affirming an identity, questioning the homogenizing tendencies of that identity, recognizing its constructedness and diversity, before endeavouring to capture these in a more fluid idea(l) – has also been followed, though in diverse fashion, within gay and lesbian politics. The major difference, however, is that this trajectory has been marked in the latter by a certain shift in terminology: from talk about homosexuals, then to gays and lesbians, and most recently to queers. It is certainly not the case that all in the movement have approved or followed these shifts. Indeed many, specifically older activists, have resisted the advent of queer theory and activism. The gay and lesbian movement is, like the women's movement, still an internally diverse, and at times fractious and divided, political movement. Nevertheless, it is against the background of its changing logic that Butler's work on sex, gender and sexuality needs to be positioned.

As Jeffery Weeks wrote in 1985, 'recent sexual politics has been a politics of identity'.[19] Emerging in the late 1960s, the gay and lesbian movement was very much a product of the radical politics of the time.[20] Like other of the new social movements, it conceived of itself as a political movement for the liberation of a subordinated group. In this case, the aim was to transform the oppressive social structures that defined homosexuality as a pathology. The 1960s was, after all, a time when the medical, psychological and legal systems still conceived the homosexual as a 'psychologically abnormal, morally inferior, and socially deviant human type'.[21] Gay and lesbian activists thus sought both to reject demeaning definitions of same-sex desire as abnormal and to affirm an alternative, positive identity based on sexuality, an identity moreover that was conceived of as authentic and natural. In line with other forms of identity politics, the assumption was that the identity that all gays and lesbians shared – and the belief was that there was one – was the basis for political solidarity.[22] Just as identity had posed a problem for feminism, so too it began to pose a problem for the lesbian and gay movement.

When lesbian and gay activists conceived of liberation initially, many thought that it would be based on transcending restrictive definitions of sex and gender. They assumed, in other words, that the whole of humanity – not just gays and lesbians – might be emancipated from the confines of homosexual versus heterosexual or man versus woman.[23] Increasingly during the 1970s, however, they began to think of gay and lesbian liberation 'along the lines of ethnic or racial politics'.[24] This 'ethnic' or 'ethnic nationalist' politics, as it has been called, combined elements of civil rights discourse with an emphasis on pride in one's identity.[25] It worked in at least one of two ways. First, some activists began to campaign for the right to equal treatment of gays (and later gays and lesbians) as a *distinct minority* within the wider population. Here the work of pressure groups such as the Gay and Lesbian Activists Alliance (GLAA) in the US and the Campaign for Homosexual Equality (CHE) in Britain was central.[26] Clearly influenced by a liberal agenda of assimilation, the purpose of such groups was not to overthrow a so-called 'oppressive social order' but to ensure the inclusion of lesbians and gays within the *existing* system on equal terms with their heterosexual counterparts. Second, some lesbian feminists began to pursue a separatist agenda. They endeavoured, that is, to create spaces away from men within which women could flourish. This separatist politics was inspired largely by the work of one group of lesbian feminists who started to argue in the early 1970s that far from lesbianism being grounded in the natural and unalterable sexual desire for another woman, it was, in fact, a political identity based on 'woman-identification'.[27] This proved to be a highly contentious move. Other lesbians and lesbian feminists resisted this characterization of lesbianism. They argued that it desexualized lesbianism and that, politically, it served to exclude those lesbians for whom same-sex desire was a fact of nature and not a political choice.

Increasingly, during this period, therefore, gay and lesbian politics began to experience kinds of internal dissent parallel to those that feminism was also experiencing. Criticisms were levelled that the movement promoted white, middle-class values, thus occluding the experiences of gays and lesbians of colour. Tensions between gays and lesbians increased, with some lesbians becoming increasingly critical of the masculinism of gay culture. Lesbians divided further during the 'sex wars' of the 1980s when, as Shane Phelan notes, the 'sex radicals' (those lesbians affirming the value of practices such as sado-masochism and pornography) found themselves allying with 'nonlesbian "sexual minorities"' against those lesbian feminists committed to a view of women as 'inherently life-affirming, gentle, and egalitarian'.[28] As with feminism, it appeared that the solidarity and collective identity envisaged by earlier gay and lesbian liberationists was fracturing under internal discord. Identity was becoming a problem.

One of the ways in which this problem was addressed within this movement was to begin to conceive of gay and lesbian identities not as operating according to a 'natural and universal' logic but as working within a 'social and historical' logic: that is, to see identity as socially constructed.[29] From the early to mid-1980s, therefore, in some quarters at least, there was yet another shift in lesbian and gay politics. Drawing on the work of Michel Foucault, this reoriented gay and lesbian politics was characterized, first, by a refutation of essentialist identity claims, including the idea of a unified homosexual identity, and, second, by a greater attention to how particular kinds of sexual identity are produced as contingent and historical effects of power and discourse. In this context, as Steven Seidman notes, the idea of a unitary gay identity came to be seen as both normalizing and disciplinary.[30] It was this shift to a social constructionist understanding of identity that marked the beginnings of *queer* theory and politics. It would be wrong, however, to see this as the sole basis for the emergence of this most recent phase in gay and lesbian politics. There are a number of other relevant factors.[31]

There was the challenge that bisexuality posed to understandings of the relation between sexuality and politics as bisexuals demanded inclusion in gay and lesbian organizations and communities. There was the impact of deconstruction within academic work both by and about lesbians and gays. Finally, the kinds of political activism that emerged within the gay community in response to HIV/AIDS were also central. Of particular note here is the work of the militant American group the AIDS Coalition to Unleash Power (ACT UP), who combined 'direct action politics and activist glamor' in spectacular political interventions and events – die-ins, for instance – designed to publicize the US government's funding failures with regard to AIDS research.[32] It is this theatrical and direct action style of politics that informs Butler's work and that she appears to advocate.[33] The combination of all of these elements, therefore, gives rise to 'queer' theory (associated most strongly with the writings of Eve Sedgwick, Diana Fuss and, of course, Judith Butler) and to the queer politics of organizations such as Queer Nation and the Lesbian Avengers, who have continued and, indeed, developed the often dramatic activist politics of ACT UP. Although Butler has observed in interviews that her association with the beginnings of queer theory and politics was unwitting ('GP': 32), as will become clear in the forthcoming chapters, there is no doubt that her work has been seen as central to the advent of queer politics, with *Gender Trouble* regarded as one of its foundational texts.

The influence of poststructuralism

Poststructuralism is notoriously difficult to pin down. First, some authors sharply differentiate poststructuralism from the associated term, postmodernism. So, for instance, Roy Boyne and Ali Rattansi in the introduction to their collection *Postmodernism and Society* contend that postmodernism is a term characterizing a set of aesthetic projects, while poststructuralism refers to work in literature, history and philosophy that stresses issues of plurality and provisionality.[34] In Boyne and Rattansi's terms, Butler is a poststructuralist. Others, however, refer to such philosophical work as 'postmodern', making no distinction between aesthetic projects and other ones. The difficulty is that in using the term 'postmodern' they obscure one of the important facets of this philosophical work: its relation to structuralism. Second, the authors grouped together under whichever label a critic deploys can vary considerably. For instance, Christine di Stefano limits her discussion of 'postmodern' ideas to the works of Richard Rorty, Jean-François Lyotard, Michel Foucault and Jacques Derrida, interestingly occluding the contribution of female philosophers, such as Julia Kristeva, to its genesis and evolution.[35] By contrast, Teresa Ebert presents a more capacious understanding of 'postmodernism', finding space for Foucault, Lyotard and Derrida as well as for Alice Jardine, Donna Haraway, Ernesto Laclau, Luce Irigaray and several others, including Butler.[36] Next, regardless of whether the range of authors referred to is limited, as with di Stefano, or more expansive, as with Ebert, considerable difficulties arise from bundling together quite diverse theoretical approaches. Although there are surely some similarities in the themes these authors cover, there are also marked differences between them. They differ, not least, in terms of the political consequences of their respective analyses and in how they understand the subject (if they discuss this at all). While a 'careful reading' of specific authors is generally, in my view, preferable to a general overview of poststructuralism (for the reasons already given), in order to contextualize Butler's work it will nevertheless be necessary to tender some general remarks on this otherwise protean mass of ideas.[37]

The simplest way to conceive poststructuralism *in general* is to see it as a negative or critical philosophical position. It is, in other words, anti-essentialist, anti-foundational, suspicious of grand narratives, opposed to the idea of history as linear and progressive, and distrustful of metaphysics. It is often wary of any appeal to the stable unified subject, and doubtful of the possibility of certainty in meaning. It is, in this way, I would suggest, more of an interrogative than normative mode of inquiry, challenging and contesting received ideas and norms rather than attempting to resolve problems and prescribe solutions. Certainly aspects of all of these elements are more or less present in the work of Butler, as we will see. Moreover, poststructuralism, as its name suggests, defines itself in relation to structuralism, with the prefix 'post' suggesting that it either goes beyond structuralism in some way or, more simply, comes after it. Either way, it is informed by it. Indeed, the trajectory from structuralism to poststructuralism can be seen, it has been suggested, in the intellectual careers of thinkers such as Foucault, who, it is alleged, began as a structuralist before becoming a poststructuralist.[38] So what is structuralism?

Itself an internally variegated theory, structuralism can be characterized, amongst other things, by its critique of the human subject and by the endeavour to apply the methods of 'science' to an understanding of social and human phenomena, ranging from language to human psychology, and from anthropology to literary theory. Central to its approach, therefore, is its emphasis on the 'subject' (or even 'Subject') rather than on the individual. The idea of the individual was shorthand for the notion of a rational, self-conscious, coherent and stable actor. By contrast, the idea of the subject conveys the notion that human reality, the unconscious and our inner selves are, in fact, constructions or products of 'signifying' activities.[39] The second key point to note is that the core task of structuralism, as its name implies, was to 'isolate the general structures of human activity'.[40] So, for instance, the structuralist linguistics of Ferdinand de Saussure emphasizes the 'structural' relation between signifier (sound-image) and signified (concept) that makes up the signs that constitute language. Structuralism was interested, therefore, in general laws and universal 'systems'. Importantly, the subject was conceptualized as an effect of these structures; thus, for Lacan, for example, language constitutes the subject.

Poststructuralism differs from structuralism in a number of ways. First, structuralists conceived of the structures they analysed as stable and invariant, that is, operating in the same way at all times. Poststructuralists, in comparison, reject the idea of general laws and universal systems and, instead, stress instability and indeterminacy. So, where structuralists thought meaning was relatively stable, because, to refer to Saussure again, the link between signifier and signified was fixed (even though it was a conventional rather than natural relation), poststructuralists like Derrida argue that meaning can never in fact be fixed. Signifiers can change into signifieds, signifieds can commute into signifiers. Moreover, in the poststructuralist account of language, one signifier always implies (signifies) another in an endless chain of signification. Language is thus a *temporal* process in which ultimate meaning is perpetually deferred.[41] Second, both structuralism and poststructuralism jettison the idea of a unified and self-contained subject. Structuralism concentrates on identifying the moment at which the Subject comes into being – when, as Althusser argues, it is 'hailed' (or interpellated) by the policeman – poststructuralism, however, does not. As a consequence of its dismissal of the idea of general laws and invariant structures, poststructuralism in its Foucauldian form looks to the variable and historically specific ways in which subjects – or rather subject positions – are produced by discourse and power, while in its Derridean form it focuses on the impossibility of defining any identity (for instance, woman) because any such definition is inherently open to resignification. As such, it is 'undecidable'.

As suggested above, the impact of poststructuralism on Butler, particularly the work of Derrida and Foucault, and her own impact on the development of poststructuralist thought have been significant. Yet, interestingly, Butler began as a critic of poststructuralism;

as she comments, she 'resisted' it (*SD*: viii). Her doctoral thesis, 'Recovery and Invention: The Projects of Desire in Hegel, Kojève, Hyppolite, and Sartre' (1984), exploring the influence of Hegelian ideas in France, is noteworthy for its inattention to poststructuralist (and, indeed, structuralist) ideas. Yet when her thesis was published some three years later, matters had moved on. *Subjects of Desire* contains an additional section exploring the ideas of Derrida, Lacan, Kristeva, Foucault and Gilles Deleuze, though exclusively in the context of French Hegelianism. Where *Gender Trouble* is, without doubt, a more poststructuralist text than *Subjects of Desire*, nevertheless, the revisions Butler made to her thesis indicate the beginning of what has been her on-going engagement with and interrogation of poststructuralist theory. It is to *Subjects of Desire* that I now turn.

Hegel and desiring subjects

Described by Butler as her 'juvenilia', for which she asks the reader for 'abundant forgiveness in reserve', *Subjects of Desire* charts how certain ideas developed by Hegel in the *Phenomenology of Spirit* are critiqued and developed by two generations of French philosophers: the first, writing during the 1930s and 1940s, is that of Alexandre Kojève and Jean Hyppolite – the two thinkers who introduced Hegel's philosophy to France – Jean-Paul Sartre, Jean Wahl and Simone de Beauvoir (though Butler makes only passing reference to the last two); and the second is the generation of Derrida, Lacan, Foucault, Kristeva and Deleuze (*SD*: viii).[42] The book is organized into four sections. It begins with an exploration of Hegel's *Phenomenology*. This is the text where Hegel explains in detail the logical movement of consciousness from its most primitive mode (what he calls 'sensuous certainty') to its most advanced (which he terms 'absolute knowing'). Butler is particularly interested in the early part of the *Phenomenology*; specifically, the chapter on consciousness and the first part of the chapter on self-consciousness, where Hegel sets out the parable of the Lord and the Bondsman (or master–slave dialectic, as it is often labelled). As such, she does not discuss the full movement towards Spirit charted by Hegel. Instead, she limits herself to discussing the co-emergence of desire and self-consciousness in his work. In the second section, Butler concentrates on outlining the influential reworkings of Hegel developed by both Kojève and Hyppolite. This is followed, in section 3, by an exploration of

Sartre's examination of existential desire and the self–other relation, while the final section focuses on the so-called 'post'- or 'anti'-Hegelian revisionings of the subject of desire developed by Lacan, Derrida, Deleuze, Foucault and Kristeva.[43] The chapter ends, importantly in the light of Butler's later work, with a short critical discussion of Kristeva and Foucault and the potential for a 'major conceptual reorientation' of Hegel's desiring subject through a 'history of bodies' that both goes beyond Foucault's work and is, amongst other things, attentive to gender (*SD*: 235).

Butler's aim in *Subjects* is to plot the concept of desire as it is first articulated by Hegel, through its subsequent re-articulations in French thought. Obviously there is much that could be said about this. What I want to draw out are two general points about her reading of this intellectual history, before moving on to more substantive matters: first, Butler disagrees with those readings, commonly those of his poststructuralist interpreters, that conceive of Hegel's philosophy as a totalizing or 'ostensibly all-inclusive [and closed] system' (*SD*: 13). Instead, she prefers a reading that stresses the openness of his thought.[44] Second, she proposes that, far from Hegel's French critics escaping the Hegelianism they are attempting to refute or transcend, they remain ensnared in a dialectical relation to Hegel that strengthens rather than undermines the logic of his thought. For even as they attempt to displace or dismiss Hegel's idea of the desiring subject, they continue to give life to it. This does not mean that Hegel cannot be criticized; clearly he can be and has been (and, indeed, Butler cites examples of this by those she studies). It is that such criticism for her is itself evidence of dialectical thinking. Since Butler is also a critic of Hegel, albeit a friendly and responsive one, then logically we must assume that her own work bears a similar dialectical relation to Hegel's.

My reason for discussing *Subjects of Desire* is not, however, to appraise the adequacy, originality or otherwise of Butler's interpretation of French Hegelianism, hence my schematic plotting of the book's contents. It is to understand better how Butler's subsequent work is indebted to Hegel, even as it is also shaped by that of other authors. In what remains of this chapter, therefore, I consider four areas where Butler's work might profitably be thought of in relation to Hegel's: first, the idea of the subject of desire; next, the link between subjectivity and alterity (or otherness) set out by Hegel in the Lord–Bondsman scenario; then, the idea of dialectical thought; and, finally, the relation between Hegel's rhetorical style and Butler's own writing style.

The subject of desire

The central theme of *Subjects of Desire* is, as already noted, the relation between the subject and desire. While thinkers prior to Hegel had examined the nature of desire, few, as Allan Megill notes, had thought that there might be 'a constitutive relation between desire and subjectivity', as Hegel did, and it is this constitutive relation that both interested his French critics and continues to interest Butler.[45] Hegel's *Phenomenology*, as stated, examines the way in which desire and self-consciousness emerge side by side. For Butler, the *Phenomenology* is not to be read as offering a philosophical truth; it is to be read as a series of 'instructive fictions' in which the relation between subjectivity and desire is plotted (*SD*: 21).[46] The journeying consciousness on its way to absolute knowledge is, she suggests, like a cartoon character who in his willingness (and it is a he [*SD*: 20]) to continue on a journey beset by one failure after another appears to be like the myopic 'Mr Magoo whose automobile careening through the neighbour's chicken coop always seems to land on all four wheels', ready to travel somewhere else to fail all over again (*SD*: 21).[47] Although the desiring subject might gain intermittent comfort from moments of recognition, and be tenacious enough to continue when what he believes is true is revealed as illusory, he is never destroyed by his experiences of negativity. Instead, he journeys onwards 'with compulsive metaphysical honesty toward his ultimate dialectical harmony with the world' (*SD*: 22).

In contrast to other readers, Butler declines to understand the *Phenomenology* as an account of a subject who is progressing neatly from one 'ontological place to another'. This is not the tale of a subject on its way to journey's end, to the attainment of absolute knowledge, she claims. It is not, to recall the Mr Magoo analogy, the story of a subject who lands on all four wheels and stays put. It is the story of a subject who must forever careen (*SD*: xv). As Butler interprets it, the *Phenomenology* charts the story of a subject that 'must suffer its own loss of identity again and again in order to realize its fullest sense of self' (*SD*: 13). This is the narrative, therefore, of what Butler calls, echoing Martin Heidegger, an 'ek-static' subject, a subject outside itself, or, to put it differently, a subject that is not self-identical. It might, of course, be objected, and perhaps fairly, that Butler is only able to present the Hegelian desiring subject as an incomplete ek-static subject because she does not engage with the whole logic of Hegel's system. She suspends the narrative, that is, before the journeying consciousness encounters reason or spirit.[48] I leave that to others to debate. For the purposes of this particular book, what I want to emphasize is that the idea of ek-static subjectivity, derived, however loosely, from Hegel, continues to inspire Butler's work to date, although the form it takes is one increasingly informed, in large part, by psychoanalysis. For this reason, far from the comic subject of desire she attributes to Hegel, Butler's subject is a melancholic figure.[49] (I will examine this in more detail in Chapter 4.) Finally, where Hegel assumes a masculine subject, Butler focuses, as I demonstrate in the next two chapters, on the regulatory processes that generate sexed and gendered desiring subjects.

In the next section, I move on to consider another element of Hegel's thought that has influenced Butler (and, indeed, *many* others): the encounter with the other sketched in the section of the *Phenomenology* where Hegel explores the struggle for recognition between Lord and Bondsman. For now I will just set out the terms of the struggle and indicate where it is salient for Butler's work. I will examine Butler's critique of recognition more fully in Chapter 6.

Subjectivity and alterity – the tale of the Lord and the Bondsman

Hegel's account of the parable of the Lord and the Bondsman, which introduces the idea of intersubjective recognition, follows on from the episode in which self-consciousness attempts to secure confirmation of itself through the 'negation', in this case the consumption, of material objects. The problem with attempting to satisfy desire in this way is that it entails a 'constant activity of negation' (*SD*: 39), since to consume an object is to destroy it, which means that desire has repeatedly to find more and more objects to consume. Self-consciousness realizes, therefore, that what it needs is a 'being like itself' (*SD*: 40), another self-consciousness (an other), that can affirm its existence as a self-conscious, and autonomous, being.

When self-consciousness begins its encounter with the other, it does so from a presumed situation of independence; it believes itself to be sovereign. This illusion is soon shattered as self-consciousness comes to realize that in its desire to be confirmed by the other it has become dependent on them. So, just as in the encounter with the material world, the Subject attempts to assert its supremacy by 'negating' the other, but here the other, in order to preserve its own autonomy, resists. A 'life-and-death struggle' thus ensues in which each tries to negate – to kill – the other. The difficulty is that if one self-consciousness succeeds in this task, then it will lose its chance at recognition by another self-conscious being. So instead of slaughtering his opponent, the 'winner' enslaves him: 'Domination, the relation that replaces the urge to kill, must be understood as the effort to annihilate within the context of life.' The slave must '*live its own death*' (*SD*: 52). In this way, the two equal self-consciousnesses are replaced by one that is independent (Lord) and one that is dependent (Bondsman) and 'whose essential nature', as Hegel notes, 'is simply to live or to be for another'.[50] Truncating (Butler's recounting of) Hegel's argument, the net result of the struggle is not, in fact, the affirmation of the self-consciousness of the Lord, because the Bondsman as a slave is not the Lord's equal but is rather his subordinate. As such, his recognition is not enough, for the Lord is recognized only by a demeaned, objectified consciousness. Moreover, the Bondsman also fails to gain recognition because he is enslaved. There is no ideal reciprocal relation here. The irony is, however, that it is the slave who gains most from the relation with his master, for having experienced the fear of death, he has experienced full consciousness of his own existence. Plus, by being compelled to labour on the objective world, he is able to transform it, thereby enabling him to objectify his own identity. No longer engaged merely in consumption, the desire of the Bondsman is satisfied rather through 'the re-creation of natural objects into reflections of their maker' (*SD*: 57).

Although Butler pays very little attention in her subsequent writings to the way in which labour constructs the material world, she does return again and again to the theme of recognition. Her work is thus threaded through with her own distinctive attempt to pursue Hegel's claim that it is through recognition that persons are engendered as 'socially viable beings' (*UG*: 2). Where her account differs most from that just sketched, as I show in Chapter 6, is that it concentrates on the question of the cultural (and thus variable) norms that determine who counts as a being that qualifies for (social) recognition in the first place. Butler also draws on the Lord–Bondsman narrative in another way: she derives from the tale the idea that the first encounter with the other is always one of 'self-loss'. This she construes as meaning that 'the self never returns to itself free of the Other'; instead, 'its "relationality" becomes constitutive of who the self is' (*UG*: 148). This reinforces the notion, covered in the last section, that the subject is an ek-static subject; one that is always outside – or other to – itself. It is this understanding of the subject and its relation to the other, as I show, that underpins, amongst other things, Butler's examination of the differential values placed on disparate lives and deaths; her treatment of what counts as a liveable life; her exploration of the constitutive role of mourning in the production of the psyche; and her discussion of the precariousness of all life.

The narrative of the Lord and the Bondsman should be thought of as a narrative of dialectical movement. In fact, one of the most influential features of Hegel's work has been the idea of the dialectic or, rather, of dialectical resolution. But what does this mean, and how is it relevant to Butler's work? The purpose of the next section is to address precisely these questions.

The dialectic

As is well known, Hegel was particularly concerned with the oppositions – or antinomies – found in traditional philosophical thought; pairings such as reason and emotion, freedom and determinism, universal and particular. He argued that, far from being incompatible with each other, the two terms in opposition are, in fact, intimately connected. First, he claimed, one term in the pair actually requires its opposite in order to define itself; it depends on the term that appears to negate it: thus reason requires emotion, freedom requires determinism, universal requires particular. Second, both terms of the binary are, in fact, compatible with one another when brought together in another, higher-order, idea that resolves, or, in Hegel's language, 'sublates', the opposition between them. This relation of sublation is also referred to by Hegel as *Aufhebung*. *Aufhebung*, in Butler's words, 'cancels, preserves, and transcends the apparent differences it interrelates' in the direction of a more inclusive identity (*SD*: 41). This process of dialectical resolution is captured in the formula: thesis, antithesis, synthesis. A concept (thesis) implies its opposite (anti-thesis), which through dialectical resolution (the so-called 'negation of the negation') produces a synthesis. The two contradictory elements are integrated in a more inclusive idea. It was this 'logic' that underpinned Hegel's account of historical development as the human species moved towards the final dialectical synthesis, when what he termed 'Absolute Spirit' is realized.

Butler certainly draws on Hegel's idea of the dialectic in her own later work. One example should suffice to show how. This concerns the way in which Butler conceives the relation between heterosexuality and homosexuality. Commonsense might suggest to us that the two positions are fundamentally incompatible; that if one is heterosexual one cannot also be homosexual. By contrast, Butler argues that heterosexuality in fact requires homosexuality in order to exist.[51] As such, heterosexuality is actualized only insofar as it is 'mediated through that which is different' (*SD*: 18). Simply put, therefore, heterosexuality exists only in opposition to homosexuality. While Butler's work is dialectical in the way just noted, where identity and difference are co-implicated, it is nevertheless clear that Butler does not adhere to all the elements of the Hegelian system. Far from it: she expressly argues that there is a need to reflect critically on 'the limitations of dialectical opposition' ('GP': 35). Part of this critical reflection involves her in attempting to understand what is excluded from the construction of any binary pairing: that is, in her own words, 'how a field is produced in which there are these two mutually exclusive and mutually defining possibilities'.[52] This, in turn, compels attention to the broader historical and cultural context within which binaries appear. Part of this critical reflection also entails Butler rejecting the idea of full dialectical synthesis and, in this way, her work is much closer to that of Foucault and Derrida, as she describes them in *Subjects of Desire*, than to Hegel. For she, like them, holds on to the idea of the critical force of negativity but refuses to link that force to the idea of a dialectic that retains the 'power of synthesis' (*SD*: 183); in other words, she subscribes, like Foucault and Derrida (on her reading, at least), to what might be called a non-synthetic dialectic.[53] What, then, are the characteristics of this non-synthetic approach?

First, Butler contends that Derrida and Foucault both subscribe to the idea that difference cannot be incorporated into identity, as Hegel had assumed. Instead, particular differences, whether historical or linguistic, are 'insuperable' differences (*SD*: 183). They cannot be overcome. *Aufhebung* is impossible. There is, thus, in the example just given, no chance of homosexuality and heterosexuality being synthesized into a more inclusive and more progressive ideal of sexuality. Second, the implication of this is clearly that when an identity is posited, difference has not been overcome; rather it has been denied. Arguably, for Butler, as we will see in the next chapter, this is what happens when feminists try to posit a single identity for women. Finally, in this non-synthetic dialectic the priority of identity over difference is reversed. Difference is thus championed as that which can displace 'the metaphysical impulse from its totalizing goal' (*SD*: 183). According to Butler, this is what happens in

Derrida's case when language misfires and in Foucault's when conflict appears. It is this idea of difference as being able to arrest what she calls the 'incorporative movement of domination' that leads her, in *Contingency, Hegemony, Universality*, to argue against the image of a 'monolithic and carnivorous Hegel whose "Spirit" incorporates every difference into identity' (*CHU*: 174).

This understanding of the dialectic, in my view, explains why Butler's critique of compulsory heterosexuality is based on revealing the dependence of the privileged term (heterosexuality) on the lower term (homosexuality) – because politically it is the most effective way to challenge and subvert the dominant gender order. The stress on difference as vital to political struggle is reflected too in Butler's adoption of Derrida's idea of iterability (discussed in more depth in Chapters 3 and 5), where the difference fundamental to signification for Derrida becomes the site of critical and, possibly, transformative political practice for Butler. Further, it also explains why she adheres (not always successfully) to Foucault's ideas of historical specificity and why the idea that Foucault once rather cryptically referred to as 'we are difference' – different subjects, in different discourses, at different times and in different places – finds some unexpected echoes in Butler's work.[54]

Having indicated three substantive areas where Butler is clearly although *critically* indebted to Hegel, let me now turn to the fourth, and final, area: the parallels between Hegel and Butler in terms of writing style.

Language and rhetoric – performative texts

Butler describes Hegel's *Phenomenology* as a *Bildungsroman*, a narrative tracing the development of its hero. This story of becoming does not simply narrate what happens to 'a journeying consciousness'; rather, it is, she declares, 'the journey itself' (*SD*: 21), a 'pilgrimage of the spirit', as she puts it (*SD*: 17). This is a journey that Butler believes is captured in Hegel's very writing style: 'Hegel's sentences', she posits, '*enact* the meanings that they convey' (*SD*: 18). How they are written is integral to what they say: the elusiveness of Hegel's grammar thus signifies the elusiveness of the desiring subject; the lack of a progressive linear narrative opens the reader to multiple meanings that move, shift and change as they are brought into conjunction with other terms. In essence, Hegel's writing style embodies the dialectical movement of his phenomenology. To understand the travelling subject, reading itself becomes a way of travelling to a destination that never arrives. It is not, however, the relation between language and desire in Hegel's work that is of interest to us; it is how this relation plays out in Butler's work. Here two factors are worth noting. The first concerns the political value that Butler attaches to difficult language; and the second the way that Butler's writing also performs the project it is advancing.

One of the most frequently voiced criticisms of Butler's writing style concerns its opacity. Martha Nussbaum makes this a central charge of her somewhat bad-tempered critique of Butler in *The New Republic*. It is also reflected in the prize for 'bad writing' that Butler was awarded by the journal *Philosophy and Literature* in 1998.[55] There is some truth in these claims. Butler's work is not easy to read. It is replete with questions, qualifications, conditional statements, hyperbole, allusion, and it makes reference to a wide range of texts in philosophy, literature, psychoanalysis and feminist theory, to name but four disciplines. In the 1999 Preface to *Gender Trouble*, Butler directly confronts this issue of her writing style.

Style, she suggests, is a complex issue. First, the styles that are available for use are not solely up to the author. Second, language (including grammar and style) is not 'politically neutral' (*GT*: xviii). To be able to communicate intelligibly with others requires that a certain set of grammatical rules are learned and followed. This process is one that Butler construes as a normalizing process: a process, that is, of being inducted into a specific set of norms. Failure to conform to these norms – grammatical rules – means that one's speech risks being unintelligible to others. The issue for Butler is that grammar does not simply constrain how language may properly be used; it also limits what can be thought (about 'reality', sexuality, the subject, and so on), and this is a problem, for it impedes the expression of radical ideas. A style, therefore, that adopts a 'critical relation to ordinary grammar' and that somehow challenges ordinary language use, while irritating and obtuse, may nevertheless be necessary in order to oppose taken-for-granted assumptions and to contest commonsense understandings of the world around us.[56] Butler sees her aim, therefore, not as defending 'difficulty for difficulty's sake' ('CS': 327) but as defending it because, as her own reading of 'difficult' thinkers such as Hegel, Heidegger and the critical theorists Adorno and Marcuse revealed, it can open up 'new' or alternative ways of thinking about the world ('CS': 327–30). Of course, in arguing the case for difficult language, Butler is distancing herself from those, like Nussbaum, who contend that feminists have a responsibility to convey ideas in a lucid and transparent way that is accessible to all women, not just academic women. What Butler is doing that is valuable, however, is highlighting how the very norms of accessibility or transparency that Nussbaum and others champion may themselves serve certain interests or obscure the operations of power.[57]

This brings me to my second point. This radical use of language and grammar in Butler's work has a similar effect to Hegel's use of rhetoric as outlined above. Butler's writings also appear to enact the theoretical positions that she is articulating; they are, in this sense, performative.[58] I have already given one indication of this above. This is the way in which her critical relation to grammar and language parallels her critical relation to normalizing discourses. Her attempts, that is, to denaturalize normative sexuality are enacted through her denaturalizing use of language and grammar.[59] In addition, her challenges to what she terms 'the conceptually proper philosopher' often involve her in the deliberate use of 'what the Habermassians call a performative contradiction'. Instead of operating within a '*conceptually* satisfying' philosophical framework, where all ideas have their appropriate place, she purposely conjoins contradictory notions in order to problematize them ('HB': 280). Furthermore, the significance of contingency to Butler's philosophical position is enacted through her interrogative style – the use of questions in the place of normative assertion in order to open up a field rather than to close it down. It is also made manifest in the numerous revisions of and qualifications to her work over time. Thus *Bodies that Matter*, she confesses, was written, in part at least, as a 'rethinking of some parts of *Gender Trouble*' (*BTM*: xii). Her turn to Althusser and Austin, and her decision to write *Excitable Speech*, were, she notes in an interview, driven by a desire to attend to some of the limitations of the Foucauldian account of constitution operative in both *Gender Trouble* and *Bodies that Matter* ('OSRM': 164).[60] And so on. Finally, the potential for linguistic resignification is also given expression in Butler's reiterative, thus variable and repetitious, use of specific terms throughout her work, not least the idea of performativity itself, which is articulated first in terms of bodily acts and practices, then appears to have evolved into a purely linguistic notion by the time of *Excitable Speech*, only to be reconfirmed as combining the linguistic and corporeal in *Undoing Gender*.[61]

Postscript

Before I begin my examination of Butler's theory of gender in the next chapter, it is necessary to make clear how in the coming chapters I will be dealing with her interpretations of those whose work she draws on. Butler has been repeatedly characterized as offering 'idiosyncratic' readings of other authors.[62] Her readings can certainly be off-centre. Sometimes, it seems, this eccentricity is manifested in the way she by-passes major concerns of a thinker in order to make her own point.[63] At other times, it is revealed in the way she draws on a particular aspect of a writer's thought and makes it stand for his or her whole position.[64] Sometimes her readings are conditioned by particular debates taking place in her own geographic locale.[65] Her use of particular terminology can be far from faithful to how it was originally deployed.[66] Finally, Butler dips in and out of her source material, rarely venturing anything like a systematic analysis of it. This was the case, as noted above, with her interpretation of the drama of desire in Hegel's *Phenomenology*; it is based on only part of the text and, thus, on only part of the drama.

Lynne Pearce offers one explanation for Butler's reading strategy: that it is a form of queer deconstructionism. Although deconstruction, in its American mode at least, has traditionally centred on identifying the binary oppositions found in a text and unpicking them in order to 'untie' the text, 'central to the success of the theoretical *argument* being pursued' by Butler, Pearce argues, is 'the *re-narrativization* of the textual action' under discussion. '[Q]ueer texts', she suggests, 'depend on the (re)construction of queer stories.'[67] Pearce traces this style of engagement back to Butler's 'disciplinary roots in literary criticism' with its emphasis on 'close textual analysis'.[68] This, however, is clearly misleading since Butler's disciplinary roots are in philosophy not literary theory (though arguably close analysis of texts can also be found in philosophy). There is also, as noted above, an issue with pigeonholing Butler simply as a queer theorist. Pearce's concerns are, furthermore, framed by a particular issue: how contemporary feminism illustrates its theories by way of literary texts. And, although Butler does interpret certain such writings in her work, not least Willa Cather's *My Antonia* and Nella Larsen's *Passing* in *Bodies that Matter*, most of her work actually engages with philosophical, political theory and psychoanalytic literature.

That said, Pearce's description of Butler's approach as entailing 're-scriptings' of what she reads and of her philosophy as 'unfigured' in the sense that it 'tends to eschew the use of trope and example' does appear apt.[69] So too does Pearce's contention that often during her discussion of a particular theorist's ideas, Butler will 'correct' the apparent meaning of a phrase, sentence or idea and will, thus, transfigure that meaning to suit her own ends. 'Once released from their original chain of signification,' Pearce suggests, 'these newly liberated subject-concepts are free to people their own (new) universe, giving birth to cognate terms and values.'[70] In the process, therefore, of deconstructing a particular text or argument, Butler also reconstructs it, and it is the reconstructed reading that then becomes the jumping-off point for her own theoretical embellishments, digressions and developments. On the grounds that I broadly accept Pearce's interpretation of Butler's rhetorical style, in what follows, therefore, I will neither trace all aspects of Butler's discussions of specific thinkers nor assess the plausibility or accuracy of the interpretations she offers. Instead, I will concentrate on the theory that Butler develops as a consequence of her 're-scriptings'.

2

Rethinking Sex and Gender

Near the end of *Subjects of Desire*, reflecting on the attempts by Kristeva and Foucault to overcome Hegel's desiring subject by focusing attention on the body, Butler asks: 'How do we conceive the body as a concrete scene of cultural struggle?' (*SD*: 237). *Gender Trouble* begins to offer a partial answer to this question when it sets out to trouble the categories of sex, gender and desire and, thereby, to challenge feminism's commitment to identity politics. Through her theorization of gender as performative and her advocacy of a political practice based on subverting compulsory heterosexuality, Butler not only offers a radical critique of sex as natural and innate, she also contests the viability of women as a unitary category. Needless to say, the impact of this book on feminist debate was profound for it seemed to challenge so many of the beliefs that feminism held dear. Provocative as it undoubtedly was, *Gender Trouble* is not actually the start of Butler's work on gender. In the period between the publication of *Subjects of Desire* and *Gender Trouble* she had been hard at work on a series of articles covering, amongst other things, the relation between phenomenology and performance as well as the ideas of Simone de Beauvoir. I will draw on some of this work in what follows, although my emphasis in this chapter will be on *Gender Trouble*, for the simple reason that it is here that Butler develops her most sustained critique of sex, gender and identity.

The trouble with women

Questions about the nature of Woman/women have, to recall the last chapter, been central to feminism for much of its recent history, in one form or another. Throughout the 1980s, however, they were located within a broader debate around what might be termed the 'politics of the subject', and, in particular, around the domination within feminism of a logic that conjures politics as reliant upon a subject that pre-exists it.[1] According to this mode of reasoning, feminism pre-supposes the prior presence of women *as a group* who share certain features (usually experiences) in common. This common identity then forms the basis for a feminist politics aimed at securing women's distinct interests. As indicated in the Introduction, however, the idea that all women could be said to have certain experiences or characteristics in common was challenged by both diversity and *différance* feminists. While the goal of the former was to champion various feminisms more attuned to specificity and difference, some of the latter began to contest the relation between women and feminism that had dominated hitherto. This is where *Gender Trouble* is relevant.

Butler's aim in this text is to present what she calls a '*feminist* genealogy of the category of women' (*GT*: 9).[2] She seeks to demonstrate, in other words, how the category of women has been deployed within feminism. Her purpose is not to offer a history of its deployment, however. It is to show how feminist uses of that term, far from being neutral, are deeply implicated in power relations. It is often assumed that feminism simply represents women. Represent, in this context, has one of two meanings: politically, it refers to acting on behalf of or in the interests of someone; linguistically, it means to correspond to or to typify something. In this latter sense, a representation is said to be accurate when it captures the reality of what it is endeavouring to represent. Butler, however, wants to challenge these commonsense understandings of representation as they operate within feminism. She argues, therefore, that far from feminist representations of women (in the linguistic sense) being simple reflections of what women are (that, in other words, correspond to the underlying truth of what it is to be a woman), they are, in fact, mechanisms of power through which women are themselves *constructed* as particular kinds of subject. Drawing on the work of Foucault, she argues that feminism exhibits a 'juridical' structure: 'juridical systems of power', she notes, '*produce* subjects they subsequently come to represent' (*GT*: 4).[3] The feminist subject 'women' is thus produced by the very feminism that claims to represent it, both linguistically and politically. Why does this matter? It matters because if feminist politics is juridical in structure, then the definitions of women with which it works are neither objective nor impartial. They are, rather, based on 'certain exclusionary practices', but practices that are hidden once the subject is produced (*GT*: 5). The definitions of women that feminism produces, on this reading, will thus be limited definitions that exclude some of those whom they purport to represent both politically and linguistically.

Clearly, Butler could not hope to cover all versions of feminism in her genealogy of women. As such, her focus is limited to examining those that anchor their understanding of women within the context of what she terms 'the heterosexual matrix' in *Gender Trouble* (*GT*: 9), re-terms 'heterosexual hegemony' in *Bodies that Matter*, and what I will call, following Michael Warner, 'heteronormativity': the institutions, modes of understanding, norms and discourses that treat heterosexuality as natural to humanity.[4] This is a position that Butler associates closely with sexual difference feminism. Popular in literary theory in the US in the 1980s and indebted to what has become known, somewhat problematically, as 'French feminism', this form of feminist theory assumes 'the fundamental difference between masculine and feminine' (*UG*: 207).[5] The problem with such thinking, from Butler's point of view, is that its reliance on sexual difference limits the meaning of gender to 'received notions of masculinity and femininity' and as a consequence both denies and delegitimates non-heterosexual 'minority gendered and sexual practices' (*GT*: vii, viii).[6] *Gender Trouble* is, therefore, motivated by a specific political aim: to contest the way in which particular idealizations of the sex/gender relation determine, to borrow language from Butler's later work, who counts and who does not. This, in turn, necessitates interrogating how sex is implicated in gender, how desire is implicated in sex, how subjectivity is implicated in sex, gender and desire, and how all are implicated in 'heterosexual necessity'.[7]

As the reader of *Gender Trouble* soon discovers, however, in order to develop her critique of the sex/gender relation (or rather the sex/gender/sexuality relation), Butler does not limit herself to an analysis of 'French feminism' in any sense; she ranges far more widely than that, engaging critically with psychoanalysis, in both Freudian and Lacanian variants, with the work of Foucault on sex and sexuality, with that of Monique Wittig on sex, gender and the lesbian, with Esther Newton's writings on drag, as well as with the structuralist anthropology of Gayle Rubin. She also draws considerable inspiration from Simone de Beauvoir's arguments in *The Second Sex*. In this chapter, therefore, I will concentrate on Butler's interpretations of Foucault, Wittig and Beauvoir, leaving aside her discussions of

Newton, Rubin and psychoanalysis to later chapters. In order to situate Butler's work, it is helpful first to outline how sex and gender had been conceptualized within feminism hitherto.

Feminism and the sex/gender debate

Throughout the 1970s and 1980s within the Anglo-American context, one term came gradually to dominate the feminist lexicon: gender. As Donna Haraway points out, gender was a concept 'developed to contest the naturalization of sexual difference in multiple arenas of struggle'.[8] It was developed specifically to rebut the assumption that a woman's biology determined not only her psychological make-up but also her role in life. The deployment of the concept of gender by feminists was a way of rejecting the idea of biological determinism (that 'anatomy is destiny', as it was often described). As Ann Oakley puts it in an early piece, '"Sex" is a word that refers to the biological differences between male and female', whereas '"Gender" . . . is a matter of culture: it refers to the social classification into "masculine" and "feminine".'[9] Sex is thus assumed to be constant, an unchanging biological fact; it is natural. Gender, by comparison, is conceived of as neither constant nor natural. Gender differences between men and women vary both over time and across cultures; they are thus socially conditioned, an effect of the process of socialization whereby differently sexed individuals are converted into either masculine or feminine persons. In *Sex, Gender and Society*, Oakley concentrated on showing how psychological differences between men and women were produced. Later feminist work added to this by exploring the role of education, the media, the family, child-rearing practices and religion in the process of gender acquisition.[10] In addition, while Oakley's work focused on gender *difference*, subsequent writers concentrated increasingly on gender as *hierarchically* organized, where women's oppression is regarded, that is, as a direct result of this organization.[11] This was a crucial move in the evolution of feminist politics. It meant that women's subordination was systematic, not natural or accidental.

The text that introduces the concept of a sex/gender *system* was Gayle Rubin's 1975 essay 'The Traffic in Women: Notes on the "Political Economy" of Sex'. At the time Rubin wrote 'Traffic', the dominant paradigm for thinking about women's oppression had been Marxism. The problem with Marxism for Rubin was, as she comments retrospectively, that it simply 'could not get at some core issues which concerned feminists: gender difference, gender oppression, and sexuality'.[12] For this reason, she turned her attention to both structuralist anthropology (the work of Claude Lévi-Strauss) and psychoanalysis, for, despite their limitations in terms of explaining women's oppression, both focused on sex and gender. Developing an 'implicit critique' of the work of Lévi-Strauss and Freud, in particular, therefore enabled Rubin to understand the 'sex/gender system'. This she defines, 'for lack of a more elegant term', as the 'set of arrangements by which a society transforms biological sexuality into products of human activity, and in which these transformed sexual needs are satisfied'.[13] The detail of the argument need not detain us at this point (I'll come back to it in Chapter 4), but what is noteworthy about Rubin's analysis is that she sees the sex/gender system as the culturally variable way that 'the biological raw material of human sex and procreation is shaped by human, social intervention'.[14] In other words, *patriarchal* society takes certain features of male and female biology and turns them into a set of gendered characteristics 'that serve to empower men and disempower women'.[15] These characteristics are then presented as the natural attributes of males and females, respectively.

The notion of the sex/gender system thus establishes the idea that male and female genders are not only different; under what came to be called 'patriarchy' they are hierarchically structured in such a way that the masculine is privileged over the feminine. Without necessarily following Rubin's argument as such, many other feminists deployed this idea of a hierarchical relation between the genders in their own work. Object relations theorist Nancy Chodorow, for instance, used the notion of a sex/gender system to understand the social organization of motherhood under patriarchy and why women want to mother even when they do not need to.[16] Others, including Genevieve Lloyd, set about unpacking the way that the oppositions between male and female, as well as masculinity and femininity, were thoroughly integrated with a series of other oppressive dualisms (mind/body, nature/culture and heterosexual/homosexual) at work in Western philosophical and political thought.[17] Whatever the differences between individual writers, and some are quite considerable, the ability to designate gender as socially or culturally constructed was an important milestone in feminist thinking, for to see gender as constructed meant that, far from being fixed, it could be changed through political struggle. Indeed, some thinkers, including Rubin as well as Shulamith Firestone and Kate Millett, went further: gender *per se* could be *eradicated*. For them a liberated future for women was a future without gender.[18]

Although from the outset, as Gatens points out, there were some feminists who rejected the distinction between sex and gender, by the 1980s the concept of gender had become central to contemporary feminist thought.[19] Indeed, such is its prevalence that when Butler developed her own critique of the sex/gender dichotomy, it was not to refute the importance or to contest the value of focusing on gender; it was to challenge what another feminist thinker, Christine Delphy, has called feminism's 'unexamined presupposition: that sex *precedes* gender'.[20]

Denaturalizing sex *and* gender

Chapter 1 of *Gender Trouble* opens with five synoptic quotations taken from the work of Simone de Beauvoir, Julia Kristeva, Luce Irigaray, Michel Foucault and Monique Wittig, respectively. These quotations encapsulate various themes developed in Butler's work.[21] The first two cast doubt on the idea of woman as an essential category; the third contests the link between women and sex; and the last two seek to problematize the naturalness of sex. In developing these themes, Butler certainly engages with the five thinkers just named, and draws considerable inspiration and insight from them. Ultimately, however, she rejects their final theoretical positions and all for the same reason: that is, for their reliance on certain pre-discursive or naturalist assumptions. Consequently, when she articulates her own theory it is one in which sex, sexuality, desire, gender and the body are *all* regarded as discursively constituted; where, in other words, none of these features is treated as a natural fact of human existence. To get to this position, however, because of her critical-dialectical approach, Butler has to work her way through some of the core claims of the five thinkers just named. It is her discussion of Beauvoir, Wittig, Foucault and Irigaray that will be my concern in the next part of this chapter. (I look at her treatment of Kristeva in Chapter 3.) I begin with her discussion of Beauvoir and Irigaray and, in particular, how they understand the sexed body.

When Butler turns her attention to Beauvoir and Irigaray, what concerns her is less how they theorize gender (masculinity and femininity) than how they deal with sex difference. Both Beauvoir and Irigaray can, according to Butler, be seen as offering accounts exploring the construction of asymmetrical relations between men and women; or, in a different lexicon, how male domination is produced. In *The Second Sex*, Beauvoir thus explores how man is positioned in Western thought as the subject: independent, capable of transcending his body, and able to exercise freedom. Furthermore, she reveals how 'man' stands for humanity. He represents 'universal personhood' (*GT*: 13), while Woman, by contrast, is the other. She is always defined in relation to man and, as such, is conceived of as dependent, as imprisoned in her body – she is sex – and, because of this, limited in her capacity to exercise freedom. Woman is, quite simply, man's inferior. Like Beauvoir, Irigaray (in texts such as *This Sex Which Is Not One*) sets out to show how Western culture is gendered in favour of the male subject. Rejecting Beauvoir's idea that man is the subject and woman is the other, Irigaray argues that both subject and other are masculine constructs of what she calls the 'phallogocentric' symbolic, that is, a signifying economy based on the exclusion of the feminine.[22] In this phallogocentric system, women are not simply the inferior of men. Instead, because they are 'the sex which is not one', they cannot be represented or thought within masculine discourse.[23] They are, in other words, outside of it. What is thus needed, in Irigaray's view, is a feminine symbolic that could represent women. For Butler, the accounts offered by both Beauvoir and Irigaray are important insofar as they identify specific masculinist strategies for excluding women and the feminine, but neither is sufficiently rigorous in deconstructing the idea of the sexed body.

Even though Beauvoir posits the idea that one *becomes* (rather than *is*) a woman – an idea that Butler will take up – she is ultimately prepared to assume, Butler contends, that each individual is sexed at birth and, thus, that 'being sexed and being human are coextensive and simultaneous' (*GT*: 142). The difficulty with Irigaray's argument is that although she suggests that binary sex is a ruse masking the masculinism of the symbolic, and thus is prepared to accept that it is not a natural division, for Butler, she fails to explain how male and female bodies as such are constituted.[24] In the end, both Beauvoir and Irigaray maintain that sexual difference is a natural aspect of human existence – the very position that Butler wants to query. Whether one accepts, or not, Butler's interpretations of either Beauvoir and/or Irigaray, the question they raise is how Butler proposes to take the debate a stage further. She does so by rethinking the relation of gender to sex.

When feminists first began to theorize the sex/gender relation, the underlying assumption was that sex was both logically and chronologically prior to gender.[25] Culturally determined gender norms, in other words, were conceptualized as secondary to natural sex. Gender was thus what was inscribed onto sex in some way. It is the priority of the relation between sex and gender that Butler problematizes. Rejecting the idea of a causal relation between sex and gender (where sex determines gender identity), Butler comments: 'If gender is the cultural meaning that the sexed body assumes, then a gender cannot be said to follow from a sex in any one way' (*GT*: 10). Taken to its logical conclusion, this means there is no reason why masculinity should accrue only to male bodies or femininity to female bodies or, even assuming binary sex, that gender should be limited to just two modalities, namely femininity and masculinity. All that is required in this setting is that a sexed body has a gender. Given this, gender might be best conceived of as a 'free-floating artifice' (*GT*: 10) and the sexed body simply as its 'arbitrary locus' ('SG': 35). If, however, there is a more determinate relation between sex and gender, then what is it based on? Since Butler rejects the idea that gender is an expression of sex, then the only alternative is that sex, far from being one of the determinants of gender, is actually one of its effects. Butler thus reads gender as the productive mechanism through which the sexes are themselves instituted (*GT*: 11). Gender, in other words, is the apparatus through which binary sex is produced. It is this gender apparatus that constructs sex as prior to discourse, and thus as natural or pre-discursive.

As Butler makes clear in *Bodies that Matter*, however, her point is not simply that sex is gendered; it is that sex is 'from the start, normative'. It operates as 'what Foucault has called a "regulatory ideal"' producing 'the bodies it governs' (*BTM*: 1). Sex (or the discourse of sex) functions, in other words, to bring into material being the very bodies it claims only to describe. Crucially, sex as a regulative ideal thus also operates to exclude – or pathologize – those whose anatomy does not fit its normative parameters. It might be objected that Butler's argument in this regard is unoriginal; after all, Foucault had already put into question the idea of naturalized 'sex' when he demonstrated in *The History of Sexuality* that sex is the effect of a historically sedimented regime of sexuality and that the so-called 'truth' of sex that every subject is supposed to exhibit is, in fact, manufactured by a constellation of regulatory and productive discourses of sexuality. Butler is certainly influenced by these ideas of Foucault's, but where his concern was to illuminate the relation between sex and sexuality, with gender playing little or no part in his thinking, she is explicitly interested in gender and its relation to sex and sexuality.[26] In this regard, Butler is not just content to argue that sex is a gendered effect and thus to re-theorize the sex/gender relation in this way. Instead, following Wittig, amongst others, her purpose is to demonstrate how sex and gender are deployed within a particular framework, namely, that of heteronormativity (where men are opposed to women, masculinity to femininity, and heterosexuality to homosexuality). This takes us on to one of the core concepts of Butler's work: the concept of cultural intelligibility.

Cultural intelligibility – contesting heteronormativity

In the 1999 preface, Butler declares that one of the factors motivating her writing of *Gender Trouble* was to contest the way that the presumption of heterosexuality in certain feminist work served to delegitimate specific minority sexual and gendered practices. This leads to the idea of cultural intelligibility. Cultural intelligibility, as Butler deploys it, refers to the production of a normative framework that conditions who can be recognized as a legitimate subject. Butler uses it in her earlier writings as a way of thinking about how normative ideals of sex and gender circumscribe who can be conceived of as subject. She also draws on it in her later texts (particularly *Undoing Gender* and *Precarious Life*), to demonstrate how the human is normatively produced within particular racial and cultural frames. On both occasions, Butler ties the idea of cultural intelligibility to the possibility of a liveable life (that is, a life that is recognized as having value and legitimacy).[27] Before any individual can live a 'liveable' life, she argues, they have first to be recognized as a viable subject. If they cannot be recognized in this way (because they deviate somehow from the norms determining viable subjectivity), then their lives will be '"impossible", illegible, unreal, and illegitimate' (*GT*: viii). They simply will not matter. Any regime of cultural intelligibility thus hinges on what she calls in the 1999 preface 'normative violence' (*GT*: xx): that is, the violence that is done by certain norms in the generation of liveable lives and in the constitution of subjectivity. It is this interest in how normative violence relates to cultural intelligibility and how both relate to liveable lives that drives her politics. In Chapter 6, I will consider this politics in terms of the relation between normative violence and mourning, amongst other things. Here I want to concentrate on the argument developed in *Gender Trouble* and its implications for a gender politics.

Butler contends that gender is rendered culturally intelligible at present through what she terms the 'heterosexual matrix' (*GT*: 9). In developing this idea, she borrows from a range of different theories and concepts.[28] The first is Wittig's concept of the 'heterosexual contract'. This is the idea that binary sexual difference and heterosexuality are the political effects of a social contract underpinning male–female class relations: 'what makes a woman', according to Wittig, 'is a specific social relation to a man' (and vice versa).[29] The heterosexual contract thus works by confining gender identities within the orbit of heterosexual desire. As Butler interprets Wittig: 'gender not only designates persons, "qualifies" them, as it were, but constitutes a conceptual episteme by which binary gender is universalized' (*GT*: 28). The second element is Adrienne Rich's essay 'Compulsory Heterosexuality and Lesbian Existence'. Here Rich sets out her argument that heterosexuality should be conceptualized as a '*political institution*' that enables male dominance and that compels women (both through force and ideology) to assume a heterosexual identity.[30] Finally, Butler's description of the heterosexual matrix as a 'grid of cultural intelligibility' appears to echo, knowingly or not, Foucault's notion of a 'grid of intelligibility' deployed in the *History of Sexuality*.[31] Foucault uses the term to refer to the particular schemas (including power) through which we make sense of the social order. The heterosexual matrix should thus be thought of as the specific framework of meaning through which to make sense of sex, gender and desire. So, how are sex, gender and desire signified within it?

According to Butler, the matrix generates a series of ideal relations between sex, gender and desire such that gender is said to follow naturally from sex and where desire (or sexuality) is said to follow naturally from gender. 'Sex' in this sense can be thought of as a natural substance that is given expression in both femininity and masculinity, *and* in specific 'modalities of desire and pleasure' ('GB': 259). Consistent with the grid, maleness entails masculinity, and masculinity is expressed in sexual desire for a woman, whereas femaleness entails femininity and is expressed in sexual desire for a man. Gender and desire are thus seen as aspects of sex. As such, '"Intelligible" genders are those which in some sense institute and maintain relations of coherence and continuity among sex, gender, sexual practice, and desire' (*GT*: 23). These relations of coherence and continuity are not natural; they are the effect of the constitutive and violent work of certain gender norms.[32] A coherent – and culturally intelligible – subject, therefore, is one in whom sex, gender and desire flow in the way just described. Where, however, sex, gender and desire line up in a different way (say, where a man desires another man), the individual in question is regarded as culturally unintelligible and, as such, as not a viable subject. In terms of the matrix, he might be thought of, that is, as 'unnatural' or as not a 'proper' man. If, therefore, according to the terms of heteronormativity, to be human is to be heterosexual, then consequently anyone who is not heterosexual (be they gay, lesbian or bisexual, for instance) is not (fully) human. As non-human or less-than-human, they lack social, legal and political validity. Exposing the regulatory and fictive nature of compulsory heterosexuality is thus central to a gender politics, such as Butler's, that seeks legitimation for non-normative sexual minorities.

The idea that sex is constructed is, as we have seen, an idea that Butler derives from her critical readings of Foucault and Wittig. She takes from Rich and Wittig the broad notion of presumptive heterosexuality as a political institution. Drawing on these positions in combination thus allows her to develop her argument that binary sex is the construct of a particular gender regime that structures normative sexuality and, consequently, to challenge 'those feminist positions that maintain sexual difference as irreducible' ('VSG': 139).[33] Although she is indisputably indebted to Wittig and Rich in her thinking, it is clear from her critique of Wittig – she is strangely silent about Rich here – that she rejects the type of politics Wittig deduces from her analysis of heterosexuality, that is, one grounded in lesbianism (a view also shared by Rich). As Wittig puts it: 'Lesbian', for her, 'is the only concept I know of which is beyond the categories of sex (woman and man), because the designated subject (lesbian) is *not* a woman.'[34] As such, the lesbian is outside the heterosexual contract (which sets up men and women in relation to one another) and is thus, following the logic of her argument, free from oppression. There is something odd about this claim, however, for having developed a social constructionist argument to explain sex, gender and women, it now appears that Wittig is relying on the idea of an identity – the lesbian – that is somehow independent of the process of construction. This has led critics, including Butler, to speculate that Wittig is falling back on certain pre-discursive or naturalist ideas about lesbianism.[35] If this is so, then it would appear that Wittig is reproducing the very logic of identity (with regards to the lesbian) that Butler is at pains to deconstruct, one that rests identity on certain essential qualities of the individual.[36]

The primary political aim of *Gender Trouble* is to make life possible for those who, within the terms of the dominant heteronormative regime, are presently unintelligible. In addition, therefore, to exposing the shortcomings of existing descriptions of sex and gender, discussed above, Butler needs to set out an alternative theorization of gender. This must avoid the essentialist pitfalls of, for instance, Wittig's approach as Butler reads it. It must also be capable of revealing simultaneously how a subject acquires a gender identity and how heteronormative idealizations of gender can be challenged. Here Butler's own question seems especially apt: 'How . . . does gender need to be reformulated to encompass the power relations that produce the effect of a prediscursive sex and so conceal the very operation of discursive production?' (*GT*: 11). The answer, for Butler, is to see gender as performative.

From phenomenology to performativity

Gender performativity is, undoubtedly, the idea for which Butler is best known. The term 'performative', however, is not one that she originates. It derives from the ordinary-language philosophy of J. L. Austin, and his distinction between 'constative' and 'performative' utterances. When Butler deploys the idea of *gender* performativity (and its cognate terms 'performance' and 'performative') in *Gender Trouble*, there is no mention of this prior work. Nor is there any mention of a paper by Jacques Derrida that Butler has frequently had recourse to when discussing performativity, namely, 'Signature Event Context', where Derrida proffers his powerful deconstructive critique of Austin. Indeed, on the basis of her claim in the preface to the second edition of *Gender Trouble* that the idea of gender performativity was suggested to her by Derrida's reading of Kafka's 'Before the Law', it might appear that these earlier articulations were, in fact, irrelevant to her thinking.[37] Perhaps in terms of her initial formulation of performativity they were. Certainly by 1993, with the publication of the essay 'Critically Queer' and her book *Bodies that Matter*, however, things had changed. She now begins to situate her own account of performativity in relation to Austin's and to Derrida's, a situating that is given its fullest expression with the publication in 1997 of *Excitable Speech*. What interests me here is less why Butler fails to discuss either philosopher in

Gender Trouble – other critics have already furnished plausible explanations for this omission[38] – than why the account of performativity that she does provide concentrates far more heavily on bodily practices and gestures than on language, as in her later work. My argument is that one reason for this, and perhaps the main one, is Butler's indebtedness to Beauvoir and to existential phenomenology.

In the period prior to the publication of *Gender Trouble*, as noted earlier, Butler published a series of articles and chapters on gender.[39] A common theme in all of them is the work of Simone de Beauvoir. Butler is particularly interested in three aspects of Beauvoir's work: first, her apparent distinction between sex and gender (and I say apparent here because Beauvoir herself does not use the word 'gender' in her work);[40] second, her understanding of the body; and, finally, the idea that one *becomes* a woman. Without going into too much detail, as an existential phenomenologist Beauvoir is particularly interested in exploring 'experience and its meanings';[41] or, more specifically, as a feminist existential phenomenologist, in exploring 'social and political phenomena: with disclosing the "lived experience" of being a woman'.[42] This means that Beauvoir, like other existential phenomenologists, pays particular attention to embodied existence and, within this, to the discourses and practices through which people make sense of, and live, their lives. It is vital when approaching Butler's theory of performativity to be aware of this debt to Beauvoir and to existential phenomenology in general, with its emphasis on 'grounding theory in lived experience' ('PA': 522),[43] for Butler, quite literally, would have been unable to develop her account of gender performativity without this work. Let me give one example. In the early papers, Butler presents Beauvoir's phenomenological account of gender as a '*stylized repetition of acts*'. In *Gender Trouble*, these same words are used by Butler to describe *her* own (ostensibly) non-phenomenological theory.[44] Interesting as it might be to plot the twists and turns of Butler's various re-scriptings of Beauvoir's work, I will not do so here. Instead, I will set out in broad terms how Butler develops her theory by exploiting Beauvoir's discussion of the three themes noted above; how she pursues, that is, what she perceives to be their most radical implications.[45]

The phrase that Butler concentrates particular attention on in all of her engagements with Beauvoir is the latter's remark that 'one is not born, but rather becomes, a woman'.[46] It is the notion of gendering as a dynamic and corporeal process that appears to attract Butler. 'To be a gender', according to Beauvoir's theorizing, Butler writes in 'Sex and Gender in Simone de Beauvoir's *Second Sex*', 'is to be engaged in an ongoing cultural interpretation of bodies, and, hence, to be dynamically positioned within a field of cultural possibilities'. As such, gendering is 'a modality of taking on or realizing possibilities' ('SG': 36). It is, in other words, a process of appropriation, interpretation and reinterpretation of the cultural norms *of embodiment* that define gender.[47] Understanding gender thus entails understanding how the human body acquires its gendered form. It is how Beauvoir conceptualizes the body that especially appeals to Butler.

According to Butler, when Beauvoir talks about the body, she does so in a very specific way. As a phenomenologist, she conceives of the body not as 'a natural fact but as an historical idea' ('GB': 254): that is, as an entity that has come to have a specific meaning within a determinate historical context. The body is thus not an abstract object but an historical construct. Moreover, as such, it is always what existential phenomenologists refer to as a 'situated body' or a 'lived body'. As Iris Young defines the lived body, it 'is the unified idea of a physical body acting and experiencing in a specific sociocultural context; it is body-in-situation'.[48] This means for Butler that, as Beauvoir understands it, the body is 'a material reality which has already been located and defined within a social context' ('SG': 45). Translated to the question of sex and gender, Butler interprets Beauvoir's thesis to indicate that there is no way to know or to experience the natural body – since all we know and experience is the *historical* body: that is, the body as it is 'signified within an historically specific discourse of meaning' ('GB': 254). So, for Butler, 'lived or experienced "sex" is always gendered'. It is always understood as mediated through historical specificity. If, therefore, the 'unstated consequences' of Beauvoir's statement are pursued, Butler surmises, then the idea of biological sex as natural is hard to sustain ('SG': 39, 45). We have already seen in the earlier part of this chapter how Butler develops these 'unstated consequences', albeit through the optic provided by Wittig and Foucault, to argue that sex is a gendered construct.

The question that this still leaves Butler with, however, is what it might mean to actually 'embody an historical idea' ('GB': 254). What, in other words, does Beauvoir mean when she says that one '*becomes*' a woman (or, in fact, any other gender)? In these early articles, therefore, Butler ponders how Beauvoir uses the verb 'to become'. This takes her straight to the question of agency. One of the merits of the idea of becoming a gender is that it suggests that gender is not to be thought of as imposed on subjects, as it is sometimes characterized within feminism (as when authors talk of women being 'culturally constructed'). Consequently, as a way of thinking, the idea of becoming a gender poses a challenge to the idea that gender is passively produced by patriarchy or forced on subjects by the phallogocentric symbolic. Becoming implies, rather, that gendering is an achievement of some kind that gendered subjects themselves engage in. In this sense Beauvoir suggests gendering the self (becoming woman) involves 'a purposive and appropriative set of acts, the acquisition of a skill' ('SG': 36). It is 'a project, a skill, a pursuit, an enterprise, even an industry' ('GB': 256). For these reasons, the concept of gender as becoming introduces the idea that gendering, in part at least, is a 'self-reflexive process' ('SG': 36). Moreover, if it is a self-reflexive process, this means that the courses of action open to us are never entirely constrained. There is always the possibility that the process of becoming contains 'emancipatory potential' ('SG': 36, 41). Indeed, the very idea of becoming hints at what Butler, in 'Variations on Sex and Gender', calls a 'theory of gender invention' ('VSG': 139).

The difficulty with reading 'becoming' entirely in this way, according to Butler, is that it might appear to suggest that the subject (the 'I') somehow precedes its gender and that it orchestrates entirely its own becoming as a gender. And, Butler comments, there are moments when Beauvoir appears to give 'becoming' a voluntarist slant by implying that gender is a process of self-construction undertaken by an agent (or *cogito*), who could, in theory at least, vary the gender they choose ('SG': 36, 40). This is patently in tension, however, with Beauvoir's construal of the body as always situated or lived – the idea, that is, that 'the body is always already gendered' ('GB': 255). Given this, Butler concludes, it cannot be that Beauvoir actually means that the acquisition of gender is an 'unsituated Cartesian act'; one that is decided entirely according to the subject's own volition ('SG': 37). If, as it clearly is, agency is involved in becoming a gender, then it must be a form of agency that is embodied. And this means that it is one that is always in some way constrained by the historical discourses that invest our bodies with meaning. When we endeavour to become a particular gender we aim, by and large, to approximate the historical and cultural norms that define what that gender ought to be: how it should look, walk, talk, sit, and so forth. As such, our becoming is always constrained by cultural norms, taboos, conventions and even laws. This is why those who fail to approximate the gender ideal, either deliberately or unintentionally, may be severely punished for their failure.[49] Does this mean, however, that no alteration in the norms of gender is possible? No, it does not.

Although the choices the subject makes in becoming a specific gender are not free choices – they are constrained – the very fact that gender is a *process* means that there is no end to it. Gender as a way of becoming is thus an incessant activity, 'a daily act of reconstitution and interpretation' ('SG': 40). Since the body is the primary site of gender, the place where received meanings are reproduced, it is also the place where the norms of gender can be varied, where it is possible to 'interpret received gender norms in a way that organizes them anew' ('SG': 40). In terminology that prefigures that of *Gender Trouble,* Butler concludes that the reinterpretation of gender norms 'through the proliferation and variation of corporeal styles becomes a very concrete and accessible way of politicizing personal life' ('SG': 45). The idea of agency contained within Beauvoir's theory of becoming, according to Butler, is thus one that should be thought of in terms of a dialectic of constraint and freedom. Gender norms are culturally conditioned, but in the process of appropriating those norms, space is generated for their transformation. Having initially argued that Beauvoir successfully reconciles the relation between constraint and choice through her conceptualization of agency as always embodied, much to the perplexity of her critics, in *Gender Trouble* she rejects this view. Instead, she now argues that Beauvoir, in fact, adopts too voluntaristic a conception of agency because she adheres to a Cartesian view of the subject in which the body is subordinate to the mind.[50] Whether or not the reader is persuaded by Butler's altered judgement of Beauvoir, there is an interesting irony here, for the very issue that Butler contends ultimately mars Beauvoir's account of agency – its tendency towards voluntarism – is one that critics would also accuse Butler of. What it points to, of course, is the difficulty in producing a version of agency capable of negotiating between constraint and freedom, a theme I will return to in the next chapter.

The final aspect that Butler takes over from phenomenology into her articulation of the theory of gender performativity in *Gender Trouble* is an emphasis on acts: recall that she characterizes gender performativity as the *'stylized repetition of acts'*. Here I want to look briefly at the article 'Performative Acts and Gender Constitution'. In this paper, Butler explores the discourse of acts within philosophy. She is particularly interested in the phenomenological discourse of acts because it concentrates on the routine ways in which 'social agents *constitute* social reality through language, gesture, and all manner of symbolic social sign' ('PA': 519). The problem with certain versions of phenomenology, however, is that they operate with the assumption of a constituting agent: that is, an agent who directs and controls their own acts. There is, nevertheless, within other species of phenomenological thought 'a more radical use' of the doctrine of acts which takes the social agent 'as an *object* rather than the subject of constitutive acts' ('PA': 519). This, in Butler's view, is the understanding of acts to be found in Beauvoir's work, where, as Butler puts it, Beauvoir conceptualizes gender identity as the effect of a series of 'bodily gestures, movements, and enactments of various kinds' ('PA': 519). This analysis accords with Butler's own preferred reading of gender, where the body 'becomes its gender through a series of acts which are renewed, revised, and consolidated through time' ('PA': 523).

Despite her obvious support for Beauvoir's thesis, and, in particular, for the idea of the gendered body as the result of a set of acts, Butler nonetheless worries about some of the implications of how phenomenologists (including Beauvoir) construe acts. Specifically, she worries that emphasizing individual acts – how a woman enacts her gender – might undermine the potential to explicate the 'scale and systemic character of women's oppression' ('PA': 525). She thus proposes to supplement a phenomenological analysis of acts with a more 'theatrical' sense. To think of acting in this context is to think about a collective experience: 'As a given temporal duration within the entire performance, [theatrical] "acts" are a *shared* experience and "*collective* action"' ('PA': 525, my emphasis). During a performance there is, in other words, an experience of shared sociality. Moreover, the theatrical conception of acts introduces the idea of historicity and conventionality.[51] Just as a dramatic script both outlasts the actors who use it but also requires them to follow it in order to convey a particular character, so the gender script also outlasts those who enact it but nevertheless requires them to follow it in order to convey a particular gender. Just as actors in a play act for an audience, so gender is also publicly enacted. In this respect, 'act', as Butler uses it, conveys both an individualistic *and* a collective (public) element.[52]

In this section, I have explored how in tracing through some, in her own words, of the 'unstated consequences' of Beauvoir's thesis Butler 're-scripts' Beauvoir. It is this 're-scripting' of Beauvoir's work that is pivotal to the genesis of Butler's own theory of performativity. When Butler articulates this theory, as we will see in the next section, all explicit reference to phenomenology has disappeared and Butler has revised her understanding of Beauvoir's conceptualization of the body.[53] Repudiating any reliance on natural or prediscursive phenomena, Butler now presents a radical constructivist theory of gender.

Performing gender

Butler's aim in *Gender Trouble* is to problematize the idea that gender is an expression of sex. To do this, she reverses the logic that usually pertains. Instead of regarding sex as the origin of gender, she contends instead that gender produces sex. Furthermore, both sex and gender are produced within a heteronormative matrix: both are its effects. Accordingly, when Butler sets out to define gender, she does so by stipulating that '*gender* is not a noun'; it is, in contrast, 'always a doing'. Gender does not describe something that *is* (an essence), rather it refers to a process – a series of acts. In this sense, a gendered identity is made manifest only at the moment of its enactment. Implicitly recalling her own concerns that certain forms of phenomenology rely on the idea of an autonomous agent, Butler stresses that her understanding of the subject is somewhat different. Quoting Nietzsche, she notes that 'there is no "being" behind doing, effecting, becoming: "the doer" is merely the fiction added to the deed – the deed is everything'. Gender is thus a 'doing' – an activity – but not one undertaken by a subject 'that might be said to pre-exist the deed' (*GT*: 33). Indeed, it is the 'doing' that produces the gendered subject. As a consequence, there is no such thing as a natural (gendered) body; the gendered body is a construct of the acts that generate 'its reality' (*GT*: 173). The 'trope of interiority' (where the sexed body is seen to *cause* gender) is, rather, an effect created by the repetition over time of these gestures and enactments (such as walking, talking, sitting, eating and dressing) that are thought of as expressive of a particular gender.[54] One never 'is' one's gender, therefore, but only in a condition of 'doing' it; moreover, doing it interminably.[55] Seeing that one of the goals of Butler's rethinking of sex and gender is to contest the norms defining viable subjectivity and what counts as a liveable life, then the question raised by her reconceptualization of gender as a form of doing (or as act-based) is exactly how it helps in combating heteronormativity. Relevant here is Butler's discussion of drag.

Frequently misunderstood, and often pilloried, Butler's assessment of drag has been the cause of much debate within feminist circles. One reason for this is that drag has not been universally applauded within feminism. Quite the reverse: it has either been interpreted as fundamentally demeaning to women or, when performed by lesbians, as based on an unthinking and, hence, unacceptable appropriation of heterosexual norms and practices (as in butch/femme relations). Critics who have read Butler's account have often rejected it because they have assumed that it is *the* template for the gender politics that performativity is thought to entail: politics as cross-dressing.[56] Yet if we examine the context in which the idea is initially articulated by Butler, we can see that it is central to her argument disputing that gender identities originate from a psychological 'core'. It is, that is, part of her critique of heteronormativity. Indeed, as Butler interprets it, drag is meaningful only within the context of heteronormativity. She deploys the idea of drag in order to reject the opposition between 'true' and 'false' genders and to demonstrate how the impression of a gender identity is established. If there is one thing that drag illustrates, and graphically at that, for Butler, it is the fallacy of assuming that a primary gender identity exists. Why and how?

A particularly clear explanation is offered in *Undoing Gender*. Here she recalls that while watching drag in a bar, she suddenly realized that 'some of these so-called men could do femininity much better than I ever could, ever wanted to, ever would'. What is more, they confirmed her sense that femininity is not natural to women but is rather an effect of specific practices. They gave expression to, that is, what she calls 'the transferability of the attribute' (*UG*: 213). Heteronormativity naturalizes a set of relations between sex, gender and desire that drag, in effect, denaturalizes. As Butler puts it in *Gender Trouble*, drag *as a practice* divulges a series of discordant elements that ultimately undermine both the assumption of heterosexual coherence and the idea that heterosexuality is original. There is not only a clash between the sex (maleness) of the drag performer and the gender (femininity) he is performing but, following Esther Newton,[57] Butler also assumes that the gender identity of the performer is at odds with both his sex and his performance. (We have no way of knowing from what he does whom he desires.) To the degree that it creates a 'unified picture of "woman"', drag as a practice successfully demonstrates the fictive nature of gender coherence; it shows, that is, how it is fabricated. '*In imitating gender, drag implicitly reveals the imitative structure of gender itself – as well as its contingency*' (*GT*: 175).[58] When drag successfully challenges heteronormativity, it does so in a particular way: it reveals *all* gender as *parody*. Drag, on this interpretation, does not involve the '*ex*propriation or *ap*propriation' of a gender that rightfully belongs to a particular sex, for there is no gender that naturally belongs in that way. It, rather, connotes the 'mundane way in which genders are appropriated, theatricalized, worn and done' by everyone ('Imitation': 21). It shows, in other words, that the 'original' (heterosexuality) is itself a construct, and thus that 'gay to straight [is] *not* as a copy to the original, but, rather, as copy is to copy' (*GT*: 41). Both rely on the repetition of those acts decreed within the heterosexual matrix to signify a particular gender; thus heterosexual identity and drag are both performative (*UG*: 209).[59]

Drag is important to Butler's argument not because she conceives of it as *the* practice most likely to undermine heteronormativity, but because it is *a* practice that sheds light on how heteronormativity naturalizes the relation between sex, gender and desire. It is significant because of its capacity to denaturalize all three constitutive elements (sex, gender and desire) of the 'law of heterosexual coherence', as well as their relations to one another (*GT*: 175). As a practice, therefore, it can be tied back to the question of cultural intelligibility. A gendered identity, as an effect of the heterosexual matrix, is generated only through the necessary and perpetual repetition of particular acts and gestures. Precisely because gender identity relies on repetition, however, it is inherently unstable. Drag exemplifies how this instability can be exploited. It symbolizes a way of resisting prevailing gender norms such that it exposes the work of fabrication that takes place in the production of any identity – coherent or not. Consequently, as a resistant practice, drag has the capacity to open up space for a critical gender politics, the contours of which I examine in the next chapter.[60] In what remains of this chapter, however, I want to consider what the implications of Butler's re-theorization of sex and gender are for feminism; particularly what it means for the idea of women.

Women in/and feminism

Earlier we noted that *Gender Trouble* was written at a time when the category of women within feminism was under scrutiny. In the essay 'Gender Trouble, Feminist Theory, and Psychoanalytic Discourse', published in the same year as *Gender Trouble,* Butler comments that the task facing feminism is thus 'either redefining and expanding the category of women itself to become more inclusive' or 'to challenge the place of the category as a part of a feminist normative discourse' ('GTFT': 325). Without a doubt, Butler is engaged in the second of these two projects. She does so by contesting the supposition of many feminists that gender assumes the pre-existence of sex. By arguing that sex, gender and, indeed, desire (which I will revisit in Chapter 4) are all effects – that is, that none of them are natural – and that gender identity is performative (produced through the repetition of certain practices or acts), she challenges the opinion that a stable and unitary conception of women can be the basis for feminist politics. Going further, far from regarding the category of women as essential to feminist politics, she views it as a limit on that politics. This judgement arises, in part, from Butler's critique of representation. Here she rejects the premise that the subject exists prior to its representations, instead arguing that it is generated through them. Feminism, in other words, reifies certain views of what it is to be female, with the net result that it actually regulates women in a manner contrary to its goals of democratic inclusivity. The concept 'women' thus becomes a coercive category, normalizing femaleness and femininity in restrictive and exclusionary ways. Given this normalizing tendency within feminism, together with the difficulty of developing a definition of women able to span all the other axes of identity (race, class, sexuality, and so forth) that separate women, Butler concludes that attempts to elaborate a more inclusive and complete category of women will not work. In fact, they are more likely to produce factionalization within the women's movement.

This is even true of 'strategic essentialist' accounts of women, of the kind advocated by Gayatri Spivak. This is where feminists, aware that there is no single definition of women, nevertheless deploy such a notion in order to advance particular political claims. Butler contends that approaches of this kind must also be resisted because, even as they accept that the category of women is 'not fully expressive' (that is, does not cover all women), they still work by setting up a regulatory and exclusive ideal of women ('GTFT': 325). For these reasons Butler concludes that 'it is no longer clear that feminist theory ought to try to settle the questions of primary identity in order to get on with the task of politics. Instead, we ought to ask, what political possibilities are the consequence of a radical critique of the categories of identity?'(*GT*: xxix).[61] Butler's argument that the female subject, *per se*, is not an appropriate starting point for feminist analysis and action thus presents an important challenge to those feminist theories that assumed that a common identity was necessary for a collective politics.[62] Needless to say, not all feminist critics accepted her position. As Lynne Segal notes, some reacted 'with bewilderment or exasperation to Butler's claim that both sex and gender, including any notion of the "female" or of "women", are but regulatory fictions'.[63] This included those such as Martha Nussbaum concerned that Butler's approach denied the 'real situation of real women' and, hence, the 'material suffering of women who are hungry, illiterate, violated, beaten'. There was, she concluded, 'no victim' in Butler's work.[64] Others, such as Seyla Benhabib, sought to defend the position that feminism requires the category of women in order to ground its politics because feminism, as a political movement by, of and about women, makes no sense – ideological, political or logical – without such a category.[65]

Since then, without retracting the basic tenets of the position laid out in *Gender Trouble*, Butler has backtracked a little. In the essay 'Contingent Foundations', for instance, she observes: 'it seems as if there is some political necessity to speak as and for *women* and I would not contest that necessity' ('CF': 15). She appears to accept the pragmatic necessity for using the term in order to make demands on behalf of women. She still insists, however, that attempts to define the term in such a way as to try to be all-inclusive – such as when womanhood is equated with maternity, for instance – will inevitably spawn division. For this reason, in *Bodies that Matter*, she states her preference for an 'anti-descriptivist perspective' where 'women' are understood as a 'permanent site of contest, or as a feminist agonistic struggle' (*BTM*: 221). So, while feminists can mobilize the term 'women' in political and legislative action, provisionally constituting an identity as they go, in order to reduce the tendency towards exclusion inherent in identity politics and to maintain feminism as a *democratic* movement, they need to accept that 'women' 'designates an undesignatable field of differences' ('CF': 15). Feminists need to accept that 'women' is an open, contingent and resignifiable concept. The term can be deployed, in other words, as long as that deployment is accepted as both nonfoundational and contestable.[66]

Conclusion

As a feminist, Butler is clearly not alone in examining the relation between sex and gender. So how is her approach different? First, she questions the idea that sex precedes gender. Where most feminists had simply accepted the idea that biological sex exists independent of culture, Butler rejects this premise. Like feminists such as Wittig and Delphy, as well as those influenced by Foucault, she seeks to show that sex is an effect of a specific set of power relations. Sex is, in other words, a *political* category. This rejection of the idea that sex is natural and its reconceptualization as a social phenomenon lead inevitably to the conclusion that, far from sex being the basis for gender, as those such as Oakley or Rubin had asserted, it is one of its primary effects. Much of Butler's work is aimed, therefore, at a denaturalization of sex.

Although there are similarities between Butler, Wittig and Delphy – indeed, Butler is deeply influenced by Wittig – there are significant differences. Both Wittig and Delphy develop materialist analyses of sex/gender. They take their theoretical co-ordinates from Marx and, as such, they conceive of gender inequality as embedded in social practices, including those such as housework or childcare. They also emphasize women's economic dependence. Finally, their goal is to isolate the causes of male domination and female subordination; they thus focus on systems of oppression.[67] Butler is clearly not a materialist in this Marxian sense: she is not concerned with class relations, with economics or with structural inequality, though the role of practices is critical to her understanding of gender performativity. So, the second element that distinguishes Butler's approach from other feminist approaches is that she offers a non-materialist account of sex and gender. Or, rather, she offers a non-materialist account of sex and gender and *desire*. This locution is important.

Butler has been criticized for focusing on sexual difference rather than on sexual hierarchy; that is, for failing, as she puts it (paraphrasing her critics), to attend to 'the continuing cultural and political reality of patriarchal domination' (*UG*: 210).[68] This judgement, of course, is based on the assumption that feminism's central concern is male–female relations (or, rather, male domination and female subordination). If, however, it is conceded that feminism ought also to be concerned with sexuality, then it is far harder to contend that Butler's work neglects questions of hierarchy and inequality, for this is precisely what her critique of the heteronormative ordering of sex, gender and desire forefronts. To paraphrase Butler's paraphrase, her concern is with 'the continuing cultural and political reality of hegemonic heterosexuality'. It might then be objected that this just proves that Butler is a queer theorist before she is a feminist. I disagree. Part of the importance of her work is that it contests the idea that sexuality as an object of study is the sole preserve of gay and lesbian theory (or what has increasingly come to be called 'sexuality studies', to distinguish it from 'women's studies'). Questions of sexuality are deeply relevant to feminism.[69]

The final aspect of Butler's work to note is her understanding of gender as performative. This is, perhaps, her most original claim. Developed out of her radical reading of Beauvoir, the idea that a gendered identity is produced only as it is enacted had a profound influence on both feminist and queer thought. Although, at first sight, it might appear that the theory of performativity resembles the sociological idea of sex-role socialization (adopted by several feminists in their explorations of gender), the two are, in fact, quite distinct. The reason is that they are based on different assumptions. Socialization theory assumes that a gendered identity is acquired by sexed subjects learning certain gendered practices. This means, first, that sex is seen as prior to gender, a view that Butler rejects, and, second, that logically there must be a time when sexed subjects are un-gendered – the time before they learn the gendered practices in question. For Butler, however, to be a person is always already to be gendered. The declaration at a child's birth of its sex is a gendered (and gendering) declaration. It constitutes them as male or female. (Indeed, with advances in ultrasound, this occurs *before* birth now.) The theory of performativity is distinct from socialization theory in a second way, in that the latter assumes the very presupposition that performativity contests: that there is a 'doer behind the deed'. Gender is performative, for Butler, because it exists *only* in the acts that constitute it. Or, to put it less obliquely, a gendered identity is produced through specific bodily gestures, practices, declarations, actions and movements. A gendered identity is thus an effect of doing gender. The theory of gender performativity thus permits Butler to advance an innovative theory of subjectivity.

Hitherto my discussion of Butler's theory has concentrated on the broad terms of her critique of sex, gender and desire (though I will return to the psychoanalytic elements of this in Chapter 4) and on her theory of gender performativity. So far I have said little about the kind of gender politics that ensues from this understanding of gender or the difficulties it might entail. In the next chapter, therefore, I will explore Butler's gender politics.

3

Towards a Subversive Gender Politics

Gender Trouble ends with a conclusion entitled 'From Parody to Politics'. It is no exaggeration to say the one feature of Butler's work that has generated controversy and misunderstanding aplenty is the idea of parody. Taken by some to signal a politics of dressing up, by others to mean a hyper-voluntarist politics where subjects can switch gender as easily as they can change clothes, and by yet others as sanctioning a mode of identity grounded in 'commodity culture', parody as politics has been both vigorously advocated and stringently rejected.[1] The first aim of this chapter, therefore, is to examine the relation between parody and politics that Butler sets out. My argument is that Butler does not sponsor a politics of parody; rather she advocates a politics of subversion focused on contesting the norms that sustain heteronormativity. The second aim of this chapter is to examine Butler's discussion of agency. Here I focus on a particular paradox: that Butler is read by her critics as supporting *both* a voluntarist politics where the subject is fully autonomous *and* a form of determinism in which the subject as the product of power/discourse has no scope for autonomous action. I will contest both interpretations and instead will demonstrate how the introduction, in *Bodies that Matter*, of the idea of iterability as integral to performativity allows Butler to develop a non-voluntarist account of agency. Since many of Butler's readers found her account of the body slightly perplexing, the final section of the chapter concerns the place of the body in Butler's theory of gender. It focuses specifically on the notion of materiality. I will explore the relation between discourse and materiality, paying particular attention to the concept of materialization. I will also consider briefly the idea of abjection and how Butler uses it to identify the bodies that matter politically.

From parody to politics

In the original preface to *Gender Trouble*, Butler sets out her political stall thus: 'As a strategy to denaturalize and resignify bodily categories, I describe and propose a set of parodic practices based in a performative theory of gender acts that disrupt the categories of the body, sex, gender and sexuality and occasion their *subversive resignification and proliferation beyond the binary frame*' (*GT*: xxxi, my emphasis). We saw in the previous chapter that Butler believes that drag exposes the imitativeness of gender *per se*. She thus deploys the example of drag to cast doubt on the naturalness of what is being imitated. Instead, she argues that the original is itself a parody of the idea of an original gender identity (*GT*: 41). This would imply, therefore, that *all* gender is parodic. What does it mean, then, to contend that 'a set of parodic practices' forms the basis for the subversion of gender norms, especially if parody is also central to the naturalization of gender? Moreover, how can the practice of subversive repetition usher in what Butler calls a 'new configuration of politics'; one not based on the belief that politics must express the pre-given interests of a 'set of ready-made subjects' (*GT*: 189)? How, in other words, do we get from parody to politics?

Here it is worth returning briefly to the essay 'Performative Acts'. In this essay, Butler explains what she means by the 'politics of performative acts'. This politics, she writes, relies upon two elements: a redescription of current gender identities and a 'prescriptive view about the kind of gender reality there ought to be'. In the previous chapter, we explored how Butler redescribes gender identity as a set of performative practices. What, though, of the 'prescriptive' aspect of such a politics? First, she notes, it has to recognize that the elements producing an identity-effect (gestures, acts, corporeality, clothing, physicality, etc.) '*express nothing*' about that identity. After all, Butler rejects theories of gender where gender is said to be an expression of sex. Second, it has to be a form of politics that can recognize the present 'complexity of gender' and allow it to flourish 'without punitive consequences' ('PA': 530). It has, that is, to be able to validate already existing though currently pathologized forms of gendered subjectivity. The politics of performative acts is thus a politics focused on challenging the naturalness of heterosexuality. It is a subversive politics.

Hitherto, feminists have typically adopted one of two broad approaches to politics: either reform or emancipation. Those committed to reform, typically liberal feminists, saw the role of feminist politics as bringing about changes in the economic, political and social condition of women in order to render them equal to men. They thus sought to eradicate gender-based discrimination primarily through legislation. So reform feminists campaigned for a variety of laws designed to ensure women's equality, including most notably sex discrimination, equal opportunities and equal pay legislation. In short, reform feminists concentrated their efforts on petitioning the state for particular rights. Their political goal was to transform the system from within. In contrast, other feminists, including radical feminists, argued that the only way to transform gender relations was to overthrow the existing gender order.[2] Their political objective was, therefore, to emancipate women from the dominant sex/gender system. As Wendy Brown notes, revolutionary feminism was thus committed to 'seizing the conditions through which gender is made' and transforming them.[3] The existing sex/gender system had to be eliminated and a new order 'beyond gender' created. We saw in the previous chapter that Rubin, Firestone and Millett all aspire to a post-gender order of this kind where androgyny would replace binary sex difference. Revolutionary feminism assumes, therefore, that it is possible to gain control of the conditions producing sex and gender and to knowingly and intentionally overhaul them. It is thus a utopian project: a form of what Lucy Sargisson, following Lyman Tower Sargent, calls 'social dreaming' based on the desire for an alternative and better future.[4] Butler refuses both these options. As will become clear, she neither seeks to challenge heteronormativity by demanding rights for excluded sexual minorities nor argues for an overthrow of the current gender system and the inauguration of an alternative in its place.[5] Instead, as already indicated, the politics of performative acts as she understands it is a subversive politics. Butler is not alone in favouring subversion over reform or revolution. Before we examine the contours of her particular account, therefore, it is helpful to consider an alternative formulation, albeit one Butler rejects, namely Kristeva's.

Subversive gender politics

Chapter 3 of *Gender Trouble*, entitled 'Subversive Bodily Acts', begins with Butler's discussion of Kristeva. The issue that concerns Butler is Kristeva's account of the semiotic. In her work, Kristeva fuses together ideas drawn from semiology (the study of sign systems) with some from Lacanian psychoanalysis. In particular, Kristeva takes over Lacan's idea of the symbolic. This is the realm of language, of social order and law. In psychoanalytic terms it is post-oedipal: that is, it refers to the time when the child becomes conscious of itself as an individuated subject and when it enters the realm of language, culture and law, when it is able to follow rules. This is where the so-called Law of the Father prevails. Kristeva contrasts this with the semiotic. This is the pre-linguistic or pre-symbolic space, and is associated by psychoanalysts with the pre-oedipal phase when the infant child cannot distinguish between its own body and its mother's body. The semiotic, as a consequence, is intrinsically connected with the maternal body, a body that furnishes the first source of movement, touch, sound and rhythm for the child. When the child enters language, according to Kristeva, the semiotic is repressed; it is shunted into the unconscious realm. For Kristeva, however, this repression is never complete – and this is where it gathers its political significance – for the semiotic is always capable of disrupting the symbolic.[6]

The issue that concerns Butler is that Kristeva sees the semiotic as furnishing a *feminine* site of subversion against the patriarchal law of the symbolic. Kristeva is only able to make this argument, however, because she conceives of the maternal body and maternity as prior to culture, an argument Butler contests. Butler's critique of Kristeva thus contains three elements, two of which I will just state here since they are dealt with in the next chapter. First, Kristeva fails to contest the structuralist claim that paternal law itself generates culture. Second, and following on from this, she simply assumes the cultural necessity of heterosexuality and, as such, projects homosexuality outside of culture as psychosis. Thirdly, and this is the key point for our current discussion, while Kristeva concedes that the symbolic can be disrupted by the semiotic, it cannot be transformed by these disruptions. In this respect, the semiotic cannot be understood as a 'rival cultural possibility' to the symbolic that might replace it (*GT*: 108) but is rather always subordinate to the symbolic (*GT*: 112). As Butler interprets her, Kristeva's aim is simply 'to validate those experiences within the symbolic that permit a manifestation of the borders which divide the symbolic from the semiotic' (*GT*: 108–9). Moreover, given that semiotic subversion is intermittent and transient, it can never be a 'sustained political practice' (*GT*: 103). So what is it precisely that leads Kristeva, in Butler's estimation, to develop such an apparently ineffective politics?

The answer, for Butler, is quite straightforward. By designating the semiotic – the pre-linguistic and pre-symbolic realm – as the site of subversion, Kristeva locates subversion outside of culture and this immediately negates its political potential. Because semiotic subversion is not an 'effective or realizable cultural practice' (*GT*: 112) it cannot alter the terms that determine the legitimacy or intelligibility of any particular subject. As a way of exemplifying this, Butler considers Kristeva's account of the female body. The drive-dominated female body, according to Kristeva, is prior to signification. Butler disagrees. Drawing on Foucault, she argues that the body is, in fact, a cultural construct, both prone to cultural variation in how it is understood and amenable to alternative cultural possibilities.[7] The idea of the female body as dominated by drives is the effect of 'an historically specific organization of sexuality' (*GT*: 118): one that establishes motherhood as mandatory for all women. The problem with Kristeva's account, according to Butler, is that it effectively conceals the relations of power through which compulsory motherhood is generated and extended. Consequently, her theory simply reproduces heterosexual maternity as inevitable and necessary.

Butler is not quibbling with Kristeva's contention that culture negates women's bodies; she accepts this. She is challenging the way Kristeva positions the radical element in her work (the semiotic) fully outside of culture (*GT*: 117–18). It is not only Kristeva who comes in for this criticism, however. Ultimately, Wittig, Foucault, Lacan and Žižek are all accused of the same error. By conceiving subversion as outside of culture, whether in the imaginary (Lacan), the real (Žižek), pre-discursive libidinality (Wittig) or pre-discursive heterogeneous bodily pleasures (Foucault), all mask rather than illuminate the cultural operations of power,[8] for, as Butler theorizes it, one of the ways in which discourse works is to construct an element as outside of – or prior to – culture. This element is then presented as natural or incontrovertible, when in actuality it is neither. It is an effect of discourse presented as if it were not. This raises an obvious question. If subversion cannot be located outside of culture, since the idea of the outside is the artificial construct of discourse within a specific ensemble of power relations, then where does it take place? The answer is equally obvious. Effective subversion must be immanent to culture. It must be a form of *cultural subversion*. How, then, does Butler develop this idea with respect to heteronormativity?

Performativity and subversion

One of the problems in endeavouring to assess Butler's own conception of subversion is that it is developed almost entirely in the context of her critical readings of other theorists; in terms, that is, of her genealogical feminism.[9] We have, therefore, to read between the lines in order to identify what Butler perceives as subversion's essential features. Given that she reprimands Kristeva for advocating an account where the symbolic is able to recuperate that which disrupts it (semiotic subversion), Butler's own account must surely be one where subversion has the capacity to transform the symbolic in some way. Secondly, where Kristeva appears content to accept that certain gender identities (the lesbian, for instance) belong to, and will remain within, the pre-cultural realm, Butler is not. Her aim is rather to seek cultural legitimacy and intelligibility for those presently denied it under heteronormativity. Finally, as noted above, since Butler criticizes Kristeva et al. for locating subversion outside of culture, subversion as she understands it must be a cultural practice. So what are the key elements of Butler's version of a politics of subversion?

Agency, as Butler presents it (and I will return to this in Chapter 5) is intimately connected with signification. Signification, according to her, refers to the process that establishes the terms of intelligibility or meaning. Signification is thus a practice. Moreover, it is a practice based on repetition. It is precisely the repetition of acts, gestures and discourses that produces the effect of an identity at the moment of action. Agency, for Butler, might be thought of, then, as an effect of signification and resignification. The possibility of producing 'alternative domains of cultural intelligibility', in particular non-heteronormative domains, rests on this necessity to repeat and on the potential to repeat differently. Indeed, for Butler, 'it is only *within* the practices of repetitive signifying that a subversion of identity becomes possible'. It is the only way to challenge the 'rigid codes of hierarchical binarisms' that sustain heteronormativity (*GT*: 185). What, therefore, might count as a subversive repetition capable of contesting the naturalization of heterosexuality? The short answer is those 'parodic styles' (*GT*: 176), as Butler terms them, that are patently imitative; that denaturalize what they are performing by displaying explicitly the ways in which the natural is produced. These are repetitions, in other words, that openly reveal their status as performative constructions. Here I want to pause briefly to consider the case of drag, since this is a topic upon which Butler's critics has expended much time and ink.

Drag is an obvious example of the way that the constructedness of gender might be exposed. Additionally, it is an example, as we have seen, that Butler herself refers to when seeking to demonstrate that all gender is imitative. Were readers right then in assuming, as Eve Sedgwick puts it, that drag as a practice had a unique and central place in the 'idiom' through which heteronormative gender could be subverted?[10] Was a subversive politics necessarily, or primarily, a *politics of drag*?[11] Intriguingly, drag actually figures comparatively little in the pages of *Gender Trouble,* and not once in the book's index. So why did her readers assume parody/subversion meant drag? Two factors, in my view, are relevant here: first, the proximal discussions of parody and drag in the text; and, second, the context in which the book was composed.[12] I will deal with each in turn.

Butler's initial discussion of parody follows immediately on from her consideration of the practice of drag (considered in the previous chapter). When she returns to parody in her conclusion, therefore, it appears some of her readers assumed that parody equated directly with drag. So when Butler advocated a subversive politics predicated upon the parodic (that is, imitative) nature of identity, this was taken (by some) to mean that drag – or, more loosely, dressing up – symbolized subversion *per se*. Further confirmation for such an interpretation appears to be offered in the original preface to *Gender Trouble,* where Butler considers John Waters' film *Female Trouble* about drag star Divine. Butler's treatment of Divine takes place in the context of her discussion of the idea of gender *trouble.* From this it is easy to infer that drag is a way to trouble – subvert – gender norms. So one of the reasons readers were led to interpret subversion as a politics of drag is an effect of certain ambiguities in Butler's argument in *Gender Trouble*. Does this mean, however, that drag is *never* an example of subversion? In my view, it does not. Drag under the right conditions (see below) might well be subversive. The point is that it is not *ipso facto* subversive. Furthermore, subversion cannot be reduced to drag for there are other ways to contest the norms that sustain the heterosexual matrix.

There is, however, a second factor that may have influenced not just some of her readers but Butler herself. This returns us to an issue discussed in the first chapter: developments in gay and lesbian politics. Sexuality cannot simply be read off the body. For this reason, as Cvetkovich notes, various 'codes and conventions', including 'performances', were deployed amongst gays and lesbians in order to convey their identity to another.[13] One gay practice of note here is camp, which David Halperin describes as a form of 'parody, exaggeration, amplification, theatricalization, and literalization of normally tacit codes of conduct'.[14] When Butler discusses drag in *Gender Trouble* she draws directly on writings on camp, most notably Esther Newton's book *Mother Camp*. Moreover, when she considers parody, Butler expressly refers to existing parodic 'cultural practices' such as drag, cross-dressing and 'the sexual stylization of butch/femme identities' (*GT*: 174) to exemplify her argument. *Gender Trouble* is thus, without a doubt, influenced and informed by what was happening within sexual minority politics at the time of its composition.[15] Since, in this context, 'camp', broadly speaking, was perceived as a 'form of cultural resistance', then it is perhaps no surprise that readers interpreted Butler's discussion of drag as a subversive political practice challenging heteronormativity.[16] Even though Butler subsequently modifies her discussion of drag, her understanding of radical gender politics nevertheless remains indebted to and continues to be inspired by the political forms practised within gay, lesbian and queer circles. In particular, the types of theatrical performance central to the 'antihomophobic strategies' of groups such as ACT UP and Queer Nation figure repeatedly in her work over time.[17] But where does all this leave us in understanding the relation between subversion and feminism?

Subversion is made possible by the necessity to repeat that is essential to gender performativity. Such a repetition is more likely to be subversive, according to Butler, when it exposes what is taken to be natural or authentic to a particular sex as simply an effect of the reproduction of particular norms, acts and gestures; in other words, when it compels us to question what is real. At such a time, the norms that define gender are not simply resisted; they are also (potentially) reworked. It is thus feminism's critical undertaking, according to Butler, to identify 'strategies of subversive repetition' (*GT*: 188). Feminists, in other words, have to identify how to destabilize gender norms. They have to determine when and where to intervene in practices of repetition so as to displace the norms facilitating repetition. They have, as Butler notes in her final sentence of the book, to identify 'local strategies for engaging the "unnatural"' in order to denaturalize the heteronormative gender order (*GT*: 190). A subversive gender politics, for Butler, on my reading, thus consists in three inter-related phenomena: agency understood as (re-)signification, denaturalization and the critical labour required to identify when and where gender norms might be challenged. Its aim: to create the space within which non-normative genders, sexes and sexualities might thrive.

Free will versus determinism

Demonstrating that subversive politics, for Butler, is not reducible to drag addresses one of the worries that critics had about her work, but it still leaves us with another. To what extent could a performative subject, that is, one produced through doing certain acts, contest heteronormativity? Some interlocutors, including the sympathetic, regarded Butler as legislating a voluntarist (even hyper-voluntarist) politics where subversive gender identities could be fabricated and reshaped at will; where subjects could deliberately make 'gender trouble'. Paradoxically, others argued that performativity was a form of determinism where, depressingly, subjects were inextricably locked into oppressive relations of power but unable to change them. Contemplating this paradox Julia Walker comments that Butler's theory 'appears to be premised upon a contradictory model of agency'. On the one hand, it suggests a limited, discursively constituted subject, while, on the other, it implies 'a voluntarist subject capable of exerting a parodistic will'.[18] Before I offer a possible explanation for this paradox, it makes sense to pause to consider how other feminists have conventionally understood agency, since this will assist our evaluation of the controversy sparked by Butler's writings.

Within feminism the dominant way of thinking about agency has been a (quasi-)Kantian one: that is, where actors are assumed to be independent of the socio-political world around them and where agency is construed as the capacity both to envisage particular projects and then to implement them according to one's free will. This is certainly the view that underpins both the emancipatory and reformist accounts of feminist politics discussed earlier. Both perspectives assume that humans are capable of making their own history and, thus, of shaping their own futures, though reformism ties that making and shaping to smaller-scale incremental change while revolutionary feminism yokes them to the possibility of constructing a social and political world according to a specific feminist blueprint. The net effect of this is that feminists have typically assumed that *collective* political action and social transformation *require* autonomous, self-directing, agents, a view that is put into doubt by Butler's theory of subjectivity. It would, however, be wrong to assume that the account of agency I have given exhausts all the formulations found within feminism. As Brown notes, feminists influenced (variously) by Beauvoir, Marx, psychoanalysis and Foucault have all been compelled to abandon the illusion that the world can be reshaped at will.[19] The specifics of the arguments vary but all of these accounts share an idea in common: that humans are 'deeply embedded or "situated" in social life'.[20] That is, their range of action is limited by factors such as their cultural location, their class position, their place in the sexual division of labour and/or their imbrication in the norms and practices through which social life is organized. Even though such thinkers tend to believe that human action is *conditioned* rather than *determined* by these factors, in that they hold on to the idea that there is some scope for agency rather than assuming that the subject is entirely controlled by their circumstances, nevertheless they all refuse the possibility that subjects can be completely emancipated or liberated from their situation. This is not to say that it is not possible to transform this situation; it is. It is rather to say that the situation cannot be deliberately and intentionally overhauled at will. This position is, as will become apparent, much closer to that adopted by Butler; the difference is that some of the latter accounts, as Barvosa-Carter notes, assume that there is some feature of the self that escapes conditioning and that this is the well-spring from which agency arises. They rely, that is, on something *pre-discursive* to ground agency.[21] This, of course, is a possibility that Butler rejects. So how does she conceive of agency, and what explains the paradox identified at the outset of this section?

The first reason why commentators could not decide categorically if Butler is a voluntarist or a determinist is because of the tension in her work between performativity understood as constitutive of the subject and a more theatrical sense of performance where an actor volitionally plays a part. This can be seen readily in Seyla Benhabib's early influential response to Butler in 'Feminism and the Question of Postmodernism'. Erroneously assuming that Butler's account of performativity was indebted to that of sociologist Erving Goffman, Benhabib reads Butler as advancing an understanding of gender performativity as a form of 'self-constitution'.[22] For Goffman, identities derive from the performance of socially approved roles. In this 'dramaturgical' approach, the individual is able consciously to use her/his body to produce different effects.[23] They are able to produce an identity. Thus when Benhabib writes: 'If we are no more than the sum total of the gendered expressions we perform, is there ever any chance to stop the performance for a while, to pull the curtain down, and let it rise only if one can have a say over the production of the play itself?', it is clear that she has interpreted Butler as offering a theatrical model of performance.[24] To recall the argument of the previous chapter, in so doing Benhabib is not entirely wrong, for Butler's theory of performativity is informed by an account of theatrical acts. This theatrical model, however, was deployed by Butler not to exemplify how gendered identities are produced but to explain the *collective* dimensions of performativity.

A second reason for the paradoxical readings of Butler (both as voluntarist and as determinist, two mutually exclusive positions) has to do with the assumptions of her critics concerning what a feminist conception of agency and politics ought to contain. Benhabib thus contends that Butler's view of the subject as performatively constituted effectively puts an end to the idea of feminist emancipatory politics because it leads to the 'reduction of female agency to a "doing without the doer"'. Benhabib, that is, assumes that feminist politics requires a self who has some capacity for autonomous action – a doer. While herself acknowledging that the self is 'situated' in a specific historical and cultural context, Benhabib nevertheless believes that it can act to change its conditions. The self, as Benhabib understands it, can, in other words, determine its own future and make normative judgements about the nature of the oppression it suffers. A performatively constituted subject, however, lacks these essential capacities; it is, she remarks, without 'selfhood, agency, and autonomy', and the reason for this lies in the very notion of performativity, which reduces the subject 'into yet "another position in language"'.[25] In other words, the performative subject is fully determined. It has no scope for autonomous action.[26]

A similar position is adopted by one of Butler's other reviewers: Allison Weir. On the assumption that feminist politics requires a subject with the ability to act deliberately and consciously to change its situation, Weir concludes that Butler's analysis of gender suffers because it is grounded in a 'metaphor of identity and of language which effectively undermines any possibility of the subversion of repressive identities' since it conceives of language as entirely repressive. Indeed, Weir charges Butler with making identity 'so omnipotent and intransigent that subversion becomes impossible'.[27]

As a result, Butler's theory lacks a 'meaningful concept of agency'.[28] Oddly, it is precisely the thing that Benhabib and Weir see as central to a feminist conception that they declare absent from Butler's work, namely the presence of an autonomous and reflective human being, that other writers discern there and proclaim problematic. As Amy Allen observes, when individuals are viewed as 'capable of performing heterosexist norms' so as to parodically denaturalize heteronormativity and deny its originality, 'the spectre of voluntarism' appears. Instead of worrying that subjects cannot act, the difficulty now appears to be that we can 'consciously and willfully' decide 'how to enact our gender' in any way we think fit.[29] This means, for Susan Bordo, for instance, that despite her awareness of the normalizing contexts of 'phallocentrism and heterosexism' within which her 'parodic bodily "texts" live', Butler displays 'a characteristically postmodern inclination to emphasize and celebrate resistance, the creative agency of individuals, and the instabilities of current power-relations rather than their recuperative tendencies'.[30] She is thus charged with paying too little heed to how power limits what subjects are able to do. So, how it is possible to account for these contradictory interpretations?

The answer, in my view, has to do with Butler's attempt to rethink agency. Rather than adhere to one side of the free will–determinism binary assumed by many of her critics, Butler attempts to articulate a conception of political action that overcomes or dissolves this opposition.[31] Central to this is the idea, for Butler, that the practices that produce gendered subjects are also the sites where critical agency is possible. Instead, therefore, of seeing these practices in relentlessly negative terms as what needs to be overcome or eliminated in order to liberate subjects from the strictures of heteronormativity, she sees them as the material of social transformation. We have already seen that some feminists do not follow a Kantian line in assuming a subject independent of its social world. Instead, they see the subject as embedded or situated. As noted, however, many of these latter thinkers still subscribe to the idea that agency resides in a pre-discursive element of the self that is outside or beyond culture and history in some way. While Butler is closer in her thinking to this second cohort, in her writing she emphatically rejects the idea that subversion resides in a site or quality prior to or outside of discourse. Instead she develops Foucault's insight that power relations not only limit but also enable possibilities of (political) action (*GT*: 158). It is this argument that allows her to contend that, although there is no feature of the subject that is pre-discursive, agency still exists. The gendered subject, that is, may be constituted but it is not determined.

To be determined is to lack agency. It is to be programmed to behave in a particular way without the space to improvise or to change that behaviour. Constitution, for Butler, is different. This is because performativity has a temporal dimension; it depends on the repetition of those acts constitutive of the subject. It is, in other words, an on-going and never-ending process grounded in 'the compulsion to repeat' (*GT*: 185). Constitution is distinguished from determination, therefore, by the need perpetually to reproduce the gestures and styles of the flesh that generate gender as an effect. Crucially, it is in this compulsion to repeat these gestures and styles that agency resides. Agency is not, therefore, a property of the subject (an innate quality it has); it is, rather, an element of signification and repetition. What remains unclear at this point in Butler's argument, however, is what it is about repetition *per se* that allows for variations in gender performance and thence social change.[32] How, in other words, is it possible to navigate between norms and acts so as to subvert or transform heteronormativity? Since the account of performativity developed in *Gender Trouble* is clearly insufficient to answer these questions, Butler needs to amend it in some way. This is why, I suggest, she borrows the idea of iterability from Derrida.

Enter iterability

In *How to Do Things with Words*, speech-act theorist J. L. Austin makes a distinction between language that describes the world, *constative* utterances, and language that performs an action as it is said, *performative* utterances. Although he later abandons this distinction, introducing an alternative schema to which we will return in Chapter 5, for our purposes what is significant is that Butler, via Derrida, appropriates from Austin the idea that language is performative. Butler's purpose in revisiting her original conception of performativity is, recall, to make clearer that her account of agency is a non-voluntarist account (i.e. it is not based on free will). This is why when she commences her reformulation of performativity, she argues that it must *not* be thought of as 'a singular or deliberate "act"' by which 'a subject brings into being what she/he names'. It is not, that is, the activity of an autonomous subject purposely endeavouring to create the particular gender identity they have decided upon (the voluntarist position). Instead, Butler (re)defines it as 'a reiterative and citational practice' or, as she comments a little later on, as the 'reiterative power of discourse to produce the phenomena that it regulates and constrains' (*BTM*: 2). Here, drawing on Derrida's reading of Austin, she now begins to conceptualize performativity as a 'citational' practice.

When we think of a citation, we usually have in mind the act of directly repeating the words of another; of quoting them. Derrida's use of the term is not dissimilar. He too uses it to convey the idea of repetition. One of the distinctions that Austin draws when setting out his speech-act theory is that between authentic speech-acts and so-called 'etiolations' or 'parasitic' utterances. Where the former are serious, intentional and singular uses of language in everyday life, the latter are '*in a peculiar way* hollow or void if said by an actor on the stage, or if introduced in a poem, or spoken in soliloquy'.[33] In 'Signature Event Context', Derrida takes issue with Austin's division between authentic and parasitic language. Against Austin he argues that it is not only parasitic utterances that are citations; rather, all utterances are citations – they all repeat particular terms. This is necessary for communication to take place. As he asks in a passage frequently quoted by Butler:

> Could a performative utterance succeed if its formulation did not repeat a 'coded' or iterable utterance, or in other words, if the formulae that I pronounce in order to open a meeting, launch a ship or a marriage were not identifiable as conforming with an iterable model, if it were not then identifiable in some way as a 'citation'?[34]

For Derrida it is precisely the fact of citationality (the repetition of linguistic signs) that enables us to understand what is being said, whether in real life, on a theatre stage or in a film. We are thus able to identify a marriage from the form of words, specifically 'I do', used during the ceremony (be it real or fictional). All language use, according to Derrida, involves the practice of citation and thus depends on what he terms the condition of 'general iterability'.[35] Or, to put it another way, all language operates according to certain conventions of use. Consequently, as Allen notes, for Derrida 'the performative utterance becomes a derivative citation rather than a founding act by an originating subject'.[36] Linguistic performativity, as Derrida understands it, therefore, challenges the idea of an autonomous subject sovereign over its speech, able to say whatever it wants and mean words in any way it likes. Speech is, rather, always contingent on convention (on, that is, its prior uses). This does not signal, however, that the meanings of particular signs are permanently fixed. When terms are recited, they can be recited in novel and unforeseen ways and so their meaning can change. As a result, convention only ever partially conditions the usage of specific terms.[37]

How, then, does Butler integrate Derrida's insights into her own work? Butler, as we have seen, conceives of gender as always already imitative: that is, based on repetition. In her case, what is being repeated is the particular repertoire of gestures and corporeal acts that generate the effect of a gendered identity, say femininity. The Derridean concept of citationality (or iterability) allows Butler to refine her account of performativity.[38] To think of a discourse as constitutive, she now argues, is to conceive of it as a practice of repetition; as the recycling of a specific set of conventions (*BTM*: 107). As such, discourses have to be understood as historical. Their force – or effectiveness – derives from the fact that the conventions that underpin them have accreted over time. Accordingly, to gain and/or maintain authority, a set of practices must be repeated or recited again and again. To construe gender as performatively produced, therefore, is to reject the idea that gender is the result of 'the exercise of an unconstrained voluntarism'; instead, it is to think of it as an effect of the 'forced recitation of norms' (*BTM*: 94; see also *BTM*: 231). We recognize certain behaviour as feminine, in other words, because it recites those practices that *over time* have come to acquire authority as indications of femininity, be that sitting with one's knees together, swaying one's hips as one walks or not interrupting others when they speak. The point is not, however, that the repetition necessary to performativity is 'performed *by* a subject'; it is that 'this repetition is what enables a subject' (*BTM*: 95). The feminine subject is only a feminine subject because of this repetition. Far from being chosen, therefore, femininity is an effect of the 'forcible citation of a norm' (*BTM*: 232).

Gender, on this reading, has the same citational structure as language: specific signs have to be repeated in order to produce a particular effect. It is not, however, just that certain norms are cited; it is that they are *forcibly* cited. The norms that are repeated are thus both deeply imbricated in relations of domination, reprimand and control (think of the risks that attach when gender is done wrongly) *and* they are inescapable. They operate from the very moment a child is born, when the medical authorities interpellate the child into one or other sex ('it's a boy!' or 'it's a girl!'), through all the various 'gendering' repetitions by other agencies and persons, until the moment of death. The recitation of gender norms is thus imperative if a person is to count and persist as a credible gendered subject throughout their life (*BTM*: 7–8). If Butler's earlier treatment of gender performativity had, perhaps, implied a fairly permissive understanding of the scope for change, her revised account places far greater emphasis on the constraints and limitations underpinning gender performativity. She still recognizes the instability inherent within performativity but, where in *Gender Trouble* this instability appeared to open up possibilities for destabilizing and reconfiguring heteronormativity, from *Bodies that Matter* onwards instability is *also* seen as central to the consolidation of heteronormativity.

Gender, as a performative, requires the mandatory and forced reproduction of a particular range of normalized practices – or, as Butler formulates it, it 'cannot be understood outside of a process of iterability, a regularized and constrained repetition of norms' (*BTM*: 95). When those practices are performed against the norm, at least one of two results can ensue: either a subversive denaturalization takes place where gender norms may be reconfigured in such a way as to contest and partially transform heteronormativity *or* the person who performs them is punished for behaving unnaturally. (In *Undoing Gender* Butler cites innumerable examples of the punishments meted out to those who fail to do their gender properly.) Does this enhanced emphasis on the compulsory repetition of gender norms mean that Butler also now views agency in a more restricted fashion? Has she, as it were, shifted to a determinist position? I think not.

When Butler rejects the idea of the autonomous individual free to transform their world, the difficulty she has is to explain how constituted subjects are, nevertheless, able to act. The idea that she turns to in order to enable her to elaborate her position more lucidly is Foucault's concept of *assujetissement*, usually translated as either subjectivation or subjectification, by which Foucault means 'that the subject is constituted through practices of subjection'.[39] In *The Psychic Life of Power* Butler renders this idea as 'the process of becoming subordinated by power as well as the process of becoming a subject' (*PLP*: 2). This captures the dual dimensions of subjectivation: that power acts on an individual in order to 'activate' a subject (*PLP*: 83). At the very moment at which the individual is dominated by power, in other words, he or she becomes a subject capable of action. Or, more specifically, at the moment the individual is subjected to gender norms, he or she becomes a gendered subject who can resist those norms. Subjection and agency are, therefore, inextricably entwined. One of the criticisms of Foucault's account is that he is unable to show that the subject generated in submission is not a determined subject.[40] By contrast, Butler's discussion of subjectivation, her critics claim, addresses precisely this question. She sets out, in other words, to identify the ways in which subjection by power produces possibilities for agency. Here lies the significance of citationality. The norms producing gender require repeating – reciting – in order to have effect. They are, in this sense, the condition of possibility for gendered subjectivity. Without their repetition, gendered subjects would not exist. It is also the fact that they must be repeated, however, that creates the space for them to be repeated differently and thus is also the condition of possibility for action.[41] The need to repeat thus allows for citations that contort or impair the very norms they are intended to fortify. As such, gender is constitutively unstable and it is, as Butler puts it, 'this instability [that] is the *de*constituting possibility in the very process of repetition' (*BTM*: 10).

It should be apparent that Butler's account clearly differs from those discussed earlier in terms of how it understands the relation between norms and action. The ability to act is central to a voluntarist account of agency; it is what allows norms to be overcome. By contrast, determinism stresses the operation of norms as reducing the scope for or, indeed, the possibility of action. Butler rejects both positions and plots a more complex link between norms and action in which norms both restrict and enable action. The two are, as it were, co-implicated. For this reason, agency, as Butler understands it, has no 'formal existence' as such. Unlike Weir or Benhabib, for instance, Butler does not conceive of agency as a personal attribute or capacity of the individual. Instead, agency is an effect that exists purely in its operation: it is, she asserts, *'always and only a political prerogative'* ('CF': 13) caught up within the very power relations it attempts to resist (*BTM*: 241). Agency thus inheres in the regulatory repetition of the very norms that sustain the system – heteronormativity – that is being resisted and amended. It is because such norms are not always efficacious, that is, they do not always succeed, that they can be exploited. Such exploitation creates the possibility for, though it cannot assure the success of, subversion.

The merit of Butler's revised account is that it explains more clearly why subversion is immanent and why performativity entails neither voluntarism nor determinism. In both cases, this is because of the citational structure of performativity, which means that subversion is always a form of 'reinscription of existing contexts'.[42] Gender subversion involves, that is, recontextualizing and reciting the elements constitutive of sex and gender so as to alter their meaning and significance. Butler thus folds into her (Foucauldian) account of the regulatory effect of norms an explanation of how gender works both as a mechanism of constraint and as the locus of productive (agential) activity. In so doing, she is able to steer a course between free will and determinism, between acts and norms, and thus belatedly to refute some of the criticisms levelled at her.[43] Moreover, this blending of Foucauldian and Derridean elements also allows her to lay the groundwork for the account of *linguistic* agency that she develops most fully in *Excitable Speech*, which I will discuss in Chapter 5.

Having outlined Butler's revised views on agency, I now want to return to the question of drag.

The ambivalence of drag

I argued above that in *Gender Trouble* Butler does not explicitly petition for a politics of drag, suggesting only that heteronormativity needs to be subverted politically from within. Nevertheless, some of her readers interpreted her as if she had. In order to address this misreading, Butler returns in *Bodies that Matter* to the question of drag. The denaturalization of gender norms, she now explains, building on her explanation of performative agency, can work both to subvert gender norms and to reinforce them (and sometimes both). Citing the performances of Dustin Hoffman in *Tootsie*, Julie Andrews in *Victor/Victoria* and Jack Lemmon in *Some Like It Hot*, Butler declares that types of drag articulated by 'heterosexual culture' are not subversive. Although they reveal the imitative structure of gender – and thus implicitly concede that heterosexuality is no more natural than any other form of sexuality (which is, arguably, a potentially subversive move) – for Butler, they reinforce heteronormativity. All threat of homosexuality, that is, is deflected through the heterosexual resolution of the film narrative (*BTM*: 126): the boy who is a boy gets a girl who is a girl.[44] In essence, drag in this context operates to re-idealize heterosexual norms without interrogating them (*BTM*: 231).

Even those drag performances that non-heterosexual culture produces, however, cannot be construed as *ipso facto* subversive, though they may have greater potential to function in this manner.

Examining Jennie Livingston's documentary *Paris is Burning*, about the drag balls in New York, Butler highlights some of the ways in which drag, although denaturalizing gender norms, still fails to subvert heteronormativity. One of the features of the drag balls is that the participants (Black and Latino men) compete for prizes in various categories ('Executive Realness', 'Miss Cheesecake' or 'Ivy League Student'). They are judged on their skill in achieving a standard of 'realness', which is measured by 'the ability to compel belief, to produce the naturalized effect' (*BTM*: 129). Clearly a performance that succeeds in attaining such a standard is precisely one in which the norms defining the category must be embodied in such a way that their imitativeness is *not* obvious. It is hard to see such performances as subversive. Indeed, one might argue that they effectively reinforce hegemonic gender (and race) norms. This reinforcement, at times, exacts a high price, as the plight of Venus Xtravaganza demonstrates. Driven by the heteronormative dream of finding a man, getting married and having children, Venus attempts to 'pass' as a 'light-skinned woman' in the real world but is found strangled to death. The point is not just that her failure to embody naturalized (white) femininity fails to subvert heteronormativity (because she was discovered to be male and Black perhaps) and thus supports Butler's claim that drag is not *ipso facto* subversive. It is that her failure costs her her life; she dies because the symbolic operates, as Butler comments, to 'eradicate those phenomena that require an opening up of the possibilities for the resignification of sex' (*BTM*: 131).

So, to reiterate, drag 'serves a subversive function' to the extent that it denaturalizes heterosexuality, but this denaturalization is no guarantee that heteronormativity will be weakened thereby. It might, in fact, unleash a response that seeks violently to quell any transformation of gender norms. This raises a question that has perplexed Butler's critics: how, then, is it possible to differentiate between a subversive and a non-subversive performance?[45] Butler's answer, such as it is in *Bodies that Matter*, is that subversion is more likely to follow when denaturalization 'calls into question the abjecting power that it sustains'. At these times, such 'an occupation or territorialization of a term . . . can become a site of resistance, the possibility of an enabling social and political resignification' (*BTM*: 231). This, she affirms, is what happened with the term 'queer'. Queer as a term is not in itself subversive; to the contrary, historically it has been a defamatory – heteronormative – term. In recent years, however, it has been resignified in such a way that it has come to validate the very subjects, lifestyles and practices it was originally used to denigrate.[46]

Subversion, therefore, is a problem of '*working the weakness in the norm*' that requires reiterating so as to sustain a given practice or regime. The 'critical promise' of drag as a practice, therefore, rests not with an increase of genders (as Butler seemed to imply in *Gender Trouble*) but with its potential to reveal 'the failure of heterosexual regimes ever fully to legislate or contain their own ideals' (*BTM*: 237). The same is true of queer: its current resignified usage goes beyond its conventional heteronormative usage. Commenting on its resignification, Butler observes that it involved a kind of 'theatrical' recitation that '*mimes and renders hyperbolic* the discursive convention that it also', and this is critical, '*reverses*' (*BTM*: 232). Simply denaturalizing heteronormative practices or discourses (through hyperbole and reversal) on its own, however, is not enough 'to establish and direct political struggle'. Such 'pure subversion', as Butler calls it, must be part of a broader strategy. Questions need to be asked about what counts as an 'affirmative resignification'. Thought needs to be given to the conditions necessary to 'establish and sustain bodies that matter' (*BTM*: 240). Time needs to be spent considering how to change the terms of cultural intelligibility. In this way, Butler makes far clearer how ambivalent drag is as a political practice. She also underlines the difficult political labour involved in the development of a subversive gender politics, given the constraints within which that politics must operate.

There is, however, one final area that we need to consider in relation to Butler's discussion of performativity, agency and gender politics, and this concerns the materiality of the sexed body. It is thus to Butler's discussion of materiality that we now turn.

The matter of bodies

Like other feminists of the early 1990s, Butler shares an interest in the body. The body is important to feminism for at least three reasons. First, Western thought from Descartes onwards has tended, by and large, to focus on the mind to the exclusion or devaluation of the body. One has only to think here of the Cartesian dictum 'I think therefore I am' (*cogito ergo sum*). The body here seems to have no impact on existence. Second, this mind/body dualism has been mapped more broadly onto the male/female binary, such that the body that is negated is the female body while the mind that is privileged is the male mind.[47] Women, thus, come to be associated with embodiment and lack of reason, while men are associated with rationality and body-transcendence. This, of course, is precisely the point that Beauvoir picks up in *The Second Sex*, discussed in the previous chapter. Third, and perhaps most significantly for Butler, the logic of the sex/gender distinction meant that the sexed body was construed within feminism as one of the primary sites upon which gender difference was constructed. How feminists responded to this insight varied, however. Some were content to accept that sex difference was natural, and that the sexed body was, as we saw earlier, logically and temporally prior to gender. The purpose of their investigations, therefore, was to find ways of retrieving the authentic female body from the clutches of patriarchy and liberating it to an unfettered female, feminine and/or feminist future. By contrast, Butler and others worried about feminism's essentialist reliance on the sexed specificities of the female body as the basis of its politics. Analytically, this second approach rejects sex as a natural or pre-given biological fact and sets out to explore how the sexed body is produced. In Butler's case, the sexed body is thus conceived as an effect of the heteronormative regime that regulates it. One of the factors that differentiate these two styles of thought is their ontological presuppositions about the body.

Ontology is a philosophical term that refers to the study of being. Traditionally, therefore, it has addressed itself to questions about the nature of reality – whether, for instance, an objective world exists. More recently, however, ontological concerns appear to have seeped into the social sciences and into contemporary political theories such as feminism. Here, as Stephen White suggests, ontology has come to be associated with 'a growing propensity to interrogate more carefully those "entities" presupposed in our typical ways of seeing and doing in the modern world'.[48] As such, it has become a critical tool in contesting particular ways of making sense of how society is ordered. This has led some critics, at least, to reject the idea of ontology as revealing fundamental, transhistorical or universal truths about the world. Instead, they argue that ontologies need to be historicized. In this way their assumptions can be exposed as contingent historical (discursive or linguistic) effects. Far from being objective and neutral, ontologies are political, locked into the power relations that order 'reality', and as such they are inherently contestable. One of the 'entities' interrogated in this way in contemporary thought, as White points out, has been the subject. Indeed, Butler's work on gendered subjectivity might legitimately be seen as part of this very interrogation. The entity that concerns us, however, is the body, and it too has been subject to ontological dispute, particularly amongst feminists.

Ahead of my discussion of Butler's account of materiality, I want to give a flavour of the divisions within feminism over the body by briefly reviewing some of the critical responses that her discussion of embodiment in *Gender Trouble* prompted. In *Gender Trouble,* Butler contends, amongst other things, that the body is 'never free of an imaginary construction', being '[a]lways already a cultural sign' (*GT*: 90); that there is no such thing as a 'real' body that exists outside of, or prior to, culture or, indeed, a reality that is not itself culturally instituted; and that the idea of a natural body falsely ontologizes what is actually a culturally fabricated physicality. To Butler's critics these claims are evidence that she is denying the brute facticity of the body. Martha Nussbaum thus decries Butler's inattention both to the corporeal realities of women's lives (including hunger, rape and brutalization) and to those aspects of the body that, according to Nussbaum, are not amenable to cultural manipulation, such as sex difference and women's special nutritional needs during pregnancy and lactation.[49] Commentators such as Carole Bigwood, Susan Bordo, Lynne Pearce and Lynne Segal similarly all draw attention to the apparently 'disembodied' nature of the body in Butler's writing.[50] Evidently unconstrained by any of its anatomical or biological features, the body, for Butler, seems to be an infinitely malleable entity that can 'take on almost limitless embodiments'.[51] For these feminists this misrepresents the body. Or, rather, it misrepresents the female body, since certain facts of female existence (pregnancy, childbirth, breastfeeding) curtail what that body can be or do. Sex difference, in other words, is an ontological truth of corporeality that shapes women's lives.

It might appear from Butler's own criticisms of Foucault that Nussbaum, Segal et al. are right: that Butler eschews the idea of a body prior to discourse. After all, she criticizes Foucault for relying on the idea of a pre-cultural body, 'a materiality prior to signification and form' (*GT*: 166). Further, she also contends that the body is not 'a "being"' (*GT*: 177) but is rather a 'set of boundaries' (*GT*: 44), constituted and regulated by power/discourse. The body, it seems, for Butler is a linguistic effect. Yet this is not quite correct. When Butler begins her reply to her critics in *Bodies that Matter*, she turns straight to the issue of materiality in order to confront the charge that 'surely bodies live and die; eat and sleep; feel pain, pleasure; endure illness and violence'. Here she concedes that there is something necessary and inescapable about these 'primary and irrefutable experiences' (*BTM*: xi; see also *BTM*: 66). Yet, recognizing this, she surmises, indicates nothing about how to acknowledge this necessity and inescapability. Butler is not, that is, conceding to her critics that they are right about there being particular indisputable facts about embodied existence. Her aim is to interrogate the nature of construction.

The body is not, Butler argues, reducible to discourse or language; however, it is only accessible through language. Fleshy corporeality can only be thought, spoken or written about via language, and linguistic 'constructions' are central to this process. Constructions might be thought of as frameworks for organizing and evaluating experiences; ways of understanding life. Butler is specifically interested in those constructions that have acquired an essential place in our thought processes, those that have become 'that "without which" we could not think at all' (the idea of binary sex, for example). It is the widespread acceptance of such constructions, she suggests, that means that 'bodies only appear, only endure, only live within the productive constraints of certain highly gendered regulatory schemas' (*BTM*: xi). So it is these regulatory schemas that are her focus. This helps to situate Butler in relation to those feminists noted above. Where they had assumed that sexual difference exists as a pre-cultural fact, Butler aims to demonstrate that this very way of looking at male–female relations is itself 'a cultural act'.[52] She thus seeks to problematize the very ontology of sexual difference that they presuppose *a priori* in their theories of corporeality. How does she go about this? She asks how the idea of sex difference has come to be construed as a 'sign of irreducibility' (*BTM*: 28), or what we might think of as a taken-for-granted assumption, within feminism.

Two theories have predominated in the debate over the relation between matter and ideas: idealism and materialism. Idealism, at its simplest, assumes that ideas determine the form that social, political and cultural existence takes. Ideas constitute reality. By contrast, materialism posits that matter, or objective reality, gives rise to ideas. Ideas thus reflect reality. An idealist account of the body would see it as the effect of ideas, while a materialist account would posit it as prior to and independent of ideas of the body. Butler has conventionally been read as offering a version of idealism or, in her case, of linguistic constructivism: that is, where language or discourse (rather than ideas) produces reality. The body, from this perspective, is conceived of exclusively as an effect of language or discourse, having no existence apart from them. In *Bodies that Matter*, Butler sets out to refute this interpretation of her work. She does so by revisiting the idea of construction. The point at issue, she avers, is not 'a theory of cultural construction' *per se* but what she obliquely terms 'a scenography and topography of construction'. This is the theoretical landscape wherein materiality and constructedness are construed as 'necessarily oppositional terms' (*BTM*: 28). This is because matter is conceived of philosophically as something that cannot be constructed or created by language or discourse. Butler wants to cast doubt on this opposition. (To simplify, we might read Butler as challenging the idealism–materialism binary noted above.) As Vicky Kirkby notes, Butler is faced with a difficult assignment 'for she has to juggle a critique of the discourse of construction while still defending its most basic tenets'.[53]

What are the steps in Butler's argument? She begins by clarifying her own position. She is not, she argues, either a linguistic idealist or linguistic monist (*BTM*: 6). She does not, in other words, assume that the body (or sex difference) is generated or determined purely by language. She contends that her interest in the negations that occur as a result of the heteronormative construction of bodies, sexes, genders and sexualities – remember that Butler's work is driven by a desire to contest what counts as a thinkable or liveable subject/body – means that she is not a constructivist; she is a deconstructionist. This is because her work emphasizes 'the constitutive force of exclusion, erasure, violent foreclosure, abjection and its disruptive return' (*BTM*: 8). Secondly, therefore, as a deconstructionist Butler neither denies nor presupposes materiality as an idealist or materialist, respectively, would. Her aim is to interrogate materiality: 'to free it from its metaphysical moorings in order to understand what political interests were secured in and by that metaphysical placing and thereby to permit the term to occupy and to serve very different political aims'. Since materiality means sex difference in this context, Butler's purpose is to identify what interests are served by pretending sex difference is a necessary and ineluctable feature of human existence. This ties into her gender politics. The purpose of interrogating materialism is to open up 'new possibilities, new ways for bodies to matter' (*BTM*: 30).[54] Third, and finally, therefore, Butler attempts to rethink corporeal matter.

Rejecting the idea of matter as either 'site or surface', she proposes to reconceptualize it as '*a process of materialization that stabilizes over time to produce the effect of boundary, fixity, and surface we call matter'* (*BTM*: 9). There are a number of claims that need unpacking here: that matter is the result of materialization; that the process of materialization is a temporal one – it takes place 'over time'; and that materialization produces stable, fixed and bounded matter. In the abstract, Butler's argument is somewhat opaque. Considered in relation to sex difference, however, her position becomes clearer. When Butler talks of materialization, she is talking about how particular ideas about the body come to have life, how they begin to order reality, and thence how they gather ontological force. With relation to binary sex, this means how that notion defines the body as a body. It does so through discourse. Matter, as Butler notes, cannot and does not escape signification since the body 'bears on language all the time' (*BTM*: 68); it is always already implicated in discourse. 'The body posited as prior to the sign, is always *posited* or *signified* as *prior'* (*BTM*: 30): that is, the process of signification generates the very body that is supposed to precede it. When feminists contend that the sexed body is the basis for women's oppression, their discourses produce that body as that basis. The sexed body is thus materialized through discourse as a sexed body. This is why when Butler contends that 'to be material means to materialize', she adds, 'where the principle of that materialization is precisely what "matters" about that body, its very intelligibility' (*BTM*: 32). Matter and meaning are inextricably linked. To materialize is to become meaningful; it is to fit within a particular frame of intelligibility, in this case *heteronormativity*. Heteronormativity is, as noted previously, sustained through the reiteration of regulatory norms. The materialization of sex involves normative violence. Categorizing bodies by sex is a way of imposing what Butler calls in 'Contingent Foundations' 'a duality and uniformity on bodies in order to maintain reproductive sexuality as a compulsory order' ('CF': 17; see also *BTM*: 33).[55] Repeated over time, the process of categorization fixes, bounds and stabilizes (to redeploy Butler's terms) what counts as a properly sexed body.

I began this section with a discussion of ontology, and I want to end similarly. Butler's focus is on ontology: she is concerned with the ontology of sex difference and how it secures particular effects in the world, in particular with why some bodies matter more than others and why some are accorded a legitimacy that others are denied. Like Foucault, she sees ontology as political ('HB': 278, 279). When she notes that she is 'not a very good materialist' because '[e]very time I try to write about the body, the writing ends up being about language' (*UG*: 198), Butler is not, in my view, confessing to linguistic idealism – to, that is, an ontological belief that the body *is* linguistically constructed. She is making an epistemological claim (about how we know the world) but one that, nonetheless, has bearing on her understanding of ontology.[56] Butler presupposes that it is never possible to access – or know – the reality of the entity called the body. Any attempt to think, talk or write about it, as she sees it, therefore, requires the use of language. As a consequence, all knowledge and understanding of the body is linguistically mediated. This means that it all has (to borrow words from a different context) 'a history and a historicity' that situates it (*BTM*: 67). Moreover, it all operates through exclusion. This is just as true of ontological claims as any other. It is, however, this very history/historicity and exclusiveness that, as we will see in the next section, renders specific ontologies amenable to contestation.[57]

Politicizing abjection – making bodies matter

If, as Butler speculates, violence is constitutive of regimes of intelligibility, and if the possibility for political change always inheres within culture, in what Kirkby calls 'the internal and interminable movement *within* language',[58] then Butler's body politics needs to be able to show how culturally *unintelligible* bodies are able to contest the normative violence that denies them. In setting up her argument, Butler creatively adapts Kristeva's idea of abjection. Kristeva utilizes abjection to refer to the process of jettisoning or radically excluding what is unclean, repulsive and improper in order for the speaking subject – and the symbolic – to exist.[59] Like Freud, therefore, Kristeva assumes that culture (or civilization, in his terms) is founded on the expulsion of the impure (particularly incestuous relations). What is more important for our purposes is that, unlike Freud, Kristeva contends that what has been barred nevertheless remains to haunt the security and stability of both the subject and the symbolic order.[60] The abject thus remains part of subjectivity and of culture, threatening both with potential dissolution. It is this idea that informs Butler's account of abjection.

As Butler uses it, the term 'abject' refers to those populations who are currently denied subject status, populations 'whose living under the sign of the "unlivable"', according to Butler, 'is required to circumscribe the domain of the subject' (*BTM*: 3). Abjection thus describes the process whereby certain persons are excluded from particular normative ideals of subjecthood. Abjection, then, is a question of ontology. Alongside those subjects who can 'lay claim to ontology' because they '*count* or *qualify* as real', there are those who 'do *not* have claim to ontology' and who are, in some sense, unreal. These are the abjects – or abject bodies – who fail to qualify as subjects. To illustrate: heterosexual bodies count as real within a heteronormative sexual ontology because they are constructed as natural and intelligible; homosexual bodies fail to count because the same ontology produces them as unintelligible or unnatural. So in contesting this sexual ontology it is, as Butler notes in *Bodies that Matter*, vital not just to examine how bodies are constructed and with what purpose, but also how and why certain bodies are '*not* constructed'. It is also important to explore, in her words, 'how bodies which fail to materialize provide the necessary "outside" . . . for the bodies which, in materializing the norm, qualify as bodies that matter' (*BTM*: 16). It is necessary, that is, to politicize abjection. Materialization, in Butler's sense, determines who matters. Clearly, then, in aiming to extend the 'field of possibilities for bodily life' it is necessary politically to contest the inadmissibility of particular bodies – those that fail to conform to the regulatory norms of society – to the realm of intelligibility ('HB': 277), for only in this way can questions be raised about 'what qualifies as bodies that matter, ways of living that count as "life", lives worth protecting, lives worth saving, lives worth grieving' (*BTM*: 16). This is the test that the abject poses to the dominant order. This is where the potential for radically altering hegemonic norms resides.

In saying that abject bodies fail to count as real bodies, Butler is not denying their physical existence. She is well aware that these bodies make their presence felt both 'in policy and politics'. Instead she is suggesting that the 'discursive life' abjects lead is a shadowy life, a life that has *yet* to qualify as legitimate and thinkable, as real ('HB': 277, 281). Nonetheless it is a discursive life and abjection is a discursive process.[61] This is important. The fact that abject bodies are not produced as bodies that matter in society does not mean, as Natalie Wilson appears to suggest, that they 'serve as a *material* outside' to culture.[62] Butler has not, that is, fallen back on a materialist explanation of the radical potential of abjection. Rather it is by dismantling *from within* the cultural codes through which certain bodies are projected as abject that change becomes possible. Regulatory regimes are sustained by reiteration. Reiteration lends itself to resignification. Resignification can lead to reconfiguration of the norms governing society. So, making ontological claims on behalf of those politically unimportant and unreal bodies is one way to contest, and reshape, the terms of cultural intelligibility. Discursively, a claim of this kind does not assume a particular ontology; it founds one ('HB': 280–1). In this respect, Elizabeth Grosz is surely right when she comments that in Butler's work, '[b]eing "important", having significance, hav[ing] a place, mattering, is more important than matter, substance or materiality'.[63] Indeed, for me, it is this emphasis on contesting the cultural terms that allocate value to particular groups or individuals that imbues Butler's discussion of the body with its political significance. In aligning matter with value, Butler makes clear that what concerns her is not matter *as such*; it is the mechanisms of denigration that lead certain bodies to become devalued. I will return to the question of normative violence and how it may be resisted in Chapter 6.

Conclusion

One of the areas where feminist readers have been most critical of Butler is with regard to her gender politics. Indeed, some have doubted that she has such a politics at all. The point that the debate turns on is the relation between performativity and agency. It is true that Butler rejects the idea of the autonomous agent able to stand back from their situation and decide how to intervene. This does not mean, however, that she denies the possibility of agency. She reconceptualizes it. Unlike many of her feminist interlocutors, Butler does not relate her understanding of agency to a theory of the self. She sees it as an effect of the operations of power/discourse and thus as a phenomenon that cannot be separated from context. This necessarily means that politics, as she understands it, is also related to context; this is why her politics is an immanent politics of subversion. More particularly, since norms determine which subjects count heteronormatively, the subversive gender politics she articulates is tied to reworking and, ultimately, undermining the norms and practices that produce heterosexuality as natural and compulsory. This also has a bearing on her understanding of the body. Some feminists have tried to ground feminist politics in an ontology of the female body. As we saw in this chapter, however, Butler is deeply sceptical of such moves because, for her, corporeal ontologies themselves are the products of particular historically specific discourses. Instead, therefore, of attempting to generate a theory of the body, one starting from certain general assumptions about that body, Butler explores the differential production *and valuation* of bodies within discourse. It is thus how specific bodies come to matter rather than the question of corporeal materiality that interests her. (We will come back to the body in Chapter 6.) Whether or not they agree with her, however, feminists cannot afford to ignore Butler's work precisely because it casts doubt on many of the most common assumptions about sex, gender, the body, politics and agency circulating throughout contemporary feminist thought today. This is where its importance lies.

4

Psychoanalysis and the Gendered Subject

It is no exaggeration to say that the idea of gender performativity sent shockwaves through the women's and the gay and lesbian movements. By contrast, Butler's psychoanalytic writings have had far less impact. Some readers largely ignore them. Others treat her critique of Freud and Lacan as simply an example of her broader position on heteronormativity – as no more nor less than a case-study. Amongst those who do engage with her psychoanalytic writings, several focus almost exclusively on *The Psychic Life of Power*, as if this were her only 'psychoanalytic' text. In this way Butler's psychoanalytic arguments are construed as dispensable, even 'aberrant', aspects of her overall theory. One of the difficulties for the reader, therefore, is knowing how to position Butler's engagement with psychoanalysis. Is it a wayward moment in her thought, a mere distraction from her real concerns? Or, are her interventions into psychoanalysis, in fact, central to her work? In my view, the latter interpretation is the more accurate. While Butler certainly does subject psychoanalysis to the same type of critique as other theories of sex/gender, including feminist versions, nevertheless a revised version of psychoanalysis remains central to her account of gendered subjectivity. She thus adopts a twin-track trajectory in relation to psychoanalysis: both critique and qualified endorsement. Failing to acknowledge this as a feature of her work from her earliest to her most recent writings is to fail to appreciate the full complexity of Butler's theory of subjectivity. It is this dual approach, therefore, that I examine in this chapter.

Butler touches on a wide range of psychoanalytic themes. For reasons of spatial economy, therefore, I have only highlighted those that I perceive to be the most significant. One of these is, without doubt, her extended critique of the Oedipus complex, an idea Butler consistently attempts to displace from its position of authority in psychoanalysis. Much of this chapter, therefore, will be spent exploring Butler's critical examination of this idea in Freudian and Lacanian thought, respectively. Given the link between the Oedipal scenario and the incest taboo, I also consider Butler's examination of psychoanalytic ideas of kinship, specifically in the work of Lacan, and the impact of these ideas in recent policy debates. As stated, Butler also deploys psychoanalysis in her own theory of subjectivity, so throughout the chapter I will in addition consider the key aspects of this, including, in particular, her acceptance of melancholia as the process constitutive of the (gendered) ego and her articulation, in *The Psychic Life of Power*, of an account of the psychic formation of subjectivity. The chapter ends with a brief review of some of the critical feminist responses that her psychoanalytic writings have elicited.

Gender Trouble and psychoanalysis

Desire is a central theme of Butler's work. In order to fully 'deconstruct the matrix of heterosexual desire', as Patricia Clough notes,[1] Butler needs to engage with psychoanalysis, the pre-eminent discourse of desire. Chapter 2 of *Gender Trouble* is devoted to exactly that. In it Butler offers deconstructive readings of Claude Lévi-Strauss's structuralist anthropology, which has been influential in Lacanian psychoanalysis, Joan Rivière's understanding of femininity as masquerade, Jacques Lacan's account of the relation between the incest taboo and the symbolic law, and Sigmund Freud's discussion of melancholia. She also touches on the work of Nicolas Abraham and Maria Torok, and their distinction between introjection and incorporation, as well as exploring Gayle Rubin's critique of the incest taboo, a critique that profoundly influences her own position. From the title of Chapter 2, 'Prohibition, Psychoanalysis, and the Production of the Heterosexual Matrix', a reader might suppose that the interpretation of psychoanalysis that Butler offers here will merely exemplify her broader point about heteronormativity developed throughout *Gender Trouble*: that is, that psychoanalysis is a discourse and practice oriented towards sustaining compulsory heterosexuality. In part, they would be right. Chapter 2 is concerned with the role that psychoanalysis plays in bolstering normative heterosexuality. But this chapter is also concerned with something else. Although not articulated fully at this stage, it is also concerned with developing a psychic conception of subjectivity. While this fully elaborated – psychoanalytic – theory must wait until *The Psychic Life of Power*, its beginnings can be discerned in *Gender Trouble* and, specifically, in the discussion of melancholia that Butler there enlarges upon. Before I look at this, however, it is first necessary to set the scene for Butler's own theory by examining two sets of ideas. The first relates to Gayle Rubin's 1975 essay 'The Traffic in Women', which I discussed briefly in Chapter 2. The second concerns the Oedipus complex, as defined by Freud.

Rubin and 'The Traffic in Women'

How and why is Rubin's essay so important to Butler? The answer is straightforward. In this essay, Rubin sets out a critique of the incest taboo. The incest taboo plays a pivotal role in psychoanalysis and, indeed, in cultural anthropology (Rubin's field). In terms of psychoanalysis, which is our concern, it is tied into the notion of the Oedipus complex, which I will consider shortly. In essence, the taboo establishes that sexual relations between blood relations are prohibited. As both Rubin and Butler read it, however, the taboo is not merely a benign prohibition; it is a prohibition that establishes what Rubin calls 'obligatory heterosexuality'.[2] It operates heteronormatively. Since it is Butler's ideas that are our focus, I will just sketch those of Rubin's claims that Butler draws on and identify some of the key differences between them.

Recall, Rubin is concerned with the development of the sex/gender system. Her critique of Freud, and of anthropologist Claude Lévi-Strauss, whose work *The Elementary Structures of Kinship* informs Lacan's understanding both of the incest taboo and of kinship, thus focuses on identifying how biological sex becomes the basis for an oppressive gender system. According to Lévi-Strauss there is a universal law that regulates the exchange of women in all kinship systems: this is the incest taboo, which ensures that women are exchanged between clans of men not related by blood. The incest taboo is crucial in two ways. First, as Butler puts it, it generates a non-incestuous heterosexuality (*GT*: 52), and, second, for

Lévi-Strauss and later Lacan, the taboo represents the crucial step in the transition from nature to culture. It inaugurates society. As both Rubin and Butler gloss it, the taboo leads to compulsory heterosexuality. How? According to Rubin, it does so in two ways: it 'divides the universe of sexual choice into categories of permitted and prohibited sexual partners', and it 'presupposes a prior, less articulate taboo on homosexuality';[3] two ideas Butler will take up. Rubin also hints at something else: she notes that the instantiation of the incest taboo through universal law does not allow 'enough latitude for the social structuring of the symbolic'.[4] The assumption as the basis of human culture of a single and unchangeable law against incest (which is grounded in the exchange of women) allows no space, in other words, for different ways of organizing social life. When we consider Butler's critique of Lacan, we will see that she adopts a similar position: she too resists the idea of an invariant and transcultural symbolic law.

From her analysis of the incest taboo Rubin concludes that 'it can be deduced that the world historical defeat of women occurred with the origin of culture, and is a pre-requisite of culture'.[5] Politically, her solution to women's oppression is thus to call for the elimination of compulsory sexualities and sex roles and for an androgynous 'genderless (though not sexless) society'.[6] The emancipatory utopianism of a genderless future is, of course, a far cry from the possibilities envisaged by Butler in *Gender Trouble*. Rubin and Butler also differ in their understanding of sex; Rubin plumping for the kind of biological and fixed understanding of sex that Butler contends is itself a gendered construct (and this difference is central to Butler's evaluation of Rubin in *Gender Trouble* [91–100]). Moreover, Butler argues that because Rubin believes all humans are sexually polymorphous, she adheres to an idea of 'sexuality "before the law"' rather than, as Butler would have it, sexuality as an effect of the law (*GT*: 94). And, of course, Rubin's account of kinship is ethnographically much richer than Butler's. Yet for all the differences, it is clear that much of the conceptual apparatus Butler deploys in her own analysis of Lévi-Strauss, Freud and Lacan is borrowed from Rubin's earlier text: her assumption of a prior prohibition on homosexuality, an understanding of heterosexuality as compulsory and a concern with the intractability of symbolic law.

The incest taboo is not simply of interest to anthropologists, however. As noted above it also plays a key role in psychoanalysis from Freud onwards. In the next section, therefore, I outline what

Freud calls the Oedipus complex and how he conceptualizes it. I will examine Lacan's version later on.

Freud and Oedipus

Freud drew his inspiration for the Oedipus complex from Greek tragedy, specifically the plays of Sophocles, one of which, *Oedipus Rex*, recounts the tragedy of Oedipus, who unknowingly kills his father and marries his mother.[7] Where Lévi-Strauss had been interested in the origins of the incest taboo, Freud is primarily concerned with the place of incestuous phantasies in the psychic development of the individual.[8] In Freud's estimation, all infants experience incestuous desires for their parents. How these desires are resolved determines not only the subject's future sexual orientation but also how its ego and superego (conscience) develop. It is thus a vital stage in psycho-sexual development. So what happens? Between the ages of three and five years, the child experiences unconscious desires for its mother. At the same time, it also experiences resentment of and hostility towards its father, even desiring his death. The complex is resolved for the boy, at least – the story is a little different for the girl – when under fear of punishment by the Father (which the child believes will involve castration) it renounces its incestuous desires and identifies with one of its parents.[9] A negative complex leads to the child identifying with the parent of the same sex and renouncing its desires for the parent of the opposite sex. The child is thus initiated into heterosexuality – its later object-choices being members of the opposite sex. A positive complex leads to the child identifying with the parent of the opposite sex and renouncing its desire for the parent of the same sex. The child is thus initiated into homosexuality – its later object-choices being members of the same sex.

Inevitably, Freud's thesis has been subject to considerable criticism, not least from feminists, who objected to its emphasis on patriarchal (or paternal) law; its devaluation of the place of the mother in the child's development; and to the privileged status within psychoanalysis of the penis/phallus as testified to by the fear of castration. Butler, however, takes a different tack. She concentrates on unpicking Freud's assumptions in order to demonstrate that what he conceives of as a natural and universal phenomenon is, in fact, the construct of a heteronormative discourse. In the next section, therefore, I set out Butler's innovative response to Freud.

Melancholic gender identifications

Key to Freud's account, according to Butler, is the idea of primary bisexuality. Freud assumes, that is, that all babies are born with both feminine and masculine dispositions. Butler is not only concerned to refute the idea that these dispositions are natural, as Freud contends; her aim is also to demonstrate that Freud's understanding of primary bisexuality is based on heteronormative assumptions. So how does Freud theorize masculine and feminine dispositions? A masculine disposition, he suggests, is expressed in the child's desire for its mother while a feminine disposition is expressed in the child's desire for its father. The sex of the child in question is irrelevant. It is the nature of their desire that determines whether the disposition is masculine or feminine. For Butler this can mean only one thing. Freud understands primary bisexuality heteronormatively: as *'the coincidence of two heterosexual desires within a single psyche'* (*GT*: 77). But why is this? Why is Freud unable to imagine the possibility of pre-oedipal homosexuality? Butler's supposition (echoing Rubin) is that the reason for this is that the Oedipus complex, and thus Freud's theory of psycho-sexual development, presumes a *prior prohibition on homosexuality*. In order to expose this prior prohibition, Butler sets about demonstrating that far from masculinity and femininity being dispositions that naturally inhere in persons, they are, in fact, effects of identification.

Identification refers to the process whereby an individual acquires its identity, or aspects thereof, from someone (or something) else. One of the ways in which this occurs is through what Freud calls 'introjection'. This is when the subject takes into its ego – into him- or herself – objects from the outside world in order to preserve them. Typically, therefore, introjection is a response to loss. In order to build her argument that masculinity and femininity result from identification, Butler turns to two texts by Freud: namely, 'Mourning and Melancholia', published in 1915, and 'The Ego and the Id', published in 1923. (Indeed, these texts feature recurrently in Butler's writings from *Gender Trouble* onwards.) In these writings, Freud sets out his account of how subjects respond to loss. In the first of these texts, as its title suggests, he identifies two such psychological processes: mourning and melancholia. Let us take each in turn.

Mourning takes place when an object (such as a loved one, an ideal or a country) is lost. In such cases, the libido (mental energy) that was once invested in that object gradually detaches from it and is cathected onto (invested in) another object. The subject thus comes to terms with its loss and is able to form a new emotional attachment – to fall in love again, for instance. At this point, 'the ego becomes free and uninhibited again' and the work of mourning is completed.[10] Something slightly different happens with melancholia. The individual in this case is not able to get over its loss in the usual way. Instead it incorporates the lost object into its ego. It identifies with it, taking on certain of its characteristics. As a consequence, 'a new structure of identity' is created in which certain qualities of the lost other are permanently internalized in the ego (*GT*: 74). Diana Fuss captures this process nicely when she notes that '[b]y incorporating the spectral remains of the dearly departed love-object, the subject vampiristically comes to life'.[11] Where mourning is the 'normal' reaction to loss, melancholia is a pathological response (since the melancholic subject is unable to accept its loss). By the time of 'The Ego and the Id', however, Freud has changed his mind. Melancholia is no longer regarded as pathological. Indeed, mourning is, henceforth, subsumed into melancholia. The details of Freud's evolving theory need not concern us. The salient point to note is that Freud now contends, to borrow his own words, that 'the character of the ego is a precipitate of abandoned object-cathexes and . . . it contains the history of those object-choices'.[12] The ego, to rephrase, is formed melancholically. It is an effect of its identifications. It is this idea that Butler takes over and applies to the question of gender identity. So how exactly does she use this idea to challenge Freudian psychoanalysis?

To reiterate: Butler's target is the Oedipal scenario as narrated by Freud because of its endorsement of presumptive heterosexuality.[13] When she talks of gender identity being structured melancholically she writes that 'the process of internalizing and sustaining lost loves is crucial to the formation of the ego *and its "object-choice"*' (*GT*: 74, my emphasis). It is not only the ego that is formed melancholically; it is also the subject's sexual orientation – their object-choice. That is, whether they choose an object (person) of the opposite sex to or of the same sex as themselves. According to Butler, when the child reaches the Oedipal phase, they have already been 'subjected to prohibitions which "dispose" them in distinct sexual directions' (*GT*: 82). They have already acquired heterosexual desires, albeit incestuous ones. As such the dispositions are not natural, as Freud assumed. Rather, for Butler, they are the 'traces of a history of enforced sexual prohibitions which is untold and which the prohibitions seek to render untellable' (*GT*: 82). Butler calls this the 'never-never' structure of gendered identity (*GT*: 88), which she defines in

The Psychic Life of Power as 'the "I never loved her, and I never lost her", uttered by a woman, the "I never loved him, I never lost him", uttered by a man' (*PLP*: 138). The fact that at the resolution of the Oedipal phase the boy identifies with his father, following the logic of melancholia, must mean that he has lost his father as an object of desire and has not been able to let go of – or grieve – that loss.[14] Ego formation, after all, requires the internalization of – or identification with – the lost object. Similarly, the fact that the girl identifies ultimately with her mother must again mean that she has lost her as a love object and has been unable to grieve that loss. In both cases, therefore, the lost desire for the parent of the same sex is installed melancholically in the ego. Heterosexual desire is bought, therefore, at the price of denying – or, in psychoanalytic language, *disavowing* or *foreclosing* (what we might think of as negating or repressing) – prior homosexual desire.[15] Heterosexuality thus has a melancholic structure.

When Freud tells the story of the Oedipus complex he narrates it in terms of the taboo against incest, a taboo which he, like Lévi-Strauss, though in different ways, saw as foundational to culture and society. When Butler re-tells the story, she does so in order to uncover what is hidden in Freud's narrative: that the Oedipus complex relies upon a prior taboo against homosexuality. The psychoanalytic story of desire, as told by Freud, is thus incomplete: it does not, perhaps cannot, tell of the loss of same-sex desire that exists prior to the Oedipal scene where the incestuous heterosexual love object is renounced and where the subject is initiated into both their sexual identity and the moral order.

Melancholia and performativity

From the layout of *Gender Trouble*, it seemed to many that Butler's critique of Freud was simply another example of her general critique of expressive theories of gender. It appears in a chapter devoted to the deconstruction of various psychoanalytic and structuralist accounts of sex, gender and desire. Butler sets out her discussion of performativity, by contrast, in her final chapters. Moreover, she made no attempt in *Gender Trouble* to connect performativity with the theorization of melancholia.[16] Indeed, such was the disjunction between the two arguments that some readers expressed concern that Butler denied the performative subject any interiority whatsoever.[17] With the publication of 'Critically Queer' and *Bodies that*

Matter, however, it soon became apparent that the theory of gender melancholia had a pivotal place in her theory. Indeed, from now on performativity and melancholia would be treated in tandem as crucial elements in a single explanation of gender. As Butler puts it in *Bodies that Matter*, gender is 'neither a purely psychic truth, conceived of as "internal" and "hidden", nor is it reducible to a surface appearance'; rather it is produced in the 'play *between* psyche and appearance' (*BTM*: 234). There is, in other words, a psychic dimension to performativity.

We have already seen that when Butler discusses performativity she means a process by which certain norms are reiterated by the subject, norms that both limit and enable what a subject can do. In *Bodies that Matter* she explicitly adds to the notion of normative constraint the idea of psychic constraint. As she now writes: 'what is "performed" [by a subject] works to conceal, if not to disavow, what remains opaque, unconscious, unperformable' (*BTM*: 234). In other words, what a subject can do is affected by what is barred from consciousness; from what is disavowed. In addition to discursive constraints there are also unconscious constraints. As such, what is performed cannot be assumed to express an inner truth about a person; rather, there might well be a difference between the appearance of gender and what it means (*BTM*: 234). To explore this difference further Butler returns to the example of drag, which she re-reads in terms of melancholia. Drag, she now asserts, 'allegorizes *heterosexual melancholy*' (*BTM*: 235). But what does this mean?

Melancholia is, to repeat, concerned with ungrieved loss; it results in an identification with the lost object. What loss, therefore, underpins drag? It might appear that, for the man performing femininity, it is the loss of femininity, while for the woman performing masculinity, it is the loss of masculinity. When Butler discusses melancholia in relation to gender she does so, however, in order to explain the formation of *heterosexual* desire – including what has to be foreclosed in order to produce heterosexual identity. Butler returns to drag, therefore, because she regards it as revealing the mundane ways in which heterosexuality is formed through the renunciation of homosexuality. What is lost – and thus enacted in drag – is the loss of a same-sex love object. Although Butler does not elucidate, what she appears to mean by this is that when a man drags up as a woman, what he is (unconsciously) revealing is his lost and ungrieved desire for a man. He 'becomes' a woman, in other words, so he can 'act out' this psychically unacknowledged desire. Similarly, the woman dragging up as a man is revealing the ungrieved loss of a woman. She thus 'becomes' a man in order to act this out. (Psychoanalytically, acting out means taking part in an activity that is a substitute for recalling specific events in the past.) In the case at hand, it means giving expression to the desire that has been repressed; a desire that has been erased from consciousness.

In *Bodies that Matter*, however, it quickly becomes clear that Butler is not talking simply about what we might conventionally recognize as drag, where someone of one sex dresses up as someone of the other, which is how she uses it primarily in *Gender Trouble*. She does not even restrict her use of the term to the kind of cross-gender identification we have just considered, where the unacknowledged loss of a same-sex love object is revealed by acting out as a member of the opposite sex. Instead, she proposes that heterosexuality as a melancholic structure is itself a form of drag. So, she writes, 'the "truest" lesbian melancholic is the strictly straight woman, and the "truest" gay male melancholic is the strictly straight man' (*BTM*: 235). The gender that is performed – the drag, as it were – is symptomatic of the disavowed identifications and attachments that constitute 'normal' gender identity. Normative heterosexuality does not just prohibit homosexual desire as and when it appears. It does rather more: it proscribes it from the beginning, and this suggests that 'what constitutes the *sexually* unperformable', namely, homosexual desire, 'is performed instead as *gender identification*'. Through melancholic identification, the straight man '*becomes* (mimes, cites, appropriates, assumes the status of) the man he "never" loved and "never" grieved' while the 'straight woman *becomes* the woman she "never" loved and "never" grieved' (*BTM*: 236).

The proscription of homosexuality grounding heterosexual desire does not just affect individual subjects. It also has public ramifications. The inability to grieve the loss of same-sex objects of desire, which renders heterosexuality a form of melancholia, also ensures that there are no social conventions for grieving lost homosexual loves within society more broadly (*BTM*: 236). This is why there is a public reluctance to mourn deaths within the gay community, exemplified particularly during the 1980s and 1990s by the failure to acknowledge deaths from AIDS. Psychically, according to Butler, heteronormative culture cannot admit the loss of homosexual lives as losses. It can only disavow, deny or repudiate them. In short, there is a public prohibition on grief.[18] Politically this needs to change. If gays and lesbians are to be acknowledged as subjects, then, for starters, 'collective institutions for grieving' their deaths are required. Much more than this needs to alter, however.

Community needs to be rethought and kinship and intimate relations require reconfiguration (*BTM*: 236). This reconstructive work requires, therefore, a concerted effort to displace presumptive heterosexuality from its authoritative position in discourses like psychoanalysis and in everyday life. In a later section, I will consider how Butler seeks to rethink kinship in non-heteronormative terms. For now, however, I want to turn my attention to her critique of Lacan. This returns us briefly to the Oedipal scenario, though this time its Lacanian version. The section thus begins with a short summary of the Oedipal narrative according to Lacan.

Lacan and Oedipus

While Butler's readings of Freud are often difficult to follow, her readings of Lacan are doubly so. This is because Lacan's writings themselves are complex and hard to understand. Rather than launch straight into Butler's reading of Lacan, therefore, I want to begin by sketching – and, it must be said, over-simplifying – those aspects of Lacan's theory that are most relevant to the discussion at hand.[19]

Lacan's psychoanalytic theory develops out of a reading of Freud. As Elizabeth Grosz notes, there are two central themes in Freud's work, namely, the unconscious and sexuality.[20] Lacan takes these two themes and reconceptualizes them in terms of language. Before I explore what this means, it is necessary to introduce one of Lacan's core ideas – the symbolic order, or the symbolic. Lacan uses this term to refer to the realm of language; or what is also referred to as the order of signification.[21] According to Lacan, both subjectivity and sexuality – we will leave the unconscious – are established when the child submits to the laws of language regulated by the symbolic order. This occurs at the Oedipal phase of development. Like Freud, Lacan sees this phase as central to the development of sexuality; unlike Freud, he also sees it as central to the acquisition of language. Where Freud, to some degree at least, endeavoured to link psychic sex difference to anatomical sex difference (the presence or absence of the penis), Lacan makes no such connection. What interests him is how the sexed body is signified in language, so what he talks about is the *phallus*. The phallus is not an organ (the penis); it is a signifier. Indeed, it is the privileged signifier within the symbolic order. But as a signifier it only makes sense in relation to other signifiers. This is why when Lacan talks about the acquisition of sexed subjectivity (being male or female) he talks about it in relation to either being or having the phallus. Truncating his argument somewhat, to be the phallus is to be female; to have the phallus is to be male.[22]

So, the phallus is the term that distinguishes the sexes. The relation to the phallus is a result of the resolution of the Oedipus complex. In the Freudian system, the father's threat of castration is enough to end the child's incestuous desires and set it on the path to 'normal' sexuality. In the Lacanian scheme, it is the child's submission to the Law of the Father (via what he terms the 'name-of-the-father' or *nom du père*) that has this effect.[23] At this time, the child repudiates its incestuous desires for its mother and acquiesces to the paternal law against incest. The Law of the Father is thus the 'threshold' between nature and culture according to which the individual is prohibited from having sexual relations with those 'named' as kin.[24] When Lacan talks about the incest taboo, therefore, he posits it as a 'set of linguistic laws that are foundational to gender and individuation' (*SD*: 201). Moreover, following Lévi-Strauss, he also conceptualizes it as the universal law that inaugurates culture and founds the symbolic. He understands it, in classic structuralist fashion, therefore, as a determining structure. The importance of this will become clearer later on.

We are now in a position to turn to Butler's critique of Lacan. There are two strands to this critique that I want to explore: the first is what Butler refers to as the 'unexamined framework of normative sexuality' underpinning Lacan's theory (*BTM*: 97) and the second relates to Lacan's purported assumption of an ahistoric symbolic. I will deal with each of these in turn, beginning in the next section with Butler's engagement with Lacan's account of sexual subjectivity.

Assuming sex

The issue that particularly concerns Butler is the place of non-normative sexualities in the Lacanian schema. We have just seen that the subject's sexed identity is determined in relation to the signifier the phallus. Sexed identity is thus a symbolic position – a position in language – that is assumed 'under the threat of punishment' (*BTM*: 96). Two aspects of Lacan's argument concern Butler: first, the binary nature of his framework (either being or having the phallus), and, second, an aspect of Lacan's work yet to be discussed: namely, lack. Let me deal with this point before I go on to outline

Butler's position. Like most psychoanalysts, Lacan rejects the idea of a self-sufficient subject transparent to itself. Instead, he conceives of the subject as split. Without plotting all the details of Lacan's account, what it means is that the subject can only generate a sense of itself by identifying with another (including identifying with 'political ideologies, patterns of consumption and social roles'[25]). Moreover, because it is not self-sufficient the self needs another to mirror back its identity to them. The ego is thus defined 'by/as the other'.[26] This can be demonstrated with regard to being and having the phallus: both require the desire of another to confirm these sexed positions. That is, in order to 'be' the phallus a female requires the desire of a male. In order to 'have' the phallus a male requires the desire of a female. The ego is always alienated, therefore. Even entering the symbolic and accepting paternal law cannot stave off lack. Instead, alienation is shifted onto the symbolic level, onto the realm of signification. This means that neither 'having' nor 'being' the phallus can fend off lack and so sexed subjectivity is doomed to perpetual failure. This inference is what Butler objects to both because it romanticizes failure before the Law and because it closes off the opportunity to reconfigure 'the play of desires' (*GT*: 72). It is the relation between phantasmatic identification, as it is called – phantasm signalling its unconscious and imaginary nature – and Lacan's binary framework that is problematic.

According to Lacan, subjectivity is produced in constraint, a view with which Butler broadly concurs. In his case, this constraint takes the form of a particular fear, the fear of castration central to the Oedipal drama. It is this fear that leads the child to submit to paternal law and to assume one of the sexed positions already discussed – either heterosexual masculinity or heterosexual femininity. As Butler interprets it, the fear that compels this assumption is the fear – the 'terror' – of occupying one of two other positions: namely, that of 'the feminized fag and the phallicized dyke' (*BTM*: 96).[27] These are abject positions. Since Lacan presupposes the cultural necessity of heterosexuality, homosexuality and other non-normative forms of sexuality have no place in the Lacanian symbolic. Indeed, for Lacan, they constitute forms of psychosis that require treatment (an argument Kristeva also deploys). It is in the interests of validating the lives and loves of non-normative sexual subjects that Butler challenges Lacan.

If the assumption of a sexed position requires an identification with a position already 'marked out within the symbolic domain' and if, given lack, this identification is 'phantasmatic' (a position the subject aspires to fill but never can), then the way that heterosexuality is established in the symbolic is by regulating the terms of identification (*BTM*: 96–7). It is, as it were, based on normalizing certain positions and pathologizing others. But what might happen, Butler asks, if instead of homosexuality being feared and abjected it becomes eroticized? Could this lead to a different way of thinking about how the sexual economy is conceptualized within psychoanalysis (*BTM*: 97)? In short, her answer is yes. Drawing once again on the idea of melancholia, Butler argues that Lacan's understanding of the relation between desire and identification is too restrictive. While Butler agrees that gender identity is the effect of a 'history of constitutive identifications' (*GT*: 85), this does not mean that the sexed subject can only occupy either a heterosexual position or one of its 'inverted versions' (the feminized fag and phallicized dyke). Identifications are, in fact, 'multiple and contestatory'. The boy may identify with his mother 'and produce desire from that identification' (*BTM*: 99). Women may phantasmatically desire to be and/or to have the phallus for other women; men might want to be and/or to have the phallus for other men. Women, instead of assuming the feminine position, might resist (*BTM*: 102). For Butler, therefore, a variety of forms of identification are possible that cannot be reduced to the binary structure of the Lacanian framework (*BTM*: 103).

One of the aims of Butler's work is thus to challenge the heteronormativity of Lacanian psychoanalysis: the assumption that heterosexuality is normal and that other non-heterosexual modes of sexuality are not. She also wants to do something else, namely, to argue against the idea that resistance to the symbolic must take place outside the symbolic. She thus seeks to subject Lacanian psychoanalysis to a similar critique to that deployed against Kristeva.

Locating resistance

We have already seen that a central place in Lacan's thought is given to the idea of the Law of the Father. It is the status of this Law that concerns Butler. First, Lacan sees this law as originating (society, culture, sexuality). Second, although Lacan talks of it operating 'invariably', according to Butler, what he actually means is that it operates 'inevitably'. The conditions producing binary sexuality are thus rigid, unchanging and universally determining. Finally, the assumption of the Law's inevitability appears to signal that Lacan is attempting to position the law as being indisputable or incontestable; as above criticism (*AC*: 21). This latter point is confirmed, for Butler, by the fact that Lacan locates any form of resistance capable of evading paternal law outside the symbolic realm in what he terms the Imaginary. The Imaginary realm refers to the realm of images, 'conscious and unconscious, perceived or imagined', and is approximately equivalent to Freud's idea of the pre-oedipal.[28] (It shares more than a passing resemblance to the semiotic in Kristeva's work.) It is, furthermore, the realm of what is called *jouissance*. *Jouissance* is a difficult term to define, but for the purposes of the ensuing discussion, it can be translated as a mode of bliss or extreme pleasure that is *unregulated by the Law*. The Imaginary can disrupt the symbolic but, in essence, it cannot transform it. This means that the terms of paternal law are left unchallenged and the idea of paternal law as binding and irreversible is also left unopposed. This failure to challenge paternal law results in compulsory heterosexuality being left intact as an idea(l). By conceiving resistance in this way, Lacan has unnecessarily circumscribed in advance what constitutes resistance. Moreover, when feminists construe the Imaginary as the site of *feminine* resistance to the symbolic, all they do, Butler charges, is 'reconstitute sexually differentiated and hierarchized "separate spheres"'. They leave unquestioned the 'dynamic by which the symbolic reiterates its power', with the effect that 'the structural sexism and homophobia of its sexual demands' remain unaltered (*BTM*: 106). For Butler, this is simply not good enough.

The only way to alter the symbolic realm significantly is to subvert it from within (*BTM*: 96). Resistance must be immanent. In order to displace Lacan's understanding of the Law, therefore, Butler begins by drawing on an argument Foucault makes in *The History of Sexuality* concerning the 'repressive hypothesis'. This is the idea that in the period leading up to Victorian times, 'sex' had become an increasingly taboo topic, subject to endless prohibitions. The aspect of Foucault's argument that interests Butler is the claim that the law, including paternal law, might actually produce the very desires it is alleged to repress. Instead of being merely prohibitive, it is, in fact, constitutive – of sexes, genders and sexualities. The law, in other words, gives rise to endless cultural possibilities not just one (*GT*: 96–100), and patriarchal law is no different. The reason for this is that the law is iterable.

When the paternal authority (Butler calls 'him' a judge) imposes the law, when in Lacanian terms he 'names' the subject, he does not originate the law. He cites an existing body of law. He 'consults and reinvokes the law' and so 'reconstitutes' it (*BTM*: 107). Indeed, it is the recitation of the law – the recycling, in other words, of a set of existing legal conventions – that ensures that it remains an 'authoritative force'. It is also this recitation, however, that opens up the 'possibility of its own failure'. It is in the 'practice of citation', in other words, that subversive potential resides (*BTM*: 108). For even though the law operates through prohibition (thus in the Oedipal scenario the injunction against desiring a parent), the recitation of that prohibition is precisely what generates the *'discursive occasion'* not just for resisting the law but also for its resignification (*BTM*: 109). The heterosexual presumptions of the symbolic can be contested; the range of sexed positions challenged; and the construction of homosexuality as abject can be resisted. The Law can be turned against itself and the symbolic transformed thereby. Understanding the law as iterable thus enables Butler to challenge Lacan's dual contention that it is invariable in its operations and that it is indisputable. Instead, Butler suggests, it demonstrates that the *meaning* of the law, in any given historical context, is less univocal than Lacan allows.

There is one final aspect of Butler's critique of Lacan that I want to look at before moving on to her own psychoanalytic theory, and this concerns the incest taboo. I have two reasons for looking at this idea. The incest taboo is, as already indicated, a central assumption of psychoanalytic thought, underpinning the Oedipal narrative, but the extent of its significance to that narrative is only really brought to the fore in Lacan's work. It also plays a significant role in determining how intimate relations are organized within society and is, thus, integrally connected with the *politics* of kinship.

Kinship matters

Butler's interest in the incest taboo is a long-standing one, going back to *Subjects of Desire* (201–4). It is a key part of her critique of heteronormativity. Owing to her interventions in a series of ongoing political debates around gay marriage and kinship in both the US and Europe, however, Butler's work in this area has taken on added significance. One of the oddities of contemporary life is that kinship in the heteronormative 'daddy–mommy–me' sense is in decline.[29] Divorce, remarriage, migration, exile and the movement of refugees and asylum seekers have contributed to a reconfiguration of kinship relations. There are now gay families, in both 'nuclear and non-nuclear forms', as well as 'blended' arrangements where gay and straight families commingle (*AC*: 23). All of these developments put into question what it is to be a mother or a father or a family. Yet at the same time as these sociological changes take place, the forces of conservatism, from the Vatican down, resist them. Same-sex marriage is characterized as being 'at war with the fundamental presuppositions of culture itself' (*CHU*: 146); homosexual parenting is presented as a form of 'violence and destruction' ('Kinship': 29); and the public is warned by Lacanian analysts that lesbian parenting leads to autism or psychosis (*AC*: 70).[30] It is 'regressive political claims' of this kind, and the conservative family politics they seek to legitimize, that Butler's writings on incest are designed to challenge (*CHU*: 146). While non-heterosexual and non-normative kinship relations are denied 'institutional sanction' (*AC*: 78), those within them are condemned to an illegitimate existence. One way to contest this absence of legitimacy, therefore, is to contest the way the relation between the incest taboo and kinship is conceptualized. This necessitates a turn to psychoanalysis – and particularly Lacanian psychoanalysis, given the central role it plays there in authorizing heterosexuality.

In order to illustrate Butler's position, the text I will be focusing on is *Antigone's Claim*. I have chosen this book for three reasons. First, it makes clear Butler's political position on kinship. Next, the critique of Lacan that she presents in this book is essentially the same as that articulated elsewhere in her other work. It is thus representative of her broader position. Finally, by deploying the story of Antigone, Butler is able to articulate a distinctive and original take on incest and kinship that challenges Lacan's position on these topics. To contextualize her argument, therefore, I will start with the story of Antigone.[31]

Antigone is the daughter of Oedipus. Her story is told in another of Sophocles' plays. This play, *Antigone*, traces what happens to Antigone when she buries her brother Polyneices, killed after slaying their other brother, Eteocles. While Eteocles is honoured with a military funeral, Polyneices is condemned as a traitor and, as such, fated to lie unburied on the hillside outside the city. Antigone, however, buries him. She thus defies the instructions of her maternal uncle and sovereign, Creon, who had made the injunction, for which she is imprisoned. Defiant until the end, she commits suicide. Butler is not the first thinker to take up the story of Antigone: Hegel, Lacan and Irigaray all precede her in this respect. Each of them, however, reads Antigone in a way that Butler finds problematic, for each treats her as representing kinship against the state. Each thus occludes, for Butler, the fact that Antigone's family is an incestuous family: her father is her brother since they share a mother; her mother is simultaneously her grandmother; her brothers are also her nephews and her sister also her niece. It is less kinship that Antigone signifies, to Butler, than 'kinship's fatal aberration' (*AC*: 15). Turning the story of Antigone back on Lacanian psychoanalysis thus allows Butler to contest the authoritative basis of symbolic Law.

As indicated earlier, one of Butler's worries with Lacan is that he envisages the Law as both invariant and indisputable. What we need to establish, therefore, is why paternal law has this status. The reason is that Lacan, echoing Lévi-Strauss, sees the incest taboo as the condition of culture. The taboo is a structure that defines a series of positions in language: 'mother', 'father', 'child'. Importantly, as Deleuze and Guattari remind us, these positions are quite separate from those persons 'who come to occupy them in a given social . . . formation'.[32] When Lacan talks of the prohibition on incest establishing the symbolic order he means that it establishes the order of language and sociality itself. He does not mean that it sets up this or that historically and culturally conditioned social order. Indeed, without the taboo there could not be a symbolic (*AC*: 66–7). The Law, therefore, is not just 'beyond social alteration'; it sets the 'condition and limit of all social alteration' (*AC*: 75). Butler rejects this argument. She contends that Lacan's distinction between the symbolic (as that which is necessary to culture *per se*) and the social (the variable forms of culture) is untenable. This is where the story of Antigone becomes pertinent.

According to Sophocles' tale, not only is Antigone doomed as a consequence both of Oedipus' actions in killing his father and marrying his mother *and* of her defiance of Creon, but she also dies. Read from a Lacanian perspective, therefore, we might see Antigone's plight as inevitable since, as he has it, the functioning of the symbolic depends on the suppression of incestuous relations. If, however, the symbolic is seen, as Butler prefers, as the 'sedimentation of social practices' (*AC*: 19), then another interpretation of Antigone's fate is possible.[33] It goes like this: the authority of the Law depends, as noted above, on its being repeatedly recited. Kinship, from this perspective, can thus be thought of as a 'set of practices' that are performed and 'relations that are reinstituted in time precisely through the practice of their repetition' (*AC*: 58). They acquire their 'lawlike' regularity through this repetition. By committing suicide, that is, 'by refusing to do what is necessary to stay alive for Haemon, by refusing to become a mother and a wife, by scandalizing the public with her wavering gender, by embracing death as a bridal chamber', Antigone in effect 'deinstitute[s] heterosexuality' (*AC*: 76). She chooses death over the 'normativities that might have saved her'.[34] Her choice is important: it exposes the weakness in paternal law, for that law cannot make her give up her 'impossible and death-bent incestuous love of her brother' Polyneices (*AC*: 6) or compel her to assume a 'normal' heterosexual position. As a consequence, the Law that Lacan assumes to be invariant and intractable is destabilized by Antigone's act. It is exposed as vulnerable.[35] Lacan's distinction between the symbolic and the social collapses as the symbolic is exposed as variable and contingent.

It might, of course, be objected that Antigone's resistance of heteronormativity ends badly for her, since she dies. Butler does not see it this way. Certainly, Antigone is unable to carve out a non-heterosexual sexuality for herself. What is significant, however, is that her story – and thus the drama of Oedipus – does not end with the affirmation of heterosexuality. A psychoanalytic theory beginning with Antigone, rather than with Oedipus, therefore, is not required to assume that the incest taboo leads necessarily to kinship based on either biological reproduction or the heterosexual couple (*AC*: 66). Instead it would be able to envisage alternative non-heterosexual forms of kinship. This is where the political significance of Butler's argument becomes evident. The failure, in practice, to consider kinship outside a heteronormative frame means that whole hosts of people are condemned to social opprobrium; their ways of life vilified; their living arrangements stigmatized. They lack not only social status but also recognition. Butler's attempt to reframe the psychoanalytic understanding of sexed subjectivity and the incest taboo from an Antigonean perspective is tied to her political project of garnering authorization for these allegedly aberrant modes of kinship, and for those who populate them. It forms part, that is, of the development of a new 'vocabulary' or 'legitimating lexicon' capable of accommodating those excluded by the current heterosexual familial norm (*UG*: 31).

So far I have concentrated on Butler's critique of both Freudian and Lacanian psychoanalysis. In the next part of this chapter, therefore, I want to change direction to consider Butler's own psychoanalytic account of subject formation. To do so I will concentrate specifically on *The Psychic Life of Power*, for it is here that Butler articulates the most comprehensive version of this theory to date.[36] It should be noted, however, that her explanation of psychic subjectivity is not developed exclusively through an engagement with psychoanalysis. Rather, the explanation she lays out combines a theory of power derived from Foucault with a theory of the psyche derived from Freud. She then fine-tunes it by using it to highlight gaps in the accounts of subjectivity posited not only by Foucault and Freud but also by Althusser, Nietzsche and Hegel. It is now time to examine this theory.

Psychic subjectivity

As Lisa Disch observes, 'the central problem of *The Psychic Life of Power* is contained in the dual connotations of the term *subjection*, which signifies subjectivity and subjugation at once'.[37] This is the idea of *assujetissement* discussed in the previous chapter: where the individual's formation as a subject depends on their submission to power. It is the nature of this paradox from a psychoanalytic perspective that interests Butler here. 'What', she asks, 'is the psychic form that power takes?' (*PLP*: 2). The enquiry is an important one both for individuals, in terms of how their very survival requires a continued subjection to power, and for the possibility of politics, in terms of how subjects are able to oppose the very power that sustains their existence. This cultural and political 'predicament' (*PLP*: 17), as Butler terms it, impinges directly, therefore, on questions of agency. It is typically assumed that agency requires an autonomous subject. In the previous chapter, however, we saw Butler contest this view with her argument that agency is an effect of subjectification. In her estimation, it is the iterability (or citationality) of the norms that define and regulate the subject that enables it to resist. In *Psychic Life*, she returns to the relation between autonomy and agency once again. Her aim, however, is somewhat different; here she is concerned with how the subject is formed psychically. This process, she contends, reveals just how illusory the whole idea of autonomy is, for psychic subjectivity is formed in dependence. How, though, does she establish that this is, in fact, the case?

The oddity of subjection (*assujetissement*) is that in order to continue as a subject, individuals have to submit to the very power that subordinates them. Their evident willingness to do so suggests to Butler that they have what she calls in this book a 'passionate attachment' to their subordination. It is worth pausing to consider what this might mean in concrete terms. I turn to an argument Wendy Brown makes in *States of Injury*, to explain. Here Brown is discussing what happens when political movements arise as a reaction against an experience of marginalization or exclusion, as, for instance, when feminism appeared as a reaction against the subordination of women. She notes that these protest movements become invested in the very identity that has secured their marginalization.[38] Feminists thus hold on to the identity of women even though it is as women – as that identity – that they have been harmed. This investment, Brown argues, is evidence of a 'wounded attachment'. While Brown limits her analysis of attachment to cases of identity politics, Butler, however, goes further. She draws on Brown's insights to develop an account of attachment that applies not just to oppositional movements but to subject formation *per se*.[39] She thus advances a theory that appears to have universal application. So how does this theory work?

Recall that in order to become a subject, the subject has to submit to power. Indeed, it is the submission to power that generates the subject. In *Psychic Life*, Butler examines Althusser's account of interpellation as an example of this process. According to Althusser, the subject is formed when it is interpellated – or hailed – by an authority figure. Thus, the policeman in the street calls out 'Hey, you there' and the individual, recognizing that it is being spoken to, turns towards the policeman's voice. At that moment the individual is transformed into a subject, or, rather, in Althusserian terms, into a subject of ideology in general. The turn to the voice of the law is the action that constitutes the individual's subjection by power. Subjection, as Butler summarizes it, is best thought of, therefore, through the rhetorical idea of the *trope*, or turn (*PLP:* 3). This turn, however, is figurative since it cannot be made by an actual subject – the subject only comes into existence through the turn. In Althusser's case, prior to the turn there is only the individual; after the turn there is a subject. What intrigues Butler, however, is why the individual turns in the first place; why, that is, does it respond to the voice of the law? Althusser, according to Butler, offers no explanation for this. So, she provides one.[40] Her supposition is that the individual responds to the voice of the law because it assumes that it is guilty of some infraction – otherwise why would the policeman be calling out to it? It responds, that is, because its conscience tells it to. But if the individual has a conscience prior to its subjection by the law, Butler speculates, then this can mean only one thing. The individual has already been subjected to a prior *psychic* operation of power, in which it has become both self-conscious and self-subjugating (*PLP:* 106–31). On its own, therefore, the theory of interpellation (which we might characterize as a theory of power) cannot explain subjection. What is needed here is a theory of the formation of the psyche.

Passionate attachment and primary dependency

There are three aspects to this psychic theory. Butler begins by considering primary human dependency. Her argument is very simple: in infancy all subjects develop a passionate attachment to those on whom they depend for life. If 'the child is to persist in a psychic and social sense', Butler notes, 'there must be dependency and the formation of attachment: there is no possibility of not loving, where love is bound up with the requirements for life' (*PLP*: 8). Although this initial dependency, or 'primary passion', is not political 'in any usual sense', it is important for Butler principally because it 'conditions the political formation and regulation of subjects', becoming their means of subjection. Out of a 'desire to survive' (*PLP*: 7), subjects are perpetually willing to submit to their own subordination.

The second element is foreclosure, which, as noted earlier, is one of the terms Butler uses to describe what happens during melancholia. When Butler defines foreclosure in *Psychic Life* she construes it in terms of a desire that has been 'rigorously barred' from consciousness and that produces a subject 'through a certain kind of preemptive loss' (*PLP*: 23). Foreclosure, for Butler, is thus essential to the formation of the subject, specifically the foreclosure of certain kinds of passionate attachment or 'impossible' loves. If the subject is produced in this way, it means that it is from the start 'separated and differentiated' (*PLP*: 9). It is not autonomous; far from it. It is a dependent subject, one produced in subordination and whose continued subordination is essential to its continued existence. Even though primary passionate attachments are necessary to the survival of the child, they must eventually be denied – or disavowed – if the subject is to emerge fully. Primary attachments are, that is, attachments that the subject 'can never afford fully to "see"' (*PLP*: 8). This means, therefore, that certain aspects of who we 'are must' become unknown and unknowable to us, even as they continue to haunt the subject, threatening it with its own unravelling.

Finally, Butler returns to the topic of melancholia. Here, given her concern with the formation of conscience and guilt, she deploys the idea to demonstrate how the subject's capacity for reflexivity is an effect of the foreclosure and installation of the other within its ego. It is at this point of her argument that Butler sets out to reveal just exactly how power impinges on psychic formation. Where Freudian theory focuses on the psychic, Foucauldian theory concentrates on the social or political. Butler's aim is to weave the two together. She wants to challenge the idea, in other words, that the unconscious is unaffected by the power relations that structure society (*PLP*: 88). Her goal is thus to advance a 'critical account of psychic subjection in terms of the regulatory and productive effects of power' (*PLP*: 19). She has already shown in *Gender Trouble* and elsewhere how the subject depends for its existence on the operations of particular regulatory norms. Her interest in *Psychic Life* is to demonstrate how the subject internalizes those norms. This is where melancholia fits. Melancholia is the way that the internal world of the psyche is produced; it determines both its interiority and exteriority and the boundary between social and psychic. According to Butler, it operates in this way because the psychic sphere is, in fact, organized according to the prevailing 'norms of social regulation' (*PLP*: 171). Because it is configured by social norms, the topography of the psyche is, thus, configured according to the operations of power.

The loss of the object that occasions melancholia is not just the loss of that object. The social world the object inhabited or made possible is also lost. When the ego internalizes the lost object, it also internalizes features of that social world, and this is what gives rise to its capacity for reflexivity or conscience. This takes us to a feature of Freud's discussion of melancholia that has not yet been mentioned. According to Freud, one of the consequences of melancholia is that the subject turns against itself the love or, more pertinently, the hate or anger that it had towards the lost other. It thus begins to berate itself; to judge itself. In giving voice to these criticisms, the ego engages in communication. Communication is, of course, a social phenomenon structured according to certain norms. When the ego berates itself it does so according to certain social norms of judgement. As such, in melancholia the ego does not just internalize the lost object; it also internalizes a particular 'configuration of the social world as well'. In fact, as a consequence, the psyche comes to be organized on socio-political lines: the ego 'becomes a "polity" and conscience one of its "major institutions"' (*PLP*: 181). This is not, however, the whole story.

Conscience may well be structured like a social institution, wherein the criticisms the individual directs against itself mirror those that social agencies use in judging the behaviour of social actors. The strength of the subject's conscience, however, relates rather to the way that social power determines which losses might be grieved and which might not (*PLP*: 183). In this way, the heightened conscience of the melancholic is an effect of the state's authority in regulating grief, but an effect that is dissimulated. There is no need for the state to explicitly prohibit particular expressions of grief and loss if conscience already does it. This, of course, is where the argument reconnects with Butler's concern with the cultural unintelligibility of non-heterosexual minorities. Since the social world itself is configured by norms, specifically heteronormativity, then for Butler it is clear that the foreclosures producing melancholia are themselves grounded in the regulatory – normative and normalizing – operations of power. And so the topography of the psyche must also be configured according to certain regulatory norms, and if it is, this means that the psyche is an effect of the operations of power.

There are two critical points to make before I end this discussion of Butler's theory of psychic subjectivity. The first is that it clearly challenges the idea of the autonomous subject, for it is only by internalizing – identifying with – the lost object, with an other, that the subject comes to exist at all. Indeed this suggests, as Salih surmises, that 'if anything may be said to be "essential" to the performative subject', it is loss.[41] 'Survival is', therefore, 'a matter of avowing [not denying] the trace of loss that inaugurates one's own emergence' (*PLP*: 195). What is less clear is how this helps Butler develop a non-autonomous account of agency. What is it, that is, that enables the subject not just to survive but, as Lisa Disch ponders, to transform their social and political situation?[42] Although Butler hints that the trauma of subjection contains within it resources for reworking or resignifying the painful interpellations constituting the subject, these resources are not identified or explored in any detail in *Psychic Life*. Indeed, it is unclear how the norms regulating the psyche can be reconfigured without threatening the subject with psychic dissolution.

The second critical point that I need to make in closing this section concerns the 'desire for existence'. Throughout her work, Butler has been at pains to challenge the assumption that a principle, law or substance exists outside of culture and language that forms the basis for understanding either sex and sexuality or subversion. Yet in *Psychic Life*, she appears to call on something very similar herself when she talks about the 'desire for existence' as prior to subjection and when she describes it as 'a desire exploited by regulatory power' (*PLP*: 19; see also 28). The desire for existence is, as Samuel Chambers has pointed out, a recuperation of 'Spinoza's prediscursive "desire to exist"', or the *conatus*, as Spinoza termed it.[43] When Butler uses the term here (and elsewhere), as she often does, it raises a question: where does the desire derive from?[44] According to Chambers, the answer is simple: because it is never admitted into the space of critical analysis the desire for existence must be pre-discursive – a universal and invariant form of desire.[45] I concur. This clearly introduces a tension into Butler's argument, however. By positing the desire to exist as the substance that power exploits, Butler undercuts her own argument that psychic life is always already social. If the desire for existence is pre-discursive, then it is not only immune from criticism, as Chambers indicates; it also cannot be changed by political intervention.[46] Butler, it appears, commits the very mistake she earlier charged Kristeva, Lacan, Foucault and Žižek with: relying on an element that exists outside of culture and history to ground their theories.

Resisting Butler

So how have Butler's psychoanalytic ideas been received within feminism? Compared to the proliferation of engagements, critiques and appropriations that followed the theory of gender performativity – I will talk about resignification in the next chapter – the response has been somewhat more muted. While Butler's reading of Freud's account of the incest taboo has been characterized as 'brilliant' and *Psychic Life* as one of her 'most thoroughgoing attempts to date to explain how a subject that is invested in power' can act, some of her feminist readers – primarily Lacanians – have been more critical of her treatment of psychoanalysis.[47] There are two main areas where Butler's work is considered to be lacking: first, in terms of her understanding of sex difference, and, second, with regard to the theory of subject formation that she herself develops. I want to deal with each in turn; so first, sex difference. I will begin with two Lacanian critiques before I move on to consider the argument posited by feminist philosopher Rosi Braidotti.

The first of the Lacanian critiques is that advanced by Joan Copjec. Her argument is simple: Butler mistakes the nature of sex difference in Lacanian theory. Sex difference, Copjec charges, has a purely formal role in Lacanian theory – it is a form of linguistic differentiation. As noted earlier, nothing can be deduced from this, however, about the actual social roles that actual men and women will play. When Butler concludes 'from the changing *concepts* of women something about the *being*, the *existence* of women', she does two things[48] she collapses the distinction between symbolic and social conceptions of sex difference (the former invariant, the latter sociologically variable) and she attributes 'objective reality to an idea which is valid only as a rule'. In other words, she mixes up 'a rule of language with a description of a Thing-in-itself, in this case with sex'.[49] And, in *Undoing Gender*, Butler concedes the point that sociological concepts of gender cannot be reduced to sexual difference in the formal Lacanian sense. Nevertheless, she persists in her claim that understanding sexual difference as an invariant symbolic order is deeply problematic for all the reasons outlined earlier (*UG*: 212).

The second Lacanian objection is proffered by Kirsten Campbell. This revolves around the idea of foreclosure. While Butler claims in *Psychic Life* to derive this idea from Freud, Campbell objects that it is, in fact, a Lacanian idea.[50] As such, there are certain inconsistencies and difficulties that follow on from Butler's deployment of it. For Lacan, foreclosure involves a failure in the generation of sexed subjectivity, while for Butler, as noted above, it denotes a moment in the successful construction of heterosexual identity (based as it is on the foreclosure of homosexual desire). From the logic of Butler's argument the foreclosure of homosexual desires is *pre*-oedipal because it occurs prior to the subject's experience of the incestuous desires that are resolved during the Oedipal phase. According to Campbell, however, psychoanalytically it cannot be. 'If it is pre-oedipal, then it must be prior to sexual difference', and if it is prior to sexual difference, then 'the object that is prohibited cannot be a homosexual object because a homosexual object is defined by sexual difference'. Identification with a same-sex object, in other words, relies upon the prior designation of sexual difference.[51] The foreclosure that Butler discusses must logically, for Campbell, be 'an oedipal prohibition in the register of sexual difference'. The fact that Butler does not recognize this means that her account of the way in which heterosexual identity is produced is flawed: it cannot be based on a prior injunction against homosexuality. Campbell also isolates a second related problem, which is that Butler's account of foreclosure cannot provide her with an explanation for the production of homosexual desire or identity either. As Campbell puts it, because Butler assumes a 'fundamental prohibition against an attachment to same-sex objects, then homosexual desire is always precluded', and, she concludes, because Butler sees homosexuality as unintelligible, this means that it 'cannot exist'.[52] This point has bite: Butler never adequately explains how the failure of the fundamental prohibition against homosexuality works to form certain subjects (or abjects) with homosexual desires.

The third critique of sex difference I want to consider is Braidotti's. Feminist engagements with the work of Lacan tend to focus on the fact that the social system erected on the back of the incest taboo is a patriarchal system: one that privileges masculinity (the paternal function) over femininity (the maternal function). Butler's critique is of a different order – she emphasizes the privileging of heterosexuality. It is the focus of Butler's critique that Braidotti takes issue with *politically* (*UG*: 210). As she comments, the aim of 'taking the trouble to define, analyze, and act on sexual difference' is because it is a way to symbolically empower the feminine so as 'to turn it into a platform of political action for and by women'.[53] Butler's rejection of sexual difference is thus also a rejection of the 'transformative power of the feminine' in subverting the patriarchal symbolic.[54] It is, that is, a rejection of a certain version of feminism. When Butler takes the originary psychic loss to be the loss of a homosexual love object rather than the mother or, to be more precise, the maternal body, she 'confuses and condenses' three separate issues: 'separation from the mother', 'realization of the heterosexual imperative' and the 'constitutive loss of homosexuality'. The effect of this is to erase the feminine or, rather, to reduce it to 'a pathetic effort at simulating signification on the road to nowhere', a move that Braidotti rejects for both conceptual and strategic reasons.[55]

In response to Braidotti, Butler rejects the claim that she depreciates the feminine. Instead, she contends that the symbolic that she envisages – that is, one not structured around binary sex difference – 'will be one in which femininity has multiple possibilities' (*UG*: 196). Surely this is true. Femininity freed from the imperatives of compulsory heterosexuality would be able to develop in a variety of ways. Women would no longer be tied to the imperatives of motherhood as presently constructed. They would no longer be expected to feminize themselves in ways attractive to men. Yet this is not quite what Braidotti means. As I read it, the difficulty is that because Butler is more interested in the heteronormativity of the symbolic than in its patriarchal structure, she underemphasizes the power relations that sustain male privilege and female subordination in general, only one of which is compulsory heterosexuality.

This is why Braidotti worries that Butler derogates the feminine; because her interest is not in women *per se* but in those women culturally outlawed because of their sexuality.

I now want to outline the second broad area of criticism, and this concerns Butler's theory of subject formation. The charge here is that this theory is insufficiently *psychoanalytic*. This is another argument proffered by Campbell and it concerns Butler's treatment of the primary passions and of melancholia in *Psychic Life*. The issue for Campbell is that when Butler attends to the question of the primary passions she crucially fails to address the 'psychic relations of the child and parent'. Butler, it is alleged, concentrates mistakenly on discussing 'empirically "real" relations', the parents or guardians who care for the child. According to Campbell, this means that Butler neglects the 'infant's phantasmatic relations to its specular others' or its own imagined relation with itself. The relations that Campbell identifies are those that have a central place in Lacanian thought – expressed in the idea of the mirror stage. Butler, however, is not developing a Lacanian account of subjectivity and so her neglect of these elements is entirely logical. Campbell also complains that Butler's treatment of melancholia is insufficiently psychoanalytic insofar as Butler collapses identity and subjectivity, leading her to produce a theory of identity formation rather than subject formation. The reason for this, as Campbell has it, is that Butler neglects the unconscious, the entity central to a properly psychoanalytic theory of subjectivity. This charge might seem unfair since Butler does, in fact, consider the unconscious in terms of psychic resistance to power; however, it is her general failure to examine the role of the id that Campbell finds problematic for it generates an aporia in her theory that limits its range and application both politically and theoretically.[56]

Conclusion

Throughout this chapter I have traced Butler's various interventions in psychoanalytic debates. As ought to be apparent, her interest in and engagement with psychoanalysis is a long-standing one. In this regard, it would be wrong to see *Psychic Life* as an exceptional text. It contains, rather, the crystallization of her thoughts on psychoanalysis over a long period: her limited critique of Freudian theory and her rejection of Lacanian thought. What is different about it as a text, however, is that in it Butler seeks more explicitly than in some of her earlier work to develop a fully rounded account of subjection. This account is organized around three core themes: first, an exploration of the subject's psychic investment in its own continued subordination by power; second, the place of melancholia in setting the limits of subjectivation; and finally a consideration of how it is possible to oppose and transform the social terms by which the subject is produced (*PLP*: 29). While the first two are treated reasonably fully in *Psychic Life*, Butler's examination of the latter is far less comprehensive. For this reason, as Lisa Disch has speculated, *Psychic Life* might be best read alongside *Excitable Speech*, also published in the same year, for *Excitable Speech* foregrounds the very issue of transformation that dips from view in *Psychic Life*.[57] In the next chapter, therefore, I explore these questions of agency and transformation primarily through an examination of *Excitable Speech*.

5

'Talking Back' – Resignification and Politics

As any student of political thought can testify, speech, debate and deliberation are central to both liberalism and democracy. To have this confirmed, one has only to think of J. S. Mill's defence of free speech in *On Liberty*, Michael Walzer's contention that in a democracy 'Citizens come to the forum with nothing but their arguments',[1] or Jürgen Habermas's various attempts to develop a version of deliberative democracy predicated upon communicative action. If democratic citizenship is intrinsically connected to issues of speech, then questions are immediately raised about what can and ought to be spoken, when, where and to whom. Given that not all speech is benign, almost inevitably consideration has also focused on whether all speech ought to be 'free', that is, unregulated by the state, or whether there are occasions when censorship is appropriate. It is Butler's intervention into these debates as they played out in the US that is the focus of this chapter. Throughout the 1980s and 1990s a group of thinkers, including feminist anti-pornography campaigner Catherine MacKinnon and critical race theorists Mari Matsuda, Kimberlé Crenshaw, Richard Delgado and Charles R. Lawrence III, argued vigorously that pornography and racially assaultive speech should be removed from the protection of the First Amendment (the free speech amendment) on the grounds that words wound.[2] Further, many of these same thinkers, drawing on the terms of the Fourteenth Amendment (the equal protection clause), contended that the only way to secure substantive equality and full respect for *all* citizens was actively to censor such speech, thus making it prosecutable under law. It is the work of these legal scholars and activists, and in particular the arguments set out in MacKinnon's *Only Words* and Matsuda et al.'s *Words that Wound*, that Butler sets out to critique.

While the debate itself is important, my primary concern in this chapter is to demonstrate the way in which Butler links the relation between speech and action not just to censorship and the politics of hate-speech, but also to the possibility of agency and political action more generally, thus raising issues concerning the scope of democratic politics and its relation to state power. Moreover, her work in *Excitable Speech* offers an opportunity to examine her fullest defence of an idea, earlier mooted in a piece on the Helms amendment, that the best way to challenge attempts to 'define and restrict the terms of political identity' is 'to safeguard the uncontrollability of the signified'.[3] So, we also return to Butler's long-standing interest in questions of subjectivity and, in particular, what in the constitutive conditions of subjectivity would enable subjects to contest both injury and degradation.

Words that Wound

Under the terms of the US Constitution, the First Amendment protects freedom of speech. The rationale is simple: all viewpoints in a democratic society have the right to be expressed in the 'free marketplace of ideas' for this fosters a tolerant society. Although certain forms of speech are already actionable, that is, exempt from First Amendment privileges, such as false advertising, defamation, libel, plagiarism and threats uttered to an officer of the law, most are not. This includes hate-speech. These ideas, it is argued, do not require exempting because although the views expressed are erroneous and offensive, hate-speech itself does no harm; it is simply the expression of an idea or opinion and one, at that, that may be countered by the many contrary ideas abounding in the political realm. Central to the arguments of those demanding legal regulation of hate-speech, however, is the contrary claim that some words, far from simply voicing an idea or contestable opinion, actually wound those to whom they are addressed. As the flyleaf of *Words that Wound* indicates: 'Words, like sticks and stones, can assault; they can injure; and they can exclude.' Certain words can, that is, be 'used as weapons to ambush, terrorize, wound, humiliate and degrade'.[4] To defend these words under First Amendment doctrine is thus to defend acts of ambush, terror, wounding, humiliation and degradation. Or, as MacKinnon writes, following the same logic in relation to pornography: 'Protecting pornography means protecting sexual abuse *as* speech.'[5] Assaultive speech, it is argued, ought thus to be construed legally as a form of 'fighting words'. This is a category of speech already prosecutable under US constitutional law that refers to words that 'by their very utterance inflict injury or tend to incite an immediate breach of the peace'.[6]

The central difference between the two sides in the debate concerns how they theorize the relation between speech and conduct. Where First Amendment defenders see no immediate relation between the two, pro-regulation critics argue that assaultive speech is not just speech; it is simultaneously assault. Wounding speech and conduct are inseparable. What is said metes out pain and suffering directly as it is said. Neither hate-speech nor pornography can be conceived as 'only words', therefore, because both are acts of abuse akin to physical assault. As Charles R. Lawrence III comments: 'The experience of being called a "nigger", "spic", "Jap" or "kike" is like receiving a slap in the face. The injury is instantaneous.'[7] People are not just assailed by these utterances; for Matsuda, MacKinnon and the others, they are also subordinated by them. Hate-speech and pornography do not, in other words, simply mirror prevailing relations of domination in society; they are not, as it were, 'merely referential or connotative'.[8] Each is rather what Matsuda calls 'a mechanism of subordination' enacting this domination.[9] Hate-speech and pornography are, thus, constitutive. They constitute the conditions of subordination in which marginalized groups live. 'Social inequality', MacKinnon asserts, 'is substantially created and enforced – that is, *done* – through words and images.'[10] Pornography does not represent or depict the fantasy subordination of women. It 'makes the world a pornographic place . . . establishing what women are said to exist as, are seen as, are treated as, constructing the social reality of what a woman is and can be in terms of what can be done to her'.[11] Pornography thus subordinates *all* women, not only those working in the sex industry. What applies to pornography also applies to racism: 'When the racist restaurant or hotel owner puts a Whites Only sign in his window, his sign is more than speech. . . . The sign is part of the larger practice of segregation and white supremacy that constructs and maintains a culture in which nonwhites are excluded from full citizenship.'[12] According to MacKinnon, this means that with pornography 'as sex becomes speech, [so] speech becomes sex'.[13] Likewise, as Kendall Thomas notes, individuals 'are raced' by 'racist speech'.[14] Both pornography and hate-speech, that is, are performative: generating the abuse and inequality they name.

At first glance, there are several similarities here with Butler's argument: the stress on the performativity of language, its centrality to how reality is constructed in exclusionary and inegalitarian ways, and the implied linkage between language and subjectification. There are important differences, however, and these relate to the choice of strategy selected by MacKinnon et al. for dealing with hate-speech. Butler, as will become clear, opposes state intervention; indeed this opposition is fundamental to her radical democratic vision. In order to set out an alternative and allegedly more democratic approach, therefore, she too concentrates on the relation between speech and conduct. Instead of pursuing the more common path of claiming that wounding words are just opinions that can be challenged in the public sphere of debate and deliberation, however, she turns to linguistic theory. She aims to show that structurally speech and conduct are always dissociable because they are always temporally distinct, and it is this temporal distinction that reveals the need for a different form of political engagement. It is not that Butler denies the existence or operation of injurious speech or that such injurious speech is constitutive in demeaning or harmful ways, as MacKinnon et al. charge. It is that hate-speech also constitutes an opportunity for defiant speech; and it is this defiant speech, not legal regulation, that has the capacity to defuse hate-speech of its power.

To build her critique of the critical race theorists and anti-pornography theorists, therefore, she articulates an argument connecting together a number of claims. First, she contests the characterization of hate-speech as illocutionary, that is, where speech and conduct are taken to be inseparable. Second, she refutes the idea that illocutionary performatives are necessarily successful in attaining their effects. Next, she challenges the view of sovereign agency that underpins the position of her opponents, a view that impacts not only on questions of subjectivity but also on those of prosecutability and accountability. Then, Butler argues against the assumption that the state can act as a neutral arbiter of speech, while finally she charges that a politics of resignification is a preferable political strategy for combating linguistic injury because it is vitalized by the instability inherent in all language.

The force of the performative

Excitable Speech opens with the following question: 'When we claim to have been injured by language, what kind of claim do we make?'

(*ES*: 1). Evidently one of the claims being made is that language has a certain force that enables it to injure. What is it, though, that endows an utterance with the kinds of injurious force attributed to it by those seeking to regulate hate-speech? How, in other words, does language harm? In order to answer this, Butler turns briefly to the work of speech-act theorist J. L. Austin.[15] According to Butler, assessing the force of any utterance for Austin requires the analyst to examine the 'total speech situation' in which the particular utterance is located (*ES*: 2). This is a problematic enterprise, Butler cautions, as an examination of Austin's own distinction between illocutionary and perlocutionary acts reveals.[16] An illocutionary speech act is one where the utterance does something; the saying is a doing. Austin cites, as examples, 'informing, ordering, warning, undertaking'.[17] (This is also where MacKinnon et al.'s arguments around hate-speech fit.) By contrast, a perlocutionary speech act is one where an utterance makes certain effects happen as a result of the utterance; what Austin describes as 'what we bring about or achieve *by* saying something', giving as examples 'convincing, persuading, deterring, and even, say, surprising or misleading'.[18] As Butler glosses it: 'the former are speech acts that, in saying do what they say, and do it in the moment of that saying; the latter are speech acts that produce certain effects as their consequence; by saying something, a certain effect follows' (*ES*: 3). They assume different temporal sequences.

According to Austin, illocutionary utterances are 'utterances which have a certain (*conventional*) force'.[19] In other words, they derive their power from the fact that they are underpinned by certain institutions and procedures, including the kinds of words that may be uttered, the particular persons authorized to utter them, the specific circumstances in which they may be uttered, and so forth.[20] So the conventions underpinning the marriage ceremony (one of Austin's examples), for instance, include that those wishing to marry are in a legal position to do so; that the person conducting the marriage ceremony is entitled to do so; that it takes place in a venue licensed for marriage ceremonies and at an appropriate time. Only then will the utterance of the words 'I now pronounce you man and wife' take illocutionary effect. It is the presence of specific traditions, institutions and related organizational arrangements – the conventions – that give force to any particular illocutionary utterance. If illocutionary speech-acts acquire their force from convention, then this makes it far harder to isolate the total speech situation and it suggests that the distinction between illocutionary and perlocutionary performatives cannot be sustained. If this is the case, it undermines the arguments marshalled by Butler's opponents in the hate-speech debate.

When Austin differentiates illocutionary utterances from perlocutionary ones, he does so by assuming that a different temporal structure underpins the two utterances. Illocutionary speech-acts require the simultaneity of word and deed, while perlocutionary utterances simply entail 'some consequences'.[21] Butler challenges this differentiation by arguing that the temporal structure of the illocutionary speech act is the same as that of the perlocutionary. If illocutionaries are grounded in convention, as Austin claims, then they contain a 'condensed historicity' (*ES*: 3) that jeopardizes the claim of simultaneity between speech and conduct.[22] If *any* performative act succeeds, it does so only because 'that action echoes prior actions, and *accumulates the force of authority through the repetition or citation of prior and authoritative set of practices*' (*ES*: 51; see also *BTM*: 227).[23] An illocutionary speech-act may enact its effects at the moment of utterance, but its illocutionary *force* derives from the presence of customs and structures that both precede and endure beyond that utterance; indeed 'no term or statement', for Butler, 'can function performatively without the accumulating and dissimulating historicity of force' (*ES*: 51). As such, as Lois McNay notes, in Butler's view there is no possibility of delimiting a 'single, self-contained moment of performance' as the idea of the total speech situation implies.[24] This is because the total speech situation of every utterance encompasses not only its immediate iterative context but also its past and future, neither of which can be described with any conviction (*ES*: 3). Austin's distinction between illocutionary and perlocutionary thus collapses.

How, though, does this general reading of Austin relate to the specific political problem with which Butler is concerned, namely, assaultive speech? Just as hegemonic gender relations attain and retain their authoritative force through the repetition or citation of prior norms, so, for Butler, forms of racial and sexual subordination acquire their force through reiteration, though in this case the reiteration of names. As she notes, 'injurious names have a history' or rather a '*historicity*'. This is 'the history which has become internal to a name, has come to constitute the contemporary meaning of a name', the way in which the uses of that name have accumulated so as to become intrinsic to it, 'a repetition that congeals, that gives the name its force' (*ES*: 36).[25] When that name is deployed, this historicity – or conventionality – is invoked. Hate-speech only works as hate-speech, then, because it cites itself; it is only because 'we already know its force from its prior instances' that 'we know it to be so offensive now' (*ES*: 80). If hate-speech is to remain in existence and to continue to have pernicious effects, it requires continuous repetition. Because it is the injunction to repeat that nourishes racism and sexism, the force of hate-speech resides in its citationality. Assaultive speech causes harm to its interlocutors, but, as McNay comments, that harm is not immediate because it relies for its efficacy upon 'a process of temporal deferral where its repeated effects bring into being or materialize derogated subject positions'.[26] The question of how hate-speech has acquired its injurious force (the injuriousness that is *re*-iterated each time such speech is recycled) is not, however, something Butler addresses.

Isolating and refuting the temporal structure of illocutionary performatives and exposing the gap, therefore, between speech and conduct is, of course, only the first element in the development of Butler's critique of wounding words. Indeed, so far, there is nothing to suggest that the argument that hate-speech reiterates certain conventions undermines the case for its legal regulation. The second aspect of Butler's argument is thus critical. This relates to what she perceives to be the erroneous belief by Matsuda, Crenshaw et al. in the sovereign efficacy of performative utterances: that is, that illocutionary speech-acts are always efficacious. Although it is not at all clear that this is what MacKinnon and the critical race theorists actually believe, showing that illocutionary performatives do not always succeed allows Butler to plot an alternative political course for the contestation of hate-speech.

Opposing sovereign performatives

Behind the idea of an illocutionary speech-act, such as a threat, lies what Butler calls 'the sovereign conceit' (*ES*: 16): the 'fantasy of sovereign action that structures the threat is that a certain kind of saying is at once the performance of the act referred to in that saying' (*ES*: 12). Advocates of hate-speech regulation assume this logic, Butler avers, when they argue that the one who utters sexist or racist speech does what s/he says when it is said, thus that he or she subordinates the addressee at the moment of the utterance. When, for instance, MacKinnon identifies the power of the pornographic text as bringing about the subordination of women, according to Butler, she 'engages a figure of the performative, a figure of sovereign power that governs how a speech act is said to act – as efficacious, unilateral, transitive, generative' (*ES*: 74). And, indeed, this claim seems to be substantiated by MacKinnon's own assertion that the 'power of pornography is more like the power of the state. It is backed by power at least as great, as least as unchecked, and at least as legitimated.'[27]

For Butler, however, there is a difference between the illocutionary status of an utterance (that it is a threat) and its efficacy (that it does what it intends). Relevant here is what Austin calls 'the doctrine of the *Infelicities*': that is, the 'misfires' and 'abuses' to which performatives are occasionally liable.[28] Admitting the possibility of infelicitous effects damages the claims of Butler's opponents, for if hate-speech and pornography are not always as efficacious as these pro-regulation critics contend, then censorship may not be the answer. Once again, Butler turns to Derrida. When Austin explored infelicitous speech-acts, he did so by exploring the conditions or circumstances in which they failed. So, for instance, in terms of marriage conventions, the performative 'I pronounce you man and wife' fails when the person conducting the marriage ceremony is not authorized to do so or when one of the two parties to the marriage ceremony is already married, and so on.[29] When Derrida talks of potential failure, by contrast, he assumes not that failure is a circumstantial possibility but that it is a risk 'proper to the speech act itself' (*ES*: 150). This is, to recall an earlier argument (see Chapter 3), the result of the capacity of speech to break with its existing contexts and be deployed in novel and unforeseeable ways. It is this feature of language that underpins the potential for hate-speech to be counter-signified in such a manner that its power to harm is thwarted.

To claim, therefore, as Richard Delgado does, that words 'such as "nigger" and "spick" are badges of degradation even when they are used between friends' and that '[t]hese words have no other connotation'[30] is, in Butler's view, to fail to take account of the kinds of 'redoubling of injurious speech' that occur because of the iterable structure of language (*ES*: 14). From political satire to rap music, from the kind of politico-legal critique in which Delgado is engaged to the many attempts either to legislate against or to prosecute specific speech (including the Helms amendment and 'Don't Ask, Don't Tell'), assaultive words are restaged and their uses proliferate. Exactly by endeavouring to censor pornography, activists and politicians such as Dworkin, MacKinnon and Helms are, for Butler, actively and somewhat ironically engaged in recirculating and reinvigorating the very discourses they seek to repudiate; they are demonstrating the citationality of the sign.[31] And it is this citationality, as indicated in her discussion of gender, that is at the core of Butler's proposed political response to hate-speech. Before we pursue this last claim further, there is one final aspect of her rebuttal of the sovereign conceit that needs to be considered, and this is the relation of sovereignty to subjectivity, for it is crucial to apprehending her non-voluntarist account of agency. To understand this we need, however, to return briefly to Butler's account of the discursive constitution of subjectivity.

A linguistic account of subjectivity

If there is one figure whose shadow looms over *Gender Trouble* more than that of any other, it is Foucault.[32] By the time of *Bodies that Matter*, however, Butler's writings are haunted at least equally by the spectre of Jacques Derrida and the idea of 'performativity as citationality' (*BTM*: 12) that he derives from his radical reading of Austin. The effects of this alteration in emphasis are noticeable in several areas of Butler's thought, but particularly, I want to suggest, in relation to her analysis of subjectivity. Initially, Butler's discussion of gender performativity is located very much within the context of discourse and, specifically, in an account of discourse clearly indebted to Foucault ('CR': 138). Simply put, when Foucault talks of discourse (at least, in his genealogical writings), he uses it, as McNay notes, to refer to the 'structuring principle which governs beliefs and practices, "words and things", in such a way as to produce a certain network of material relations'.[33] Discourse (or the discursive) thus always implicates the institutions, techniques and practices that generate subjects, amongst other things. Furthermore, discourse and power are inextricably connected for Foucault. Thus, he writes, 'discourse can be both an instrument and an effect of power'. It 'transmits and produces power; it reinforces it'. Critically, however, even the most hegemonic discourse is, on Foucault's account, always open and polyvalent. Discourse neither uniformly serves the interests of power nor uniformly resists them; it is more complex and volatile than this, working at once both to consolidate hegemonic power and to oppose it. In addition to consolidating power, discourse thus 'also undermines and exposes it, renders it fragile and makes it possible to thwart it'.[34]

During Butler's rebuttal of Benhabib's critique of agency (discussed in Chapter 3), she defines what it means to be performatively constituted or 'constituted by language' as 'to be produced within a given network of power/discourse' ('CR': 135). The locution power/discourse, a term that peppers Butler's account of gender performativity, is not simply a corruption of Foucault's notion of power/knowledge but a reference to the relation between power and discourse that Foucault himself establishes. Additionally, when refuting Nancy Fraser's accusation of the linguistic 'esotericism' of *Gender Trouble*,[35] Butler expressly remarks that discourse 'is not merely spoken words, but a notion of signification which concerns not merely how it is that certain signifiers come to mean what they mean, but how certain discursive forms articulate objects and subjects in their intelligibility' ('CR': 138). The heterosexual matrix within which gendered subjects are produced represents just such a discursive form, where objects and subjects are articulated into a culturally intelligible frame; it both echoes the notion of a 'structuring principle' noted above and captures the generativity of the discursive as Foucault presents it. When critics accuse Butler of linguistic determinism in her writings on gender, therefore, they conflate discourse with language.[36] That said, a small but significant shift in her argument nevertheless begins to take place when Butler starts to engage more explicitly with the work of Derrida. This culminates in her development of a linguistic account of subjectification in *Excitable Speech*. The point is not that Butler has abandoned all notion of the discursive in general. It is merely that in *Excitable Speech* she concentrates principally on the role of language in subject production – though language is always thought of by Butler as a bodily act. It is this thesis that I now want to explore.

The citationality of speech-acts is said by Butler to challenge the sovereign conceit that underpins the belief that wounding words are illocutionary. It does so in two ways: first, as duly noted, by casting doubt on the efficaciousness of illocutionary speech acts because of their potential to fail; and, second, our focus here, by problematizing the idea of the sovereign subject as both the author and origin of assaultive speech, an idea hinted at but not developed in *Bodies that Matter*.[37] So how does this latter argument work? In an original turn, Butler explains the relation between speech and subjectivity by juxtaposing Austin's understanding of illocution against Althusser's account of interpellation. Her aim: to expose the limitations of both analyses by highlighting their hidden assumptions. Noting that the positions of the two thinkers appear to be at variance since Austin assumes that the subject precedes speech while Althusser assumes that speech – or rather the interpellating call of an authority figure (the 'hey you' of the policeman discussed in the previous chapter) – inaugurates the subject, Butler suggests that, in fact, the interpellation preceding and forming the subject in Althusser 'appears to constitute the prior condition of those subject-centred speech acts that dominate Austin's domain of analysis' (*ES*: 24). To allow, therefore, that hate-speech injures those against whom it is directed, it is not enough to argue that illocutionary speech has force; it is also necessary to believe that speech has an interpellative role in the constitution of the subject (Althusser's assertion). Otherwise the claim that words wound makes no sense.

In the previous chapter, I examined Butler's psychoanalytic interpretation of interpellation. In this chapter, I want to pursue her linguistic interpretation. As noted previously, according to Althusser the individual becomes a subject (of ideology in general) when it turns in response to the voice that is hailing it. 'One comes to "exist"', in other words, 'by virtue of this fundamental dependency on the address of the Other' (*ES*: 5). Butler interprets this to mean that since subjects are linguistically constituted, they cannot 'be' independent of language. According to her, however, the subject does not actually need to turn to be interpellated as a subject. It can be constituted without being aware of it (*ES*: 33). Moreover, interpellation can occur even when the subject resists its terms, when it denies that it is the one being named. Finally, interpellation does not necessarily require an actual speaker (like Althusser's policeman) to hail the individual being interpellated. Interpellation works through other practices and institutions – 'bureaucratic forms, the census, adoption papers, employment applications', and so on. The reason for all of this is that interpellation, like illocutionary speech, is based on convention. It has a ritual form that precedes and exceeds it, with all the consequences discussed above that this conventionality entails. As such, the sovereign power thought to ground interpellation is actually more diffuse and, Butler will argue, uncertain than previously thought.

If naming is what enables the subject to 'be', then being called a demeaning name also has this effect: 'Called by an injurious name, I come into social being' (*PLP*: 104). As Butler has it, however, all interpellations – even ones that are not ostensibly harmful – injure as they constitute. This is because the terms that make social recognition possible are themselves conventional. They foreclose other interpellative possibilities, other potential namings. So the previously referred to 'it's a girl' uttered in the delivery room serves the convention-bound interpellative function of inaugurating the female subject. Likewise, the utterance of derogatory terms operates in similarly convention-bound fashion to inaugurate its interlocutor as a subordinated subject. Either way, the subject is linguistically constituted.

Linguistic subjectivity and responsibility

One of the presumptions underpinning the work of MacKinnon, Matsuda, Delgado and others is the possibility of the state prosecuting those who utter derogatory speech on the basis that such speakers are responsible for their utterances. Butler apparently takes this to imply that MacKinnon et al. assume that the subject is, somehow, independent of language; that it confronts language as an external phenomenon. Once it is recognized that all subjects exhibit the prior vulnerability to language just outlined where all require the interpellative address of the other in order to exist, and where the possibility of naming another is always dependent upon one's own prior naming, this compromises the idea of a subject independent of language. It also compromises the idea of a prosecutable subject.

When someone utters a 'violating interpellation', as we have seen, they do not initiate that term; they recite it but their recitation produces a particular effect: the '*subject who "cites" the performative is temporarily produced as the belated and fictive origin of the performative itself*' (*ES*: 49). They appear to be the originator of their own speech when, in fact, they are not. The person uttering wounding words is only able to do so because of a 'long string of injurious interpellations' that precede his or her deployment of them (*ES*: 49). This is important for it means that the speaker of hate is produced as a racist or homophobic subject by the speech it utters, just as, in turn, that speech produces the subject against whom it is uttered as 'raced' or 'sexualized'. If hate-speech is to be prosecuted, therefore, Butler asks, 'where and when would that prosecution begin?'

> If the function of the subject as fictive origin is to occlude the genealogy by which that subject is formed, the subject is also installed in order to assume the burden of responsibility for the very history that subject dissimulates; the juridicalization of history, then, is achieved

> precisely through the search for subjects to prosecute who might be held accountable and, hence, temporarily resolve the problem of a fundamentally unprosecutable history. (*ES*: 50)

While conceding, slightly later on, that 'there are probably occasions' when subjects ought to be prosecuted for injurious speech, though not specifying in detail what those occasions are, Butler contests both the juridical discourse of prosecutability and the reduction of the scene of utterance to the face-to-face encounter between the addressor and addressee of hate-speech.[38] For they have a reductive effect: they localize the political problem of assaultive speech in the relation between two or more determinate individuals (where one directly harms the other). This is precisely what the critical race theorists and anti-pornography feminists do, according to Butler, when they contend that it is individual acts of speech that cause harm. The problem is that this focus allows the broader institutional and structural dimensions of racism and sexism to disappear from sight.[39]

Butler is not claiming that those who utter hate-speech are devoid of *any* responsibility for their speech (*ES*: 34). Her point is, rather, that when racists speak, their speech recycles existing language. It is this reiteration that locks them into 'an imagined relation to an historically transmitted community of racists' (*ES*: 80). Although, therefore, they *are* responsible for repeating hate-speech, they are *not* responsible for generating it in the first place. It is not entirely clear, however, why this distinction means that those who utter wounding words ought not to be prosecuted for their speech. As Catherine Mills notes, Butler appears to assume that legal culpability – and thus the law – requires a sovereign subject to prosecute; but does it? Mills's suggestion is that it is, in fact, possible to differentiate between the idea of legal culpability for the recitation and thus reinvigoration of hate-speech and the 'philosophical' claim that hate-speech does not originate with any particular individual.[40] What is needed from Butler, therefore, is 'further explication of an alternative account of responsibility and its relation to legal culpability'.[41] It is perhaps here that Butler could flesh out her comment that sometimes prosecution might be appropriate.

So, to reprise: Butler contests the supposed temporal structure of illocutionary acts, arguing that what gives them their force is their conventionality. She also argues that performatives are not always efficacious and that the citational structure of language enables it to break with its prior context. Each of these moves has the effect of relaxing the connection between the speech-act and its effect. The implications for hate-speech are clear: wounding words do not always or necessarily harm as they are spoken. There is thus a potential hiatus between the act and the injury that can be exploited as a site of resistance. This is where counter-speech becomes possible. Even more productively for Butler, 'the gap that separates the speech act from its future effects has its auspicious implications: it begins a theory of linguistic agency that provides an alternative to the relentless search for legal remedy' (*ES*: 15). There are, therefore, two strands of Butler's argument that need examining in more detail: first, her conception of a non-sovereign account of agency, and here the claim that subjects are constituted in and through language is pivotal; and, second, her rationale for rejecting legislative politics.

Revisiting agency – politics and resignification

From the discussion in previous chapters, we can identify a number of features of Butler's account of agency prior to *Excitable Speech*: agency is contingent upon the repetition of the norms that condition social life – it is a consequence of their iterability; it is distinct from autonomy – in fact, subordination by power is essential to agency; and, for this reason, 'agency begins where sovereignty wanes' (*ES*: 16). In *Excitable Speech*, Butler extends her discussion further by considering linguistic agency. Her theory rests on the twin provisos that subjects depend for their existence on language and that language is persistently 'excitable', that is, outside the control of its user. It is the citationality of language that is the primary condition of possibility for linguistic agency and action, therefore.

To reiterate: those who argue that hate-speech is illocutionary assume that it instantaneously and necessarily harms as it is spoken. By construing hate-speech as citational, and its performative force as perlocutionary, however, Butler is able to argue that while hate-speech generates consequences, there is nothing necessary about the direction or shape they take. The idea that the subject exerts sovereign control over its utterances is thus refuted. An absence of sovereignty, however, does not betoken an absence of agency. Quite the opposite: it is because an utterance cannot guarantee a particular effect that it is open to appropriation, reversal and recontextualization (to echo Butler [*ES*: 39]). It is, in Derridean terms, such breaks with context that create the possibility of political transformation. Hate-speech can thus, potentially at least, be turned against its tainted past and be resignified. Although hate-speech injures, Butler also sees it as presenting 'the initiating moment of a counter-mobilization'. The repetition of assaultive speech does not simply reproduce and hence consolidate hegemonic (racist and patriarchal) power relations; when a term is appropriated and made to resignify in insurrectionary or mutinous fashion it can deform, reconfigure or even suspend those relations. The authority a pejorative name has garnered over time by its repeated usage can be challenged and a new, potentially authoritative, meaning engendered (*ES*: 163).[42] Two examples drawn from Butler's wider work will suffice to demonstrate how insubordinate resignification works.

When asked by a child yelling at her from a Berkeley window 'Are you a lesbian?', Butler replies affirmatively, 'Yes, I *am* a lesbian.' As she recounts it, in that moment, 'the power of my interrogator was lost': its attempt to interpellate her as an object of fear and loathing had failed, and failed miserably, because Butler had 'received the term' it threw out at her and had returned it resignified. Instead of accepting the speech as hate-speech, Butler reclaims it as a positive description of herself ('CS': 352). She defuses its pernicious potential. When Butler and the child communicate in this way, neither is the author of the speech they use; both are engaged in recycling the language that already circulates in everyday communication between people. The second example is drawn from *Bodies that Matter* and is an example already touched on in Chapter 3: the term 'queer'.

Traditionally the term 'queer' had operated primarily as a term of abuse; a 'linguistic practice whose purpose has been the shaming of the subject it names' (*BTM*: 226). As such, it was deployed to stigmatize those against whom it was directed (as part, one assumes, of a broader homophobic strategy). From the early 1990s onwards, however, the term underwent a radical resignification. The repeated use of queer 'again and again as part of an affirmative practice' by queer theorists and queer activists (including Queer Nation) worked, in Butler's judgement, to 'take it out of an established context of being exclusively injurious' ('CS': 351). The word became the locus of collective challenge; it was reclaimed, opened up and turned 'in the direction of urgent and expanding political purposes' (*BTM*: 228), and so the 'public assertion of "queerness"', Butler notes, 'enacts performativity as citationality for the purpose of resignifying the abjection of homosexuality into defiance and legitimacy' (*BTM*: 21). Celebration of homosexuality replaced its stigmatization – in *some* places, at least.

Despite what Butler, to recall, refers to as the 'historicity' contained in egregious or exclusionary speech, that speech is always, in her view, amenable to resignification: 'sullied terms' are thus vulnerable 'to an unexpected innocence' in which 'they assume a life and a purpose for which they were never intended' (*ES*: 161). Consequently, no term is ever entirely corrupted and no term ever entirely innocent; they are both at once. They make possible both the 'subject's linguistic survival as well as, potentially, that subject's linguistic death' (*ES*: 28). When Matsuda et al. construe hate-speech as illocutionary and always efficacious, they mask this possibility in language: the possibility that is, of language for appropriation and resignification, for this is where its political promise resides. 'Counter-speech', as Lisa Disch notes, provides 'a conception of agency to rival autonomy that is premised in the temporality of construction, the possibility of citing a term anew to break with its customary associations and challenge the relations of power they serve to naturalize'.[43] The agency of the 'post-sovereign subject' is thus not a personal capacity they possess but an effect of the iterability of language. This is why Butler's account focuses on the structural conditions that facilitate insurrectionary speech-acts (*ES*: 139).

A number of issues arise from this discussion of resignification, three of which I want to highlight here. First, as Butler acknowledges, resignification is a risky strategy both in the sense that it puts the speaker at ontological risk by taking up an injurious term but also because there is no guarantee of its success (*ES*: 163). In this respect, Mikhail Bakhtin's observation that not all words 'submit equally easily to appropriation' appears apposite. As he notes, 'many words stubbornly resist, others remain alien, sound foreign in the mouth of the one who appropriated them and who now speaks them', and some 'fall out' of their new context.[44] Yet there is more than risk at stake here, I think. Take the term 'nigger'. It is not entirely clear to me that this name can be radically resignified in the manner that Butler implies. While it can certainly be restaged in a court of law or in academic discourse so as to neutralize its harmfulness to specific addressees (as Butler suggests a propos Delgado), it does not follow that it can become, therefore, readily acceptable as a form of address more generally. As a term that is deeply imbricated in the history of slavery in the US, indeed which was used by the slave-master precisely in order to dehumanize the slave, it is hard to imagine that it could be used more progressively. And, although groups such as Niggaz with Attitude (NWA) have appropriated the term and sought to invest it with more positive connotations, and while some African Americans use it familiarly to address one another, the stigma attached to it historically has not entirely abated. Nigger – or the N-word, as it is more often known – remains, for many, at best a controversial term.

This ties in to the second observation, which is that for all her debts to Foucault, Butler appears to commit a very un-Foucauldian move when, as Catherine Mills asserts, she predicts 'at the level of theory' the kind of politics that can best counter subordinating speech *regardless* of the specific context of that speech.[45] In other words, Butler appears to validate resignification *a priori* as the optimum form of political intervention against hate-speech. Although it might well be 'a logically possible mode of redress' against assaultive speech, for Mills, 'it is [not] necessarily the most efficacious one, since this could only be decided *in loco*'.[46] In Butler's defence it might be argued that she favours linguistic resignification as a response to hate-speech simply because hate-speech performs a linguistic harm. In other words, because language is the site and vehicle of the injury, then it is also the site and vehicle of resistance. When, for instance, Butler debates gay marriage, she expressly does *not* argue that marriage as a heteronormative practice is best challenged by gays and lesbians appropriating and resignifying it. She argues instead that marriage must be divested of its privileged status *per se*.[47] This seems to imply that Butler recognizes that, although resignification, as a logically inescapable feature of language, has political potential, on its own it is not sufficient for an entire politics. This takes me to my third and final point.

It is a feature of Butler's work that she is deeply suspicious of any theory that assumes an *a priori* universal of any kind. Instead, in her work, she privileges contingency. This is why, as noted in the previous chapter, she is such a vigorous critic of Lacan: because he assumes the existence of an invariable structure, the Symbolic. Yet Butler's own understanding of language seems to rely on the identification of its invariant structural features – its iterability, its inherent risk of failure and its propensity to be resignified regardless of context. Here a question she directs at Žižek might profitably be addressed to Butler herself. Worried that Žižek cleaves to certain structural truths about the nature of language, Butler asks: 'How would the new be produced from an analysis of the social field that remains restricted to inversions, aporias, reversals that work *regardless of time and place*?' (*CHU*: 29, my emphasis). Reformulating slightly, we might ask Butler: how does iterability allow for the creation of the new out of resignifications that simply invert or reverse the terms they redeploy, apparently regardless of time and place? How, in other words, does Butler's account of language manage to evade the charge of invariance levelled at Žižek's?

When Butler differentiates her own approach from Žižek's in *Contingency, Hegemony, Universality*, she does so by referring to *Gender Trouble*. She notes that: 'Where Žižek isolates the structural features of linguistic positing and offers cultural examples to illustrate this structural truth, I am, I believe, more concerned to rethink performativity as cultural ritual, as the reiteration of cultural norms, as the habitus of the body in which structural and social dimensions of meaning are not finally separable' (*CHU*: 29). So, for Žižek, cultural examples merely illustrate his broader point about language, whereas for Butler performativity is, itself, cultural. Language and culture cannot, that is, be separated. What, though, of Butler's argument in *Excitable Speech*, where it is precisely language, rather than cultural norms, that *appears* to concern her? Her defence here is that language is never solely language. It is always and only ever language in its social or cultural operation; language articulated in and as norms. Here Pierre Bourdieu's take on the social dimensions of performativity, as discussed by Butler, might help shed light on this claim.[48]

Like Derrida, Bourdieu starts with Austin's account of the force of the performative. Bourdieu agrees with Austin that force derives from convention, but he contends that Austin's account conceives convention too narrowly; it presupposes an account of social power that Austin never explicates. This is what Bourdieu aims to provide. The force of the performative, he contends, derives from the social power of the speaker, from the authority they have been vested with as a result of their institutional position. This is why when they speak, when, for instance, a member of the police says 'you are under arrest', their utterance has force. Someone is arrested. The same is not true of 'imposters', those without institutional authorization to speak. They may 'recite the same formula' as the authorized individual but without effect (*ES*: 146). They can, to continue my example, utter the words 'you are under arrest' but no arrest will take place.[49] For Bourdieu, therefore, it is possible to differentiate between those legitimately entitled to speak and those who are not so entitled. Agreeing that there is a need to theorize the 'social iterability of the utterance', Butler disagrees with Bourdieu, however, about how this ought to be done. She thus broadly approves of his attempt to extend the '"ritual" sense of "convention"', and the implications of this for understanding infelicities, but disapproves, in particular, of the ensuing loss of emphasis in his account on the *temporality* of performativity (*ES*: 151).[50] She thus returns to Derrida. Performatives have effects because they recite conventional formulae. This is just as true for 'legitimate' as for 'illegitimate' utterances, in Bourdieu's terms. Both have the scope to engender new meanings for the terms that are being reiterated. This points to a particular difficulty with Bourdieu's conception of social institutions. According to Butler, he tends to think of them as operating statically to reinforce the *status quo*; as a result, he underestimates the potential of performativity for social transformation.[51]

In concurring with Bourdieu about the social dimensions of performativity, Butler is, of course, partially distancing herself from Derrida. The merit of Derrida's approach, for Butler, is that he can explain the potential for transformation, because failure is intrinsic to language. The problem is that he pays too little attention to the social nature of iteration (*ES*: 150). In other words, Derrida focuses too much on language *per se* and not enough on its social form. This is where Butler sees her own account diverging from Derrida's. She is primarily interested in social questions – heteronormativity, hate-speech, kinship, gay marriage. Her interest in the operations of language is thus always, she indicates, an interest in the concrete operations of language in particular determinate instances. Despite her protestations that she understands iterability always as social iterability, nevertheless and against all her best intentions, Butler, in my view, still pays insufficient attention to the exact power relations and to the specific social and political institutions or practices that underpin and shape actual acts of iteration and resignification. She concentrates too much, that is, on the *general* conditions of possibility for resignification and not enough on the specific *historical* circumstances within which *particular* resignifications emerge. Perhaps the principal reason for this weakness in her theory is that her conception of the social is simply too narrow and undifferentiated. She tends, that is, to use the adjectives 'social' and 'cultural' to refer to the contingency and the power-invested nature of particular norms, practices, language uses and symbolic forms.[52] This is too general, however. Take hate-speech.

In *Excitable Speech* Butler concentrates on the capacity of language for recitation. She is particularly concerned with social transformation. She ignores, however, the manner in which, as Anna Marie Smith observes, 'contemporary definitions of protected speech have emerged out of various historically specific institutions and social movements alike'.[53] She fails to explore the kinds of technologies of power through which protected speech is secured, the historical and exclusionary conditions of its emergence, or how it is tied into a particular conception of political rationality. Crucially, there is no examination of the relation between protected speech and *liberal* forms of governmentality. There is, in other words, no genealogy of protected speech. This not only suggests that for all her vociferous criticisms of the liberal state, which I outline below, Butler's argument in *Excitable Speech* is inextricably invested in 'the truth claims and problematics of liberalism'.[54] It also means that there is no examination of how the culturally and historically contingent definition of protected speech on which her critique of hate-speech draws might actually serve both to limit resignification (instead of just facilitating it, as she seems to assume) and to contain any attempt to radicalize democracy.

All that remains to be done in this chapter is to consider why Butler rejects recourse to the state, and in particular the law, as a fitting tactic for dealing with wounding words. It is thus to her critique of the liberal state that I now turn.

Against the state

Although the state barely figures in Butler's theory of gender performativity or in the subversive politics it entails, it becomes a more common theme in her writing after *Bodies that Matter*. While the account she develops initially lacks nuance and complexity, it is an important development, nevertheless.[55] It clearly signals her thinking on what has been called the legalization of politics and, in particular, its place within feminism. This is the attempt, as Butler defines it, to 'recast political opposition as legal plaint and to seek the legitimacy of the state in the espousal of feminist claims' (*AC*: 1), a move that she is deeply sceptical of, because, as will become clear, for her, democratization works best in civil society. This is particularly clear in her discussion of hate-speech.

As we have seen, those articulating the case for state regulation of hate-speech and pornography do so on the basis that such speech is illocutionary; it harms as it is spoken. They reject the claim that hate-speech and pornography simply represent opposable viewpoints, countering instead that they are both ways in which inequality is actively constituted. To secure substantive equality for oppressed groups, they counsel using censorship and state regulation. To Butler the robustness of their case for state intervention is explicitly tied to their assumption of an indissociable link between utterance and effect (or speech and conduct). Accepting that there is a gap between the two, as Butler argues, is to 'lend support', by contrast, for 'nonjuridical forms of opposition, ways of restaging and resignifying speech in contexts that exceed those determined by the courts' (*ES*: 23). For Butler this is a far 'more promising and more democratic' strategy than allowing the law to determine when – and if – speech harms (*ES*: 101). Why?

There are three aspects to her critique: first, Butler is suspicious of the arbitrariness of state power; second, she construes the regulation of hate-speech as a means by which the state can extend its power; and, finally, state regulation curtails the opportunities for resignification in civil society. Let us explore each in turn. Examining a range of legal precedents and Supreme Court decisions, Butler concludes that the state is not neutral in its adjudications. State censorship works differentially in practice. So, for instance, while narrowing definitions of 'fighting words' so as to make it harder to prosecute racist hate-speech (such as the burning of a cross on the lawn in front of the home of an African American family [*ES*: 43–70]), the Court has been willing both to extend definitions of obscenity and to exclude this enlarged definition of obscenity from the purview of protected speech. It has, in other words, determined that obscenity is a form of 'fighting words' and, in a move consonant with the advocacy of MacKinnon, accepted that 'graphic sexual representation is injurious' (*ES*: 64). The effect of this is that racist hate-speech is countenanced by the Court while representations of sexuality, including homosexuality, in particular, are castigated as obscene and thus open to prosecution (and the Helms Amendment is a case in point here). There is, thus, a clear anomaly for Butler, for where racist speech is conceived as protected speech, racially inflected representations of sexuality (as in the sexually explicit language used in rap, for example) are the most liable for prosecution.[56] In a parallel case, the very logic that is denied with regard to hate-speech (that speech performs what it describes or that words wound) underpins the 1993 'Don't Ask, Don't Tell' policy on gays in the military. In this case the phrase 'I am a homosexual' is construed as 'a homosexual act' (*ES*: 64). It is 'explicitly' interpreted, furthermore, as 'contagious and offensive conduct' (*ES*: 107), and taken to be a form of precisely the kind of 'fighting words' that the Court will not recognize in relation to race (*ES*: 65). In short, the arbitrariness of state power 'is evidenced in the contrary use of precedents on hate speech to promote conservative political goals and thwart progressive efforts' (*ES*: 62). The manner in which the law is implemented, so as 'to further reactionary political aims' (*ES*: 39), exposes the non-neutrality of the state.

Of course, Butler is not alone in her criticisms of the American judicial system. Anna Marie Smith, in a commentary on *Excitable Speech*, endorses Butler's observations concerning the judiciary's ever more conservative stance towards hate-speech throughout the 1990s, citing examples of the ways in which gay and lesbian political demands have been co-opted by Republicans for electoral purposes or used for the state's own advantage.[57] The authors of *Words that Wound* also, themselves, confess a certain scepticism towards 'dominant legal claims of neutrality, objectivity, color blindness and meritocracy'.[58] Empirically, there is little doubt that the Supreme Court has become increasingly conservative in the last decades. Butler's point, however, is more far-reaching. She asks, 'What happens when we seek recourse to the state to regulate . . . [hate-] speech?' (*ES*: 77). Her answer is that the state itself generates such speech. Arguments for state censorship usually characterize it as a *response* to offensive speech: censorship, that is, comes after the speech that it is censoring. Butler, however, argues that hate-speech is actually a 'category that cannot exist without the state's ratification', for it is '*the state* [that] *produces hate speech*' (*ES*: 77). So how does this argument work?

The state commits its harms by actively instituting a realm of publicly acceptable speech, based on differentiating between 'the speakable and the unspeakable'. Allowing the state to determine what counts as offensive speech is thus to allow it to hold on to the power 'to make and sustain that consequential line of demarcation' (*ES*: 77).[59] Permitting the state to prosecute hate-speech runs the risk of handing over to the courts the chance to 'impose a further violence of its own. And if the court begins to decide what is and is not violating speech, that decision runs the risk of constituting the most binding of violations' (*ES*: 65). It is thus the state (through the courts) that generates the act of assaultive speech, that establishes the doctrine of 'fighting words'. Hate-speech does not precede judicial intervention; judicial intervention performatively enacts hate-speech. Indeed, hate-speech only becomes hate-speech 'by yet another "act of speech" – the speech of the law' (*ES*: 96). This formative capacity of the state also has critical implications for citizenship, for state censorship inaugurates subjects. Or, more specifically, it generates certain types of (citizen-)subject, able to speak a particular legitimated language, at the same time that it disallows others and denies their speech. And, although censorship for Butler is clearly related to speech, its primary concern rather is 'to produce subjects according to explicit and implicit norms' (*ES*: 133). Ordering the realm of 'speakable discourse' is thus a way of deciding who can be a subject in the first place and, of course, this takes us back to Butler's own primary concern throughout her work, which is to extend the meaning of who counts.[60]

Although Butler acknowledges that the sexual or racial utterance that the Court is being asked to adjudicate upon is, in some sense, distinct from the state's determination of whether it counts as hate-speech, and this is her second point, seeking legal redress against assaultive speech allows the state to enhance its regulatory powers in relation to both speech *and* subjects. Hate-speech is not only one of the products of the state; it is also the legal mechanism through which the state can extend its own racial and sexualized discourses. The state is thus allowed to set the norms that determine what counts as racist and sexist speech, and, of course, to recall the previous argument, since the state tends to act in reactionary or conservative ways, to use these determinations against the very groups they are allegedly designed to protect (*ES*: 97–8). To reiterate, the state does not simply censor or limit speech; rather, in the moment of censorship or limitation, it generates the speech that matters legally. Crucially, for Butler, those who favour legal circumscription of harmful speech fail to notice the productivity of state discourse and, consequently, underestimate the potential for the law to be misappropriated or used in an anti-progressive fashion.

This takes me to my third and final claim, which concerns the way that focusing on legal redress minimizes the potential for the resignification of hate speech in non-juridical settings. According to Butler, when the law is conceived, as it is, for instance, by Matsuda, in instrumental terms as a mechanism to secure protection for those harmed by assaultive speech, even in a context where its reactionary past is taken into consideration, two paradoxes appear. First, the citational reversal allowed the law is the opposite of that allowed to pornography. Where pornography's capacity to turn an utterance against its 'original or intended meaning' is what makes it pernicious, it is precisely this capacity that Matsuda insists is positive with respect to the law (*ES*: 98). Second, while it appears that law can be resignified 'beyond any limit' (and away from its contaminated past), hate-speech cannot (*ES*: 99). Butler uses these contradictions in the work of Matsuda, MacKinnon et al. not to endorse the claim that state speech can be progressively recited, but rather to argue that reappropriation works best in the 'domain of protected public discourse' (*ES*: 101), that is, in civil society. Where attempts are made to curb speech, the potential for insurrectionary speech is simultaneously limited. Leaving assaultive speech uncensored, by contrast, actively encourages its 'radical democratic contestation' (*ES*: 108). It allows for the gap between speech and effect to be exploited and for hate-speech to take on an alternative, non-threatening, even empowering, meaning, thus potentially defusing the power of assaultive speech in a way that legal redress cannot. This is, of course, the site of non-sovereign agency discussed above.

There are a number of issues that arise from Butler's characterization of the state. By construing state intervention as necessarily reactionary or arbitrary, she occludes the fact that the state has been, and might continue to be, active in aiding progressive movements, not least against reactionary forces in civil society. Without assuming that the state can furnish the solution to all problems, as fellow radical democrats Ernesto Laclau and Chantal Mouffe note in their own work, the state is, nonetheless, 'an important means for effecting an advance, frequently *against* civil society', as for instance, 'in legislation which combats sexism'.[61] Assuming that legal regulation is necessarily reactionary leads Butler to 'miss the vagaries of the state's position within relations of power and political contestation'.[62] In addition, her presumption that legal language is politically loaded leads her to argue that it is necessarily hazardous to the less powerful in society. Critics have contended, however, that conversely it is actually because the law is not neutral, because it is linguistically indeterminate, that it is 'open to reinflection and reappropriation' even by subordinate groups.[63]

Next, there is, as Paul Passavant and Jodi Dean observe, considerable ambiguity in Butler's usage of the term 'the state' in *Excitable Speech*. At times, they note, it appears she is deploying 'a narrow version of the state, the state as judiciary, as Court, as judge'. At others, her conception seems broader, encompassing a 'variety of conflicting institutions, practices, pronouncements and discourses'.[64] The differences between a limited legal definition and a more pluralistic notion of the state are considerable. Both, however, pose Butler with problems. Reducing the state to law means that any distinction between the two is effaced and the way that the state and law conflict is erased thereby. Using a more pluralistic notion, however, undercuts Butler's presentation of the state as acting unilaterally to further its conservative impulses, for it denies actual and potential occasions of conflict between competing arms of the state and the way that progressive forces might exploit them.[65] In apparent recognition of the inadequacy of her conceptualization of the state, in 'Is Kinship Always Already Heterosexual?', Butler offers a qualified definition. The state 'is not reducible to law', she argues; it comprises plural institutions whose interests do not always coincide, and where there are, consequently, multiple sites for political resistance (27). Nevertheless, her scepticism of the state as a democratizing institution remains and her argument continues to prioritize the state's judicial and normalizing functions.

Perhaps the two most substantive criticisms, however, concern Butler's assumption of the efficacy of state power and her rejection of the potential for recycling state speech in radical directions. As Vicky Kirkby points out, Butler tends to conceive the law's power as 'the power to name, to assign and to delimit'. Moreover, as noted above, this power is seen as constituting a form of violence. Consequently, 'the law itself appears as a unified force', a force with the capacity unilaterally to impose a name, to inaugurate a subject, to violate.[66] This implies not only that the state is efficacious in its utterances, succeeding in naming through violence, but also that it is sovereign and that the power of the state is an illocutionary power to do what it says.[67] Without these assumptions, no sense can be made of Butler's charge that the legal regulation of hate-speech forecloses opportunities for resignification, because if the state failed to achieve its goals, then there would be space to protest. This view appears to be endorsed by Butler herself when she contends that state speech takes sovereign form when its utterances are acts of law (*ES*: 16). What it obscures, though, is a contradiction in her thought: thus when talking about hate-speech, Butler exposes its potential for failure, but when it comes to state-speech, this potential seems to have disappeared. Is state speech always efficacious, therefore? The answer, in short, is surely not. The state is often unable to respond in the ways demanded. This takes us on to the second point identified above: the issue of the resignifiability of state utterances.

Although Butler concedes that the state can resignify discourse, her view is that it 'only and always' reiterates 'its own law' (*ES*: 101), thus permitting it to fortify its own normalizing power. Precisely because the law needs to be recited, however, in order for it to continue to function as an authoritative discourse, then, according to the Derridean logic that Butler follows, that recitation is also always a recycling. Here it is worth adverting to an argument made in *Bodies that Matter* (and touched on briefly in the previous chapter). 'The performative speaking of the law', Butler comments, 'works only by reworking a set of already operative conventions' (*BTM*: 107). Legal conventions are iterable. And, if this is the case, it must mean that they, like hate-speech, can be decontextualized and resignified in more progressive ways. Two subsidiary points need to be made. First, as Passavant and Dean point out, Butler is wrong: it is simply not the case that only the law recites its own terms. They note, for instance, the fact that the category of hate-speech pre-exists the state's determination of it. They also remark that the work of Matsuda et al. 'circulates the term before and beyond its invocations and applications in particular cases'.[68] When the law redeploys this term, therefore, it does so in a way that is not separate from its extra-legal or social uses. And, indeed, evidence of the congruence of the social and legal is present when Butler notes that the state restages the racial and sexual slurs found in civil society but it does so as 'state-sanctioned speech' (*ES*: 101).

Second, even if it is conceded that the law recycles its own law and that this enhances its normalizing powers, does this in itself mean that that recycling is necessarily reactionary or discriminatory? One has only to think of the ways in which, for instance, the Fourteenth Amendment, the equal protection clause, has been used historically both to support and to contest segregation to see that the same legal clause can be deployed to support very different ends. The problem, as Jenkins discerns, lies in Butler's use of the words 'only and always' to describe what the law does, for these terms imply that the power of the state is both 'highly homogenous and unilateral' and singularly pernicious.[69] This not only contradicts Butler's more general critique of sovereign power developed in *Excitable Speech*, but it also leads, in my view, to a wonderful paradox. Having criticized MacKinnon and Matsuda for endowing the state with the very capacity for citational reversal that they disallow for hate-speech and pornography, Butler does the same in reverse. She allows that hate-speech and pornography can be radically recited but denies this possibility to state speech, or rather she allows that it can be recited but only in anti-progressive directions. To be true to her broader discussion of language and iteration, she ought, in my view, to allow that the weaknesses in the norms instantiated and reiterated by the state can be worked in the same way that the norms constituting heteronormativity can. Further, as Jenkins notes, and I agree, 'it seems that the field of law should be more appropriately construed as one in which perpetual and "productive" struggle between the advocates of different views and constant reinterpretation of normative "fictions" takes place'.[70] For these reasons, it would make sense politically to argue for some form of engagement with the state as part of an overall radical democratic strategy rather than simply supporting democratic activity in civil society.

Conclusion

The account of resignification that Butler offers in *Excitable Speech* appears, *at one level*, to echo the traditional liberal defence of free speech, which is that the cure for bad speech is more speech. After all, resignification is precisely about recycling existing speech, albeit in a radical and empowering direction. Where Butler's argument differs is that it is made on the basis of the philosophical presuppositions of linguistic theory and not from the ideological perspective of liberalism. Or, at least, that is how it seems. The ambiguity arises because, as I show in the next chapter, Butler conceives radical democracy as extending the terms of liberalism so as to make them more inclusive. So, it is not implausible to read her exploration of how to combat hate-speech in terms of liberal values: or, rather, one such value in particular, namely, freedom. This would help to explain why Butler is so critical of the state, because it hampers freedom by intensifying moments of subordination and regulation. Moreover, it would explain why she is so committed to securing intelligibility and legitimacy for those groups abjected by hegemonic racial, gender and sexual norms. What concerns her is their freedom to live a liveable life, a freedom presently restricted by the operation of norms defining the terms of such a life. That said, the point should not be overstated, for although committed to freedom, Butler is absolutely silent on what it means to be free, viewing judgements of this kind as the (provisional) outcome of democratic contestation rather than the purpose of political theory. Instead her aim, indeed the aim throughout her work, is to uncover how restrictive norms might be challenged. In the case of hate-speech, this is best done through 'talking back'.

6

What Makes for a Liveable Life?

Without a doubt, Butler is best known as a theorist of sex, gender, desire and the body. As *Excitable Speech* demonstrates, however, these issues are not her sole concern. Butler is equally interested in the myriad ways that subjects are subordinated racially by language. In her last three books (*Precarious Life, Undoing Gender* and *Giving an Account of Oneself*) she extends her remit even further. She turns her attention to the problem of what makes for a liveable life. This in turn leads her to the question of the human and, later on, to ethics. While the subject matter may vary, the overall approach does not. Butler's focus remains the relation between normative violence and cultural intelligibility: how, that is, culturally particular norms define who is recognizable as a subject capable of living a life that counts. There is a change, however, and it is that Butler now locates this discussion in terms of human survival. She joins, in other words, her previous examination of the way subjects are produced in constraint to a newer agenda that concentrates on discerning the conditions necessary for humans to secure their own liveability. The aim of this chapter, therefore, is to explore this argument in more detail. In order to do so, I begin by broadly considering the relation between normative violence and liveability. I then move on to a new idea in Butler's scheme of thought: the idea of corporeal vulnerability. This is followed by an examination of mourning and grief as possible resources for an ethics. Since an ethical relation requires the other to be intelligible to us as a subject, the next two sections explore Butler's distinctive take on the politics of recognition and her reasons for rejecting the state as a mechanism of recognition. The final two sections of the chapter, then, are devoted to an exploration of Butler's theory of radical democracy and its relation to a politics of liveability. A core element of this discussion is the notion of cultural translation, yet another new theoretical feature of this later work.

Normative violence and questions of liveability

In Chapter 2, I explored the idea of the 'heterosexual matrix'. This matrix, for Butler, establishes the parameters of cultural intelligibility in terms of sex, gender and sexuality. It defines the kinds of beings that can be recognized as socially and culturally coherent. It is, thus, this heteronormative framework that generates a restricted and restrictive conception of what constitutes normal sexed and gendered life. As Butler writes in *Undoing Gender*, a text that shares much of the conceptual and theoretical framework of *Gender Trouble*, the consequences of this can be profound: 'Sometimes a normative conception of gender can undo one's personhood, undermining the capacity to persevere in a livable life' (*UG*: 1).[1] The norms that define gender constitute subjects but they do so in differential ways. Certain persons, as we saw in Chapter 3, become abjected by those norms and, as such, are culturally unintelligible. In *Undoing Gender*, Butler offers several additional illustrations of what counts as an unliveable life and the norms that secure this unliveability.

Drawing on the 'New Gender Politics', for instance, Butler examines how the norms governing human anatomy work to disenfranchise the intersex population because there is no space in the dominant morphological imaginary for those who are born with mixed genital characteristics. The choice: corrective ('coercive') surgery or having an 'inconceivable' body (*UG*: 64). Butler studies the way in which the *Diagnostic and Statistical Manual of Mental Disorders*, the text produced by the American Psychiatric Association as the authoritative guide to psychiatric illness, constructs the diagnosis of Gender Identity Disorder (GID), and how it uses GID not just to diagnose transsexualism but also to check latent homosexuality in the young.[2] She continues the work begun in *Antigone's Claim* by exploring how only certain familial organizations count and only particular persons are seen as 'fit' to parent. Finally, she analyses several cases of violence against those who deviate from prevailing gender norms (including the killings of Gwen Araujo, Mathew Shephard and Brandon Teena[3]). What is central to all of these examples is the idea of 'normative violence': that is, the violence of particular norms (or normative frames) in determining what (or who) will or will not count as culturally intelligible.

The principal difference between Butler's earlier and later writings with regard to normative violence, as noted in the introduction to this chapter, is that the idea is increasingly integrated into a discussion of the question of 'liveability', or what she calls 'a politics of human life' (*UG*: 225). While this theme undoubtedly underpins her argument in *Gender Trouble*, it is made more explicit in her later texts. She now stresses how the ability to critique existing norms is tied to the 'capacity, invariably collective, to articulate an alternative, minority version of sustaining norms or ideals that enable me to act' (*UG*: 3), the goal of which is 'not to celebrate difference as such but to establish more inclusive conditions for sheltering and maintaining life that resists models of assimilation' (*UG*: 4). This is all part of the political need 'to rethink the possible' (*GT*: xx) so that those excluded from the terms regulating reality can gain admittance to them. So, discussing GID, she notes that the 'critical question' is 'how might the world be reorganized' so that such non-normative bodies could survive? (*UG*: 5). Similarly, considering kinship and marriage, she asks: 'What reorganization of sexual norms would be necessary for those who live sexually and affectively outside the marriage bond or in kin relations to the side of marriage either to be legally and culturally recognized for the endurance and importance of their intimate ties or, equally important, to be free of the need for recognition of this kind?' (*UG*: 5). The subversion of gender norms, she now explains, 'must be guided by the question of what maximizes the possibilities for a livable life, what minimizes the possibility of unbearable life or, indeed, social or literal death' (*UG*: 8).

In *Undoing Gender*, in my view, we are witnessing evidence of the subtle shift that has taken place over a number of years in Butler's work. In this period, she has developed a more expansive conception of normative violence extending beyond gender or sexed corporeality to how the limits of cultural intelligibility are also set by racial and ethnic frames and the normative violence this brings with it. This was prefigured in an early chapter on Rodney King,[4] was developed further in *Bodies that Matter*, where race and ethnicity figure more strongly than in *Gender Trouble*, and was then amplified in her discussion of racist speech in *Excitable Speech*. It receives its fullest articulation in *Precarious Life* and *Undoing Gender*. The shift is also presaged, I would propose, in *Bodies that Matter* when she explores abjection and where she begins to consider the multiple elements that contribute to the violent foreclosure of possible lives (including but not limited to sex, gender and sexuality). Although this re-positioning might, as indicated in Chapter 1, be conceived of as further evidence of the very contingency that Butler's work seeks to theorize, it has additional significance. It affects the nature of the politics she seeks to articulate. For although Butler's work has been centrally concerned with 'the question of homosexuality, and *lesbianism* in particular', once it is admitted that it is not just norms of sex, gender and sexuality that operate violently, then it becomes very difficult to prioritize sex, gender and/or sexuality over other elements ('HB': 284, my emphasis).[5] This is why, in my view, she turns her attention to the category of the 'human': because to focus uniquely on non-normative forms of sex, gender and sexuality would be to commit the very kinds of erasure Butler warned of in her own discussion of women (discussed in Chapter 2). It occludes the impact of ethnicity and race on sexual orientation (and vice versa). And it obscures the ways that, in her own words, abjection is not restricted to sex and gender but pertains to 'all kinds of bodies whose lives are not considered to be "lives" and whose materiality is not understood to "matter"' ('HB': 281).

The question begged by this apparent shift of focus is, of course, what needs to be done in order to 'rethink the possible'? Just how can the possibilities of living a liveable life be maximized? Butler's answer involves both politics and ethics. In terms of the politics, she focuses on radical democracy, contestation and what she terms the practice of 'cultural translation'. With regard to the ethics, her approach is two-fold. She reviews a wide range of ethical thinking, particularly in *Giving an Account of Oneself*, a book described on the back cover as Butler's 'first extended study of moral philosophy'.[6] A key figure in this review process is Emmanuel Levinas, whose idea of a non-violent ethics has been particularly influential in feminist ethics. Additionally, particularly in *Precarious Life* and *Undoing Gender*, Butler articulates her own account of the challenges to living an ethical life today and how they might be overcome. It is this second strand of her ethical thinking that I will concentrate on mainly, though from time to time there will be some reference to the first strand. It should be noted at the outset that Butler does not view the relation between ethics and politics as a mutually exclusive one. Like Levinas, she sees ethics as being 'in continuity' with politics.[7] To begin with, however, we need to consider Butler's notion of corporeal vulnerability.

Corporeal vulnerability

In the 1999 preface to *Subjects of Desire*, Butler notes that the constitution of any subject involves a 'radical and constitutive relation to alterity' (*SD*: xiv). In *Undoing Gender*, she writes: '*This means that the ec-static character of our existence is essential to the possibility of persisting as human*' (*UG*: 33). Ek-stasis, as noted in Chapter 1, is a Heideggerian term used to connote a 'standing outside of oneself' (*UG*: 258, n. 7). In *Precarious Life*, Butler gives some examples of what this entails: 'to be transported beyond oneself in a passion, but also to be *beside oneself* with rage or grief' (*PL*: 24). Essentially, it is to be other to the self. Two factors secure this otherness: our relations with others, and the fact that we inhabit a world governed by social norms that we have not chosen. Moreover, the latter affects the former, for if social norms constitute us as 'unintelligible' then, this will colour our encounters with others: we may desire to be rid of them rather than love them; to kill them rather than cherish them, and so on. The ek-static character of existence, therefore, is inextricably tied to questions of recognition. It might, of course, be suggested that Butler is simply highlighting how our confrontations with others have the potential to affect us in certain ways. She is not. She is making a far stronger claim, a claim that takes us back to arguments developed in *The Psychic Life of Power*. She is using the idea to do two things: first, to challenge the idea of the autonomous subject, by demonstrating just how the other is a necessary condition for our persistence and survival; and, second, to explore the kinds of ethical encounter that might be made possible by these inescapable, indeed vital, engagements with others. Let us explore how.

In *Psychic Life*, Butler establishes that the subject's existence depends on its 'primary vulnerability to the Other' (*PL*: 21): the infant's literal dependence on the care of the other for all its physical and emotional needs. All subjects thus emerge as a result of attachment to and dependency on another, but this primary relationality to the other is then repressed; it is, in psychoanalytic terms, foreclosed, though it continues to haunt the subject. It is lodged in the unconscious, and thus unamenable to conscious reflection. As Butler puts it in *Giving an Account of Oneself*, subjects are 'divided, ungrounded . . . incoherent from the start' (*GAO*: 19). In *Psychic Life*, the issue that concerns Butler is the paradox of subjection: the subject's dependence on power – its subordination to it – as the basic condition for its continued existence. As noted in Chapter 4, she examines the psychic effects of that power, not least of which is that it produces forms of reflexivity (including, in particular, guilt and conscience). At this point, her discussion of primary relationality focuses on how the subject is constituted psychically. In *Precarious Life, Undoing Gender* and *Giving an Account of Oneself,* the idea of primary vulnerability curves in another direction. Butler argues that the subject's primary dependence on others and its ensuing opacity to itself is precisely what 'incurs and sustains some of its most important ethical bonds' (*GAO*: 20).[8] To illustrate this, however, she does not focus exclusively on the psychic formation of subjectivity; she returns to the body.

The body is, of course, a central element in Butler's work. In *Gender Trouble,* her purpose is to denaturalize the sexed body – to show that it is an effect of gender norms. In *Bodies that Matter,* she extends this discussion by exploring in more abstract terms the relation between materiality and discourse and by considering how particular political ontologies of the body, such as heteronormativity, operate to determine which bodies matter. In her later writings, however, there is a small but significant shift of emphasis. Bodies, she argues, are vulnerable. This is what defines them. 'The body', she writes in both *Undoing Gender* and in *Precarious Life,* implies 'mortality, vulnerability, agency: the skin and the flesh expose us to the gaze of others but also to touch and to violence' (*UG*: 21; *PL*: 26). From the vulnerability of the infant, relying on someone to care for its bodily needs, through later experiences of love, guilt, desire, betrayal, anger, grief or mourning, our bodies expose us to one another. The body is the medium of our relations with other bodies. It is 'a porous boundary, given over to others'. As a consequence, the corpus is not just open to violation by those other bodies, but, echoing Levinas, Butler notes, it, too, can violate: that is, the vulnerability of the other might elicit a violent response from us – we might desire to kill, maim or beat them (*GAO*: 92; *PL*: 134–5). In short, therefore, bodily vulnerability is the basis of ek-stasis: it is how we open up to the other. It is this porosity to other bodies, therefore, that 'establishes a field of ethical enmeshment with others' (*UG*: 25). Like Levinas, Butler conceives of ethics in terms of the meeting of embodied subjects.[9] Before I go on to explore further the link between corporeal vulnerability and ethics, I want to pause to consider how this theorization of the body – as dependent on others – resonates with feminist concerns about the body.

Traditionally, of course, feminists have argued for bodily autonomy for women. They have demanded rights to reproductive freedom, to contraception, to abortion on demand, and to choice of sexual or marital partner. They have campaigned to outlaw rape within marriage and sexual harassment. Corporeal integrity and self-determination have been seen to go hand-in-hand within feminism. (The same is equally true of sexual minority, race and disability politics.) The argument is straightforward: a woman cannot be free to live her own life if someone else controls her body. Since her body is her own (she 'owns' it), then she ought to be allowed to determine what happens to it. This position assumes the idea of corporeal autonomy. Butler's contention that bodies are, in fact, vulnerable to and dependent on others offers a profound challenge to this idea of bodily autonomy. Although 'we struggle for rights over our own bodies' (*PL*: 26), from birth these embattled bodies are never simply *'our own'* (*PL*: 25). Butler is emphatic that acknowledging the co-implication of bodies does not mean that feminists (or others) should give up campaigning for rights to corporeal self-determination; such campaigns, she asserts, 'are part of any normative aspiration of a movement that seeks to maximize the protections and the freedoms' of their members. Rather what she asks is whether this should be the sole focus of such campaigns. Might there not, she inquires, be 'another normative aspiration that we must also seek to articulate and defend' that recognizes the ek-static quality of embodied existence (*PL*: 26)? Here, I think, there is a way to align the former feminist campaign with Butler's project.

The terms that define vulnerability, understood in its most expansive sense (that is, covering both the prospect of violation by the other and connection with them), are social (*PL*: 20). They depend upon the operation of particular norms. This is why when Butler talks about the possibility of living a liveable life, she talks of it in terms of 'the struggle with the norm' (*UG*: 13), for it is the operation of norms that determines which bodies can be loved, desired, attended to and which are at risk of harm and violation. Struggles for bodily rights, in this sense, might be reconceptualized, therefore, as struggles against the norms of embodiment. In demanding the right to reproductive freedom, feminists are also battling against the norms that define who counts reproductively. In arguing for the right to sexual freedom, gays and lesbians are struggling against the norms that define who counts as an eligible sexual partner and for whom. The difference between these two accounts of body politics, however, is that the first starts from the assumption of autonomy (that the body is – or ought to be – under the control of the individual), while the second (Butler's position) regards the body as 'invariably in community' and, as such, never entirely under individual control (*PL*: 27). The question this leaves Butler with is whether it is possible to acknowledge this human interdependency not just as a mere fact of existence but normatively. Could the recognition of corporeal vulnerability lead, that is, to a 'normative reorientation for politics?' (*PL*: 28). Could it, moreover, lead to a more ethical relation with the other? In order to answer this, I want to turn to Butler's discussion of mourning and grief in *Precarious Life*.

Mourning and grief

Precarious Life contains five essays written in the aftermath of the violent events of September 11, 2001 ('9/11'). Each, in its different way, takes issue with the Bush Administration's response to 9/11 both at home and abroad. Topics include the indefinite detention of prisoners at Guantánamo Bay, the increase in censorship (both overt and covert) and thus the growing threat to civil liberties domestically, and the politics of obituary writing. In particular, Butler is concerned with the way that 9/11 has been used to legitimize a violent, militaristic politics. Her focus is the war on terror. The central aim of all the essays is thus to imagine how the precariousness of human life – so evident on 9/11 – might become the basis not for a retaliatory politics, but for a shared ethical and radical political project, in which 'an inevitable interdependency becomes acknowledged as the basis for global political community' (*PL*: xii–xiii). So how, precisely, might the experience of loss and vulnerability lend itself to a recognition of interdependence and community? How might it replace the language of vengeance with one of non-aggression? Grief and mourning, Butler suggests, provide a possible resource here.

Butler is not interested, however, in developing an account of grief or mourning *per se*. She examines these states, rather, only because they expose the precariousness of life and vulnerability to the other, for they are symptomatic of the inter-corporeal nature of existence: the extent to which one's sense of self depends on others. As Butler notes: during grief and mourning 'something about who we are is revealed, something that delineates the ties we have to others, that shows us that these ties constitute who we are, ties or bonds that compose us'. When loss occurs, that is, 'I think I have lost "you" only to discover that "I" have gone missing as well' (*PL*:

22). Loss reveals to the subject its dependence on the other, not just for love or friendship, but for its own sense of self. In losing the other, the subject loses part of its own identity, part of what makes it what it is (the dutiful son, the rebellious daughter, the best friend). Grief and mourning are thus forms of 'dispossession' (*PL*: 28). They are occasions when one body can be 'undone' by another body, and it is the moment of undoing that reveals that our existence is always a being-with the other. This is the moment, for Butler, when ethical relations are illuminated; when 'my own foreignness to myself is, paradoxically, the source of my ethical connection with others' (*PL*: 46).

We have already seen that Butler regards the address of the other as constitutive of the self; the other (the policeman, for instance) hails – or linguistically interpellates – the subject and so it comes into existence. According to thinkers such as Levinas, the moment at which the subject is summoned into existence is also the moment that an ethical relation is established. For him, ethical responsibility arises, as Butler comments, 'as a consequence of being subject to the unwilled address of the other' (*GAO*: 85). Although Butler disagrees with Levinas about the nature of this address (he sees it as accusatory, she does not), she acknowledges that the subject's susceptibility to the other is the basis of its vulnerability to injury *and* of its ethical responsibilities (*GAO*: 91),[10] the assumption being that it is the other that invokes feelings of fear, outrage and anxiety in us and that these feeling are the basis of our response to them. Only an openness to the other, that is, can create what Butler calls 'a point of identification with suffering itself' (*PL*: 30), for if grief is to galvanize people ethically, then, for Butler, its galvanization has to be conditional on acknowledging that *all* fleshly existence is precarious; that all people suffer. In the absence of this acknowledgement, political violence will be sanctioned and human lives will continue to be lost.[11] The US will continue its 'war on terror'.

The specific case that concerns Butler in *Precarious Life* is that of post-9/11 politics. It should be obvious, however, that the logic of her argument applies equally to other acts of violence, from gay-bashing to racist murders and assaults on women. Acts of violence take place because humans are vulnerable. The ability to recognize this vulnerability is the first step on the road to halting violence. The difficulty is that before corporeal vulnerability can prompt an ethical response it has to be recognized as such (*PL*: 43). We have to be able to 'see' that someone is suffering or dying; we have to be able to recognize that the act that has taken place is an act of violence. The problem is that humans are not only dependent on the particular others they encounter for their existence, as Levinas assumed. According to Butler, they are dependent also on 'the social dimension of normativity that governs the scene of recognition' (*GAO*: 23) and it is this that conditions their capacity to respond ethically. In the next section, I thus turn to the question of recognition and consider how certain deaths count as mournable deaths, that is, deaths that permit grief, while others do not.

Questions of recognition

The politics of recognition has been a dominant theme not just in political theory since the early 1990s, when Charles Taylor published his landmark essay 'The Politics of Recognition', but also in feminism, where it has been allied with identity politics.[12] Recognition is an Hegelian concept, exemplified in the struggle between self-conscious beings in the *Phenomenology of Spirit*. The emphasis in recent theoretical work, both feminist and non-feminist, has been on finding ways to ensure that all citizens in a democracy, and particularly those from various minorities, are recognized as equal to all others. Butler takes the debate in a slightly different direction. As Patchen Markell points out, 'recognition makes the social world intelligible'.[13] It is thus the relation between recognition and social normativity that concerns Butler. To develop her argument, she returns to Hegel and to the question of the relation between desire and recognition mooted in *Subjects of Desire* (xiv).

Like Hegel, Butler sees recognition as a reciprocal not a unilateral process produced in the struggle between two 'structurally similar' self-consciousnesses (*GAO*: 26). Following her own earlier interpretation of Hegel, she also contends that recognition is a process of ek-stasis: it is 'the process by which I become other than what I was and so cease to be able to return to what I was' (*GAO*: 27). Despite the ingenuity of his account of recognition, in *Undoing Gender* Butler charges that Hegel is, nevertheless, inattentive to 'a couple of important points' (*UG*: 2). First, echoing an argument made in *Excitable Speech*, she contends that the terms by which subjects are recognized as human are 'socially articulated and changeable' (*UG*: 2; see also *ES*: 5). And, secondly, she observes that 'sometimes' the terms that define the human are precisely those that 'deprive certain other individuals of the possibility of achieving that status', leading to a differentiation between the human and the not-human or the 'less than human' on the basis of sex, bodily morphology and race (*UG*: 2). This in turn is what endows some with liveable lives and others with unliveable lives. In short, the point is that Hegel fails to acknowledge the fact that the scene of recognition itself assumes a set of cultural norms – or a normative horizon – that conditions who is recognizable as human.[14] Here Butler turns to Foucault, for despite certain limitations with his approach, Foucault is acutely aware of the role that norms play in constituting subjectivity (*GAO*: 17, 22).[15] As Butler understands recognition, therefore, it is a process based on the operation of particular norms, norms that determine who counts as human. Social normativity thus determines not only 'what I can "be"' but also whether or not I can recognize (or be recognized by) the other in the first place (*GAO*: 22). The problem, of course, is that not everyone can be recognized because not everyone figures as normatively human: that is (to recollect an argument from Chapter 3), not everyone counts as ontologically real. This has a profound bearing on the subject at hand: the possibility of recognizing as human and vulnerable particular persons or groups in order that an ethical responsibility towards them might emerge. What happens if a life that is not recognized normatively as a life is violated in some way?

According to Butler, if 'violence is done against those who are unreal, then, from the perspective of violence, it fails to injure or negate those lives since those lives are already negated' (*PL*: 33). Physical violence cannot, that is, be recognized as taking place against those who fail to qualify as humans with a life. The issue here is what Butler terms the 'violence of derealization'. This is a form of normative violence wherein certain groups fail to count as human according to the dominant regime of intelligibility. There appear to be two possible ways in which this derealizing violence takes place. The first occurs 'on the level of discourse' (*PL*: 34); the second occurs through omission. To make sense of this distinction, it is helpful to go back to an earlier distinction that Butler draws between prohibition and erasure. Discussing Jesse Helms's attack on the art of Robert Mapplethorpe, Butler observes that for Helms 'gay men exist as objects of prohibition' while the lesbian 'is not even produced within this discourse as a prohibited object'. This suggests to Butler that oppression operates not just through explicit prohibition (expressed in the fact that Helms wanted to suspend funding for the production of homoerotic works of art), but also in a covert fashion through abjection. 'Here oppression works through the production of a domain of unthinkability and unnameability.

Lesbianism is not explicitly prohibited in part because it has not even made its way into the thinkable, the imaginable, that grid of cultural intelligibility that regulate the real and the nameable' ('Imitation': 20). Butler's point is that 'erasure', as she calls it at this point, is an effect of power but not one that works 'through discourse as its instrument' ('Imitation': 30, n. 11).

My suggestion is that we read Butler's comments on derealization in parallel fashion: that derealization is produced both discursively and through erasure. In so-called '"discourse[s]" of dehumanization' (*PL*: 35) specific populations or groups are named as *inhuman* or *less than human*. In these instances, acts of physical violence carry out what is 'already happening in discourse, such that a discourse on dehumanization produces treatment, including torture and murder, structured by the discourse' (*PL*: 36). Acts of corporeal violation follow on from ideas that are already circulating culturally. We might thus read Butler's discussion of the activities at Guantánamo Bay as an example of this form of derealization and how the subject status 'detainee' accorded to the prisoners held there effectively works to dehumanize them.[16] By calling them 'detainees', the US Administration is effectively able to deny to them the rights accorded under various international conventions (including the Geneva Conventions) to counsel, to knowledge of the 'crimes' for which they are being held, to a trial, to appeal and to the possibility of repatriation.[17] In essence, to deny these rights is to deny their humanity. To talk of them as 'detainees', but to talk of them nevertheless, is thus to construct them *within* discourse as less than human.[18] Their discursive production as inhuman, secured, in part, by associating them discursively with Islamic extremism and terrorism, then enables the violence they suffer as a result of the denial of their rights.

In the second case, it is the omission from discourse that derealizes. Here 'there is a limit to discourse that establishes the limit of human intelligibility' (*PL*: 35).[19] It is not that discourse names the inhuman; it is that it dehumanizes or derealizes by failing to name. This, Butler contends, is what happens when, for instance, the US media fail to identify 'singly or collectively' the '200,000 Iraqi children . . . killed during the Gulf War and its aftermath'. It occurs in the absence of 'obituaries for the war casualties that the United States inflicts' (*PL*: 34). It takes place when, in the interests of the war effort of a particular state, its journalists fail to expose or investigate the killing of civilian targets and the 'decimation of communities, infrastructures, religious centers' (*PL*: 36). At these moments,

Butler concludes, 'it is not that a death is poorly marked, but that it is unmarkable. Such a death vanishes, not into explicit discourse, but in the ellipses by which public discourse proceeds' (*PL*: 35). Normative violence works here through 'radical effacement', thus 'there never was a human, there never was a life, and no murder [or death] has, therefore, ever taken place' (*PL*: 147; see also 146).[20] In essence, what this means is that any violence against such groups 'leaves a mark that is no mark' (*PL*: 36): that is, the violence clearly happens (200,000 Iraqi children die) *but* it is not registered in discourse as violence. Instead, by failing to represent this violence in any way, a derealizing – normative – violence occurs. Such bodies do not figure in the *reality* constructed by the media, military, state and other organs and institutions. They are erased; they simply cannot be thought within 'the contemporary order of being' as human.[21]

This presents a particular problem: for how is it possible to identify with suffering if that suffering is erased from consciousness? How is it possible to base an ethics on bodily vulnerability if evidence of that vulnerability cannot be seen? If grief is a pre-requisite for the kind of identification with suffering that Butler argues might foster ethical responsibilities towards the other, then what happens when a death cannot be grieved because it is not perceived as a death? For it is not that these deaths are irrelevant to a specific subject's social existence; rather, these disavowed deaths are just as constitutive of that subject as those it mourns. As Butler formulates it: they constitute 'the melancholic background for my social world' (*PL*: 46). Ethical questions thus arise exactly at the 'limit of our schemes of intelligibility'; at the point, that is, where the norms constituting the human define some persons as incomprehensible to us. How, at such times, is it possible to 'offer and receive acknowledgement' to and from the other (*GAO*: 22)?

What's wrong with 'desiring the state's desire'?[22]

Typically, one of the ways in which political theorists and feminists have argued that recognition can be universalized is through a framework of equal rights organized either around the individual or around groups. The state clearly has a central role to play in this process since it acts as the mechanism through which recognition is conferred and/or resources are made available to ensure equal participation in democratic governance. Indeed, this line of argument has a long tradition going back at least to Hegel. As I demonstrated in the previous chapter, however, Butler is a staunch critic of the state, viewing it primarily as a regulatory institution intent on consolidating its own power. It should come as no surprise, therefore, that she is reluctant to allow the state a central role in the struggle for recognition. To explore a little more fully why this is the case, I want to set aside the discussion of mourning for a moment in order to consider her discussion of gay marriage in 'Is Kinship Always Already Heterosexual?'

When proponents of gay marriage petition the state to recognize non-heterosexual unions, Butler argues, they construct the state as 'withholding an entitlement that it really should distribute in a non-discriminatory way, regardless of sexual orientation' ('Kinship': 16). What this argument misses, however, is that the state operates as a mechanism of normalization. It is not just that it determines how particular subjects might be recognized publicly. It also determines who is eligible for recognition as a subject – it sets the norms of recognizability. The state, thus, has an integral role in reinforcing the prevailing norms of human intelligibility. If the state is assumed to monopolize the 'resources of recognition' – because it is conceived as the primary mechanism through which recognition might be attained – then, not surprisingly, it is seen as the sole mode through which 'desire and sexuality are ratified, justified, known, publicly instated, imagined as permanent, durable' ('Kinship': 26, 22). On this basis, if a subject wants recognition from others, then it needs to be recognized, first, by the state – by, for instance, being granted marriage rights. If it fails to secure state recognition – fails to be construed as worthy of desiring the state's desire, as Butler puts it – then it is, in effect, derealized. It is not a subject. So, if the call for state recognition serves only to produce 'new and invidious forms of social hierarchy' ('Kinship': 26), and to foreclose certain modes of living, then what alternatives are there? What other ways of garnering recognition might exist that by-pass the state? How is it possible to become recognizable, in other words, without further consolidating existing (exclusionary) norms of recognition and legitimacy and without fortifying the normalizing power of the state?

Butler's solution is to argue for the radical democratic transformation of the norms that structure society. What, though, precisely does she mean by radical democracy, and how is it supposed to transform existing norms?

The politics of radical democracy

A central difficulty in assessing Butler's account of radical democracy is that it is never explicitly articulated in any detail. The reader has, rather, to reconstruct her understanding of it from various scattered remarks, some more or less sustained. There are, however, a number of features of it that can be identified. First, it is evident that Butler's conception of radical democracy is *critically* indebted to that advanced by Ernesto Laclau and Chantal Mouffe in *Hegemony and Socialist Strategy*, and that it continues to be marked by an engagement with the subsequent writings of Laclau.[23] Second, it also draws on the writings of Paul Gilroy and Jacques Derrida. Third, Butler's account is what Norval has called a 'post-structuralist conception of radical democracy'.[24] Like other poststructuralist radical democrats, Butler stresses the disruptive rather than rational nature of democratic activity; assumes power relations are intrinsic to society, including democratic society; and views radical democracy not as an alternative to liberal democracy but as a process of 'incessant contestation' over, and thence radicalization of, 'the key terms of liberalism' – equality, freedom, justice, humanity – so as to make them 'more inclusive, more dynamic and more concrete' (*CHU*: 13).[25] She also emphasizes contestation and disagreement and rejects the idea that democracy is ultimately attainable. Radical democracy is thus a constitutively open-ended rather than teleological process, sustained by its very unrealizability.[26]

Having given a very general overview of Butler's account, I now want to turn to the detail of her theory. For a radical transformation of society to take place, she notes, 'we need to know that our fundamental categories can and must be expanded to become more inclusive and more responsive to the full range of cultural populations' (*UG*: 223–4). A radical democratic project is thus one that is committed to extending to the disqualified the norms that define a liveable life. As such, radical democracy operates according to what Veronica Vasterling has called 'the political ideal of radical inclusivity'.[27] It aims to universalize the terms of inclusion. Radical democrats, however, argue that democracy can never actually be attained. This suggests, therefore, that the universal that radical democratic politics aims at developing is one that is always in some sense out of reach. Why? The reason is that the universal is always limited because it is always based on certain exclusions. So, for instance, human rights as encapsulated in the Universal Declaration of Human Rights assume a male subject and thus exclude women.[28]

Precisely because the universal is always exclusionary, however, it fuels democratic political struggle. Women have thus campaigned for human rights instruments that recognize the specificity of women's experiences as women (for instance, the Convention on the Elimination of all Forms of Discrimination against Women). Democratic activism, in other words, arises as a means to contesting the limited nature of particular universals and aims to expand them ('End': 419; *ES*: 160). Although, like many a poststructuralist, Butler once rejected any appeal to the universal on the grounds that it necessarily operates in totalizing and violent ways ('CS': 339), as part of her commitment to radical democracy she has nevertheless come to accept the political necessity of the universal.[29] What we need to consider, therefore, is how she theorizes the universal.

When Butler sets out her discussion of the universal in *Contingency, Hegemony, Universality*, she does so by differentiating her own account from that of Laclau and, to a lesser extent, Žižek, her two co-authors.[30] Since my concern is with Butler, rather than her debate with Laclau and Žižek, I will focus primarily on her account of the universal rather than comparing hers with theirs. The first thing to note is that Butler understands the universal as always a 'universal in culture'.[31] In an argument she claims to take from Hegel, she notes that the universal always relies on cultural norms for its articulation.[32] This means that it is always already shaped by the customary practices through which it is enacted. 'Significantly, this means that no assertion of universality takes place apart from a cultural norm' (*CHU*: 35). Exactly because the categories through which we understand and engage the world are 'continually remade in the encounter with the world that they facilitate' (*CHU*: 20), the universal is thus a dynamic and 'temporalized' concept (*CHU*: 24). It changes. The second point to note is that, because the universal is particular to a culture, there are competing versions of the universal in existence at any one time. Different political movements, for instance, articulate different conceptions of the universal. They articulate alternative visions of the norms needed to ensure a liveable life, and these rival visions vie for hegemony. There is no point in assuming, therefore, that 'a single political direction is necessitated by virtue of . . . [a] commitment' to expanding the terms of a liveable life (*UG*: 226). Quite the contrary: democracy thrives in a context of contestation and agonism. The point is not just to accept the existence of rival ideas of the universal as a relativist might; the task is to endeavour to generate a more encompassing universal out of these competing conceptions. It is thus a matter of 'establishing' what Butler terms *'practices of translation'* between them (*CHU*: 167).

Before we examine both what Butler means by the practice of translation and how it works to generate norms capable of sustaining a more inclusive mode of liveable life and a more expansive category of the human subject, I want to make one final comment on her conception of radical democracy. We have already established that Butler is resistant to state-centric politics. Consequently, the radical political struggles that she envisages are those occurring in 'civil society'.[33] Although her account of civil society is underdeveloped – there is no attempt to theorize what she means by the term – she uses it in a way that has become very familiar within contemporary thought. She employs it, that is, to connote an arena of political struggle distinct from the state. According to this characterization, civil society is populated by, amongst other things, associations and other non-state organizations, as well as by social movements. Here individuals and groups mobilize around particular issues of concern to them and act to change them. Given that Butler sees civil society as one of the primary sites where the norms that govern social life and human interaction are reiterated on a daily basis, and where regulatory and disciplinary processes proceed, it should come as no surprise to find her arguing that civil society is the optimum site for democratic struggle. Social transformation, she thus proposes, will take place where 'daily social relations are rearticulated, and new conceptual horizons opened up by anomalous and subversive practices' (*CHU*: 14). When Butler talks of a politics of human life, therefore, it is a politics that operates at this level: the level of everyday interactions and of the reproduction of social life.[34] And so, it must be assumed that cultural translation is also a practice that takes place in civil society.

Cultural translation

If, as Butler surmises, recognition is governed by social norms defining both what counts as an act of recognition and who may be recognized, then a potential crisis is precipitated when someone who is 'unrecognizable' demands recognition (as, for instance, when women demanded to be recognized as equal to men). This crisis puts the current norms of recognition into question and, potentially at least, sets up the possibility that a new set might be developed (*GAO*: 24). In essence, two universals clash: that currently defining recognition (a masculinist norm, in my example) and that articulated by those who are excluded from its terms (a sex-neutral norm). This is where the practice of cultural translation comes into play. But what does it mean to reconceive the universal through the 'constitutive act of cultural translation' (*CHU*: 20), as Butler proposes to do? To answer this it is necessary, I think, to ponder the genesis of the term 'cultural translation', a term that Butler acknowledges she borrows from Homi Bhabha (who in turn derives it from Walter Benjamin) ('UC': 49).[35]

Bhabha introduces the idea of cultural translation in *The Location of Culture* in order to explore, amongst other things, the question of exclusion in cultural politics. 'Cultural translation', he writes, 'desacralizes the transparent assumptions of cultural supremacy, and in that very act, demands a contextual specificity, a historical differentiation *within* minority positions.'[36] Drawing on Benjamin's idea that there is always 'an element in a translation which does not lend itself to translation',[37] Bhabha deploys the idea of translation to draw attention to what is *untranslatable* in a culture, and thus to what cannot be transformed by a translational encounter. He examines the ways that the liminality of migrant experience – the being between cultures – 'dramatizes the activity of culture's untranslatability', producing what he describes as an 'encounter with the ambivalent process of splitting and hybridity'.[38] In other words, instead of being able to assimilate minority cultures to that of the majority, the 'foreign' elements that resist translation put into jeopardy the very possibility of a communal standpoint, a shared set of values and beliefs, or a shared language. Indeed, they subvert it. Different languages, in short, are distinct 'discursive and cultural *modes of signification*' that are in 'conflict with each other, striving to exclude the other'.[39] There is thus a necessary agonism in the attempt to communicate across cultures. In the process of translation, cultural difference is staged.[40] How does this account relate to Butler's?

Butler assumes, firstly, that since universality makes 'its varied and contending appearances' in different languages ('UC': 49), there are different cultural versions of the universal rather than a single transcultural form. The absence of a cultural consensus, particularly at the international level, over what counts as a universal means, therefore, that there is disagreement about 'who may make it [a universal claim], and what form it ought to take' (*CHU*: 35). Given that the 'human' is a universal category, the result is that competing discourses of human rights (universal discourses) conceive the distribution of those rights differently. One universal may treat a given set of rights as pertaining to all humans whereas in another case 'those very rights mark the limit of universalizability'. Such, she suggests, is the case with gay and lesbian human rights, wherein 'various cultures and various mainstream human rights groups' do not view gays and lesbians as part of the 'human' to whom human rights belong ('UC': 46).[41]

Secondly, in order to develop a more substantive and inclusive conception and practice of the universal, in a context of competing universals, it is necessary to identify the exclusions and parochial ideals that ground its existing historical articulations. This is what Butler refers to as identifying the 'alterity within the norm (an alterity without which the norm would not assume its borders and "know" its limits)' ('UC': 50). This can only be done by subjecting to critical scrutiny the gendered, racial and religious frames that currently define the human so as to contest them. As Butler comments, this is when a new 'universal begins to become articulated precisely through challenges to its existing formulation'; at such times, 'the universal, far from being commensurate with its conventional formulation, emerges as a postulated and open-ended *ideal* that has not been adequately encoded in any given set of legal conventions' ('UC': 48). Cultural translation, to reformulate, subverts an existing universal by revealing precisely what is excluded from it (this is the alterity within). So, a universal predicated upon a male subject is subverted when its masculinist premises are revealed; when, that is, it is shown that women are constitutively excluded from its terms. It would be no good here to try to assimilate women to this ideal because, in essence, it is asking them to be like men.

The aim of cultural translation is thus not to posit *a priori* universal claims about the human.[42] Nor is it to impose a 'universal claim on a culture that resists it', by attempting to make that culture fit into an existing framework ('UC': 51). Nor, indeed, is it to argue that the universal emerges progressively and dialectically out of a synthesis of prior universals. Rather, the competing universals brought together in a moment of translation must both *'change in order to apprehend the other'* (*UG*: 38). Conflict arises because the same terms do not have the same meaning everywhere. To resolve this conflict, therefore, each side has to rethink its own presumptions about the human, about liveable lives, and about what counts as a universal claim. Each side, that is, has to confront the particularistic cultural limitations of its own conception of the universal and open itself up to the other before it can develop a more encompassing version.

Cultural translation is thus, necessarily for Butler, an on-going part of an evolving and inherently democratic human rights politics.

There are obvious parallels here with Bhabha's account, as set out above, in that translation in both cases is centrally concerned with cultural difference and with the problem of the incommensurability between elements of diverse cultures as they are mobilized in different 'rhetorical and cultural contexts' (*CHU*: 35). Moreover, Butler's account echoes Bhabha's in seeing the introduction of foreign elements into another culture as potentially conjuring something 'new', some kind of hybrid form (though she does not appropriate the idea of hybridity) out of the encounter between two competing 'languages' of the universal. It might even be possible to see Butler's discussion of cultural translation as inviting the same kind of examination of the forms of social contradiction and antagonism as Bhabha assigns to the experience of hybridity, where the limits of shared knowledge and understanding are exposed. There is, however, also a difference. When Bhabha and Benjamin talk about translation, they use it to refer to the practice of taking terms from one language and attempting to render them in a different language or another medium. Translation is thus a cross-linguistic practice. One of the problems with translation, as both Benjamin and Bhabha recognize, concerns the *untranslatability* of certain words or ideas, their resistance to rendering in another language or idiom. As Bhabha recognizes, it is precisely at this point that cultural difference is staged. Yet Butler does not appear to acknowledge untranslatability as an issue. Indeed, given the presuppositions of her account of resignification (which, at times, is conceptually indistinguishable in my view from her conceptualization of translation), her emphasis is on the malleability of language: its amenability to recycling, and not its resistance to such.[43]

Whatever the ambiguities of Butler's account, and whether she intends it or not, what the idea of cultural translation brings to the fore, in a way that resignification did not, is the difficult political labour necessary to construct a universal capable of encompassing groups with very diverse ideas about what it is to be human, the needs that humans have and the rights that they may require. It makes far clearer the kinds of ontological and epistemological challenges a democratic movement committed to human survival must face as it attempts to transform the terms of recognition and of *recognizability*. At its most effective, cultural translation can usher in a reconfigured and more inclusive universal, a reconfigured and more inclusive sense of the human, but it will not be an easy task. Without it, however, non-violent ethical relations with the other will be stymied. So how do Butler's concern with ethics, with recognition and with the politics of radical democracy (and its reconfiguration of the universal via the practice of cultural translation) all fit together?

Human vulnerability is, for Butler, the basis for a new, non-violent, ethics *and* politics. Our dependence on others, revealed in experiences such as grief and mourning, opens us up to them. Yet two factors hinder our ability to react ethically towards these others. First, we are unable to recognize certain individuals as human (because of the violence of derealization – or normative violence – that determines who can be recognized) and thus to acknowledge the precariousness of their existences. Second, and relatedly, the universal is always expressed in terms of cultural norms and, as such, is always circumscribed. Radical democratic politics, as Butler conceives it, is the means to tackle these obstacles: through the process of contesting, from 'myriad directions', definitions of the human that limit rather than enlarge the 'possibilities of life' (*UG*: 224, 223). This is where the practice of cultural translation figures, for it works at the cultural and social limits of particular conceptions of the universal, exposing what they exclude, and creating space for their reformulation. It is this translational practice that produces the space within which a non-violent ethical encounter becomes possible. Radical democratic politics, as Butler conceives of it (as an agonistic politics operating at the level of civil society), is thus the optimum way to extend to the currently disenfranchised the possibility of a viable life and to create the conditions for a generous ethics, for, that is, a non-violent ethics.

Conclusion

As a thinker who in 2000 confessed to being disturbed by the 'turn to ethics' on the grounds that 'ethics displaces from politics', Butler's recent interest in ethics is intriguing.[44] The explanation she offers for her disquiet is that ethics does not start from the use of power, whereas politics does. The fact that her own discussion of ethics concentrates so heavily on norms would suggest that she has found a way to reconcile the two (ethics and politics). Although she does not really subject the idea of an ethical impulse to critical scrutiny – she appears simply to assume that there is one – most of her discussion of ethics is concerned with identifying the factors inhibiting an ethical encounter. Central to this, of course, is the construction of the category of the human according to particular restrictive cultural frames. When Butler considers Levinas's idea of the face, the idea he develops to explain how the other makes moral demands on a subject (*PL*: 140–51), her focus is on how certain faces are humanized (the women of Afghanistan removing their burkas) while others are dehumanized (the faces of Osama bin Laden and Saddam Hussein, both of whom come to symbolize evil). Her exploration of ethics is thus embedded in an account of the politics – or power relations – involved in producing the human. The reason, in other words, that encounters with others do not automatically result in an ethical response towards them is because these encounters are structured by power relations: we cannot respond ethically when we cannot recognize the other as human (*PL*: 150). The goal is not, however, to eliminate politics from ethics. It is, rather, to accept that the two are continuous. Political struggles against the norm are a way of securing the possibility of ethical relations.

The idea of an ethically inflected politics is, of course, still a largely embryonic one in Butler's work and, as such, it is difficult to assess its impact at present. Nevertheless, articles have begun to appear either engaging with or deploying arguments drawn from *Precarious Life* and *Undoing Gender*, so it is probably only a matter of time before these works acquire the status of others of Butler's volumes.[45] What it is possible to say, however, is that Butler's ethical 'turn', if this is indeed what it is, raises a number of questions that have not yet been answered in full: whether the idea of an ethical impulse, as Butler deploys it, is like her account of the desire for existence, pre-discursive or not; whether there has been a shift from critiquing political ontologies to positing an ontology, an ontology of bodily vulnerability; whether the apparent emphasis on experience and the situatedness of existence returns her to the phenomenological terms of her earlier work; whether, in fact, the hopes she holds out for a reconfigured, more democratic, less violent, counter-imperialist politics are actually realizable or not;[46] whether there is a tension between the account of primary relationality set out in *Psychic Life* and that developed in the triad of books with which this chapter has been concerned; and whether sovereign agency can automatically be construed as a denial of primary dependency rather than as a means of securing oneself against human vulnerability and primary attachment.

But even though *Precarious Life, Undoing Gender* and *Giving an Account of Oneself* undoubtedly signal certain changes in the direction of Butler's thought (not just in terms of ethics but also with regard to the body), it would, I think, be a mistake to interpret them as breaking entirely with the lines of inquiry pursued in previous texts. From her earliest to her most recent writings, there are a number of themes that characterize Butler's work: a concern with norms and how the terms of both existence and resistance are constrained and yet enabled by their operation; an interest in the power relations that structure contemporary reality, establishing hierarchies of viability for human life; the issue of recognition and who counts; questions of subjectivity, language and agency; and the body. The difference is that in her first books, these themes were explored almost exclusively in relation to sex, gender, sexuality and desire. This is why Butler's ideas gained such enormous influence in feminist and gay and lesbian politics. By contrast, in subsequent volumes this emphasis has shifted. Race has become more important to her work and, gradually, Butler has begun to situate her discussions in terms of the human and the possibility of its survival. And so the appeal of her work has extended. Moreover, although gender performativity will almost certainly be the concept for which Butler is best remembered, the real strength of her work, to my mind at least, is its emphasis on norms. It is this idea that is developed so brilliantly in these last books.

Notes

Chapter 1 Introduction

1 These include Bulgarian, Chinese, Croatian, Dutch, Finnish, French, German, Hungarian, Japanese, Korean, Norwegian, Portuguese, Romanian, Russian, Serbian, Slovakian, Slovenian, Spanish, Turkish and Ukrainian. Whether it has had quite the formative influence on feminist debates outside of the English-speaking world is moot. See, for instance, Griffin and Braidotti, eds, *Thinking Differently*.
2 A full list of these books is given in the Bibliography.
3 Žižek , 'Class Struggle or Postmodernism?', p. 132 n. 30.
4 Segal, *Why Feminism?*, p. 57; Heinämaa, 'What is a Woman?', p. 20. Indeed, Butler herself claims in an interview that she is a 'feminist theorist before I'm a queer theorist or a gay and lesbian theorist' ('GP': 32).
5 Dietz, 'Current Controversies in Feminist Theory', p. 412; Hekman, 'Beyond Identity', p. 289. See also McNay, 'Subject, Psyche and Agency', p. 175.
6 See, for instance, the interview 'Changing the Subject', where Butler corrects the statement of her interviewers that she initiated the feminist critique of identity politics by noting the prior publication of Denise Riley's book (*Am I That Name?*), stating that 'it made the argument [concerning identity] in a way that I definitely profited from'. Here she also identifies the work of bell hooks, Patricia Hill Collins, Kimberlé Crenshaw and Gayatri Spivak, amongst others, as contributing significantly to the rejection of the idea of a unified feminist subject ('CS': 336). See also the list of quotations that Butler uses to open Chapter 1 of *Gender Trouble*.
7 For a personal account of the significance of Derrida's thought, see Butler's obituary of Derrida in the *London Review of Books*, 4 November

2004 (available online at: *www.lrb.co.uk/v26/n21/butl02_.html*, accessed 8 January 2007).

8 MacKinnon, *Feminism Unmodified*.

9 Grant, *Fundamental Feminism*, pp. 33–9.

10 Rowland and Klein, 'Radical Feminism', p. 271.

11 Grant, *Fundamental Feminism*, p. 23. According to Grant it is the three core ideas of radical feminism that ensure this; they are Woman, experientialism and 'the personal as political'.

12 See, for instance: Christian, 'The Race for Theory'; Collins, *Black Feminist Thought*; Haraway, 'Manifesto for Cyborgs; hooks, *Ain't I a Woman* and *Feminist Theory;* Lorde, *Sister Outsider*; and Rich, *On Lies, Secrets, and Silence*.

13 Some sense of the difficulties attached to attempting to retrieve authentic experiences of being Black and female, for instance, can be seen by looking at 'A Black Feminist Statement' by the Combahee River Collective. This statement offers an account that while attuned to the idea of oppression as a complex of multiple interlocking forces (of racism, sexism and class oppression), nevertheless assumes that it is possible to access the authentic experiences of being Black and female. Critics contended that it could not because, amongst other things, 'authentic' Blackness was inseparable from other aspects of identity.

14 De Lauretis, 'Eccentric Subjects', p. 115.

15 For further discussion of this shift, see Alcoff, 'Cultural Feminism versus Post-structuralism', p. 405; de Lauretis, 'Eccentric Subjects', p. 115; and my *Beyond Identity Politics*, pp. 5–6.

16 See, for instance, Hurtado, 'Relating to Privilege' and King, 'Multiple Jeopardy, Multiple Consciousness'.

17 Perhaps the most influential version of this thesis is Spelman's *Inessential Woman*. The term 'intersectional' is taken from Crenshaw, 'Demarginalizing the Intersection of Race and Sex'.

18 On *différance* feminism see Coole, *Women in Political Theory*, pp. 211–21; and on deconstruction feminism see Dietz, 'Current Controversies in Feminist Theory', pp. 401–14. See also my *Beyond Identity Politics*, Chapter 2.

19 Weeks, *Sexuality and Its Discontents*, p. 185.

20 In terms of Butler's context, namely the US, the defining moment in the emergence of the gay and lesbian movement is often taken to be Stonewall, which, as one commentator notes, 'has become synonymous over the years with gay resistance to oppression' (Duberman, *Stonewall*, p. xvii). Stonewall refers to the name of a bar in Greenwich Village, New York, that, on 28 June 1969, was raided by police. Its patrons protested and five days of rioting ensued, and, so the story goes, the gay and lesbian movement was born.

21 Seidman, 'Deconstructing Queer Theory', p. 116.

22 It was also the grounds for communitarian belonging. This is a community that, as Gallagher and Wilson suggest, extends back in time to

such ancestors as 'Plato, Michelangelo and Sappho' (cited in Fuss, *Essentially Speaking*, p. 106).

23 Seidman, 'Deconstructing Queer Theory', pp. 120–1.

24 Phelan, *Getting Specific*, p. 60.

25 Ibid.; Seidman, 'Deconstructing Queer Theory'; Spargo, *Foucault and Queer Theory*.

26 In fact, the GLAA and the CHE grew out of earlier rights-based movements: in the former case out of the Gay Activists Alliance and in the latter out of Committee for Homosexual Equality, both formed in 1969. It has thus been suggested that the equal rights-based strand of gay and lesbian politics was initiated, primarily, by white middle-class gay men.

27 This group was the Radicalesbians, who at the second Congress to Unite Women, in May 1970, circulated a paper, 'The Woman-Identified Woman', in which they articulated their political position. The idea that lesbians are *ipso facto* political radicals was further developed by Adrienne Rich in her 1980 essay 'Compulsory Heterosexuality and Lesbian Existence'. For a fuller discussion of the idea of woman-identified women, see Phelan, *Identity Politics*, Chapter 3. See also her *Getting Specific*, p. 21.

28 Phelan, *Getting Specific*, pp. 152, 151.

29 Seidman, 'Deconstructing Queer Theory', p. 116.

30 Ibid., p. 124.

31 See Phelan, *Getting Specific*, pp. 151–4. It should be noted that the move to constructionism in itself did not undermine entirely the idea of gays and lesbians as a distinct minority deserving equal rights.

32 Halperin, *Saint Foucault*, p. 63.

33 Butler's debt to these political organizations will become more apparent in Chapter 3.

34 Boyne and Rattansi, 'Theory and Politics of Postmodernism'. They also distinguish postmodernism and poststructuralism from postmodernity, which they use to refer to the social, political and cultural configuration of which postmodernism is a component part.

35 Di Stefano, 'Dilemmas of Difference', p. 76. For a discussion of Kristeva's role in helping both to displace the structural linguistic hegemony that had dominated French theory and to introduce an alternative poststructuralist theory of language, see my 'Julia Kristeva'.

36 Ebert, 'Ludic Feminism', pp. 6, 10. Interestingly, very few of those listed use the terms explicitly in their work (except perhaps to refuse it as a description of their theoretical endeavours, as Foucault did). The two obvious exceptions are Jean-François Lyotard, the author of *The Postmodern Condition*, and Frederic Jameson, the author of *Postmodernism: Or, the Cultural Logic of Late Capitalism*.

37 I take this term from Butler; see 'CR'.

38 Foucault's *Archaeology of Knowledge* and *The Order of Things* are classified as 'structuralist' texts. Things are not always as straightforward

as they appear to be with Foucault, however. In the case of Lacan, the same body of work has been defined as both structuralist and post-structuralist. Yannis Stavrakakis charts some of the terminological confusion surrounding Lacan's writings in his *Lacan and the Political*, pp. 13–14, and, in particular, p. 144 n. 1. I think Stavrakakis is right in his adjudication that trying to pigeonhole someone as either one or the other obscures the way in which certain thought goes beyond such reductive labels. I will, however, continue to use both terms here for heuristic purposes only.

39 Silverman, *The Subject of Semiotics*, p. 130.

40 Sarup, *An Introductory Guide to Post-Structuralism and Postmodernism*, p. 43.

41 This account is shared by Derrida, Lacan (who, recall, is thought of *both* as a structuralist and as a poststructuralist) and Ernesto Laclau and Chantal Mouffe, at least in *Hegemony and Socialist Strategy*. A good example of the perpetual deferral of meaning, mentioned by Sarup amongst others, is what happens when one consults a dictionary in order to find the meaning of a word (a particular signifier). What one discovers are simply more words or signifiers. One can, of course, look up their signifieds, but only to find further signifiers. And so it goes, on and on. Butler discusses the idea of temporalization in an interview, 'OSRM': 168.

42 Interestingly, amongst the gaps that Butler herself identifies in *Subjects of Desire* is her failure to consider the second of the chapters on self-consciousness in the *Phenomenology*, 'Freedom of Self-Consciousness: Stoicism, Scepticism, and the Unhappy Consciousness' (*SD*: viii).

43 Butler's treatment of Derrida is relatively short, largely because Derrida effectively 'excludes himself from the discourse on desire' (*SD*: 184). As such, she talks only about his essay in homage to Hyppolite, 'The Pit and the Pyramid'.

44 For a brief consideration of 'open' and 'closed' readings of Hegel, see Hutchings, *Hegel and Feminist Philosophy*, p. 32.

45 Megill, '*Subjects of Desire*', p. 124.

46 She also talks of the *Phenomenology* as a 'study in fiction-making' (*SD*: 23), interestingly presenting this reading as a 'Nietzschean' one.

47 It is, as Butler and others have noted, exceedingly unlikely that any human could actually withstand such debilitating disappointment all the time (*SD*: 23).

48 Pippin, '*Subjects of Desire*', p. 129.

49 There are some scattered references to melancholia in *SD* (36–7) but at this stage they lack the Freudian conceptual apparatus that underpins Butler's later discussion.

50 Hegel, *Phenomenology of Spirit*, §115.

51 Indeed, in her account of the way in which the psyche is constructed, she argues that homosexuality must be disavowed in order for hetero-sexuality to exist. I discuss this in Chapter 4. Butler, of course, is not

the only thinker to argue for the co-implication of homosexuality and heterosexuality; see also Fuss, ed., *Inside/Out*.

52 Ibid.

53 Butler's position, in this respect, is somewhat different from that adopted by other commentators; see, for instance, Coole, *Negativity and Politics*, p. 43 and the comments by Osborne and Segal in 'GP': 35. Significant questions are raised by Butler's idea of a non-synthetic dialectic, but as they fall outside the thematic scope of this particular book, I do not address them at this time.

54 Foucault, 'Discourse on Language', p. 131. The fact that Butler sees parodic politics as leading to a multiplication of sexes, genders, sexualities and bodies 'beyond the binary frame' that presently defines them (*GT*: xi) echoes her description of Foucault in *Subjects of Desire*, where she contends that he advances a dialectic 'in which the constant inversion of opposites leads not to a reconciliation in unity, but to a proliferation if oppositions which come to undermine the hegemony of binary opposition itself' (*SD*: 225). See Chapter 3.

55 Nussbaum, 'Professor of Parody'.

56 Butler, 'A "Bad Writer" Bites Back'; and 'CS': 327–30. Here Monique Wittig's claims, which Butler discusses in *Gender Trouble*, that grammar naturalizes gender (via the use in French, which is the language with which Wittig is concerned, of the feminine and masculine articles *la* and *le*) is apposite. As Butler reads this, to challenge gender normativity one needs also to challenge the normativizing work of grammar in producing gender linguistically (*GT*: xix).

57 For a consideration of the anti-democratic nature of calls for 'clarity' and of the ethics involved in engaging with complex texts, see Salih, 'Judith Butler and the Ethics of Difficulty'.

58 See ibid. and Pearce, *Rhetorics of Feminism*, pp. 160–5.

59 See her own reflection on this: *GT*: xx.

60 In fact, Butler's interviews are a particularly fecund source for examining the contingency of her thought, as are the later prefaces added to earlier works.

61 Indeed, at one point she suggests reiteratively that 'performativity' might also be 'psychic' (*GT*: xv).

62 Hood-Williams and Harrison, 'Trouble with Gender', p. 85. Their comment is specifically about Butler's reading of Freud.

63 This is the claim Stevi Jackson makes in relation to Wittig (*Christine Delphy*, pp. 136–7). I discuss this again in the next chapter.

64 For Hood-Williams and Harrison this occurs in relation to Derrida: by emphasizing citationality over undecidability, Butler, it is charged, fixes 'the very undecidability that wants to set, and keep, in motion'; 'Trouble with Gender', pp. 81–2.

65 Heinämaa makes this claim when she argues that Butler's reading of Beauvoir is influenced by debates in Anglo-American feminism that do not pertain to Beauvoir's work; 'What is a Woman?'

66 This is what happens, in my opinion, with relation to Foucault's discussion of power when Butler treats his analytic of power as a theory of power, and when she conflates the distinction he draws between juridical and discursive power in her definition of juridical power. See Chapter 2, fn. 3 below.
67 Pearce, *Rhetorics of Feminism*, p. 180.
68 Ibid., p. 179.
69 Ibid., pp. 10, 6, 218 n. 12.
70 Ibid., p. 27; see also pp. 25–6 for a discussion of particular examples of Butler's rhetorical style in *Bodies that Matter*.

Chapter 2 Rethinking Sex and Gender

1 Elam, *Feminism and Deconstruction*, p. 70. For a fuller treatment of this topic see my *Beyond Identity Politics*.
2 The term 'genealogy' derives from Nietzsche's *On the Genealogy of Morality*, though Butler takes her inspiration from Foucault (who adapts his account from Nietzsche). The principal difference between Foucault and Butler is that Foucault treats genealogy as a form of historical investigation that concentrates on how particular phenomena (such as punishment or sexuality) emerge from chance and contingent events whereas Butler sees genealogy as investigating what she describes as 'the political stakes in designating as an *origin* and *cause* those identity categories that are in fact the *effects* of institutions, practices, discourses with multiple and diffuse points of origin' (*GT*: xxix). Where Foucault concentrates on historical documents, often obscure ones, Butler seeks to unpick the assumptions of certain theoretical texts in order to demonstrate that what one has assumed to be necessary relations between elements (e.g. sex, gender and desire) are, in fact, non-necessary. As Anna Marie Smith notes, Butler is, in fact, engaged in problematization, which is only one aspect of genealogy in Foucault's sense ('Words that Matter', p. 391). The result of this, as I will show later, is that Butler often fails to attend to the historical conditions that both make possible and limit the very phenomenon that she is exploring. On this issue of historicity see also Ebert, 'Ludic Feminism'; my 'Radical Democratic Activism'; McNay 'Out of the Orrery?', p. 145 and *Gender and Agency*, p. 59; Mills, 'Contesting the Political'; and Smith, 'Words that Matter'. For two accounts that explore the relation between Butler and Nietzsche (via Foucault), see Schrift, 'Reconfiguring the Subject'; and Stone, 'Towards a Genealogical Feminism'. For a discussion of Foucault's changing approaches to history, see Thacker, 'Foucault and the Writing of History'.
3 See also Butler's discussion of Foucault in *SD* (222, 225, 227). Butler claims to derive this understanding of the relation between feminism and women from Foucault's understanding of juridical power. She

reads this as meaning that the juridical subject prior to the law is in fact a product of the law, deployed in order to legitimate law's disciplinary role. There is, in my view, evidence of conceptual confusion in how Butler uses the term 'juridical'. Foucault explicitly distinguishes between different empirical forms of power – specifically disciplinary and juridical – in order to show that power operates differently in certain contexts, times, spaces. To complicate matters, however, he also conceptualizes power, in general, as productive, labelling this broader understanding of power 'juridico-discursive', bringing together the two empirical forms he has identified (*History of Sexuality*, p. 82). When Butler uses the term 'juridical', it seems that she actually means juridico-discursive.

4 Butler does occasionally talk about 'patriarchy', especially in *Gender Trouble*, but Warner's term, which first appears in his 1991 essay, 'Fear of a Queer Planet', seems more appropriate. Significantly, additional support for the use of this idea is provided by the French version of *Gender Trouble, Trouble dans le Genre*, where normative heterosexuality is explicitly translated (after consultation with Butler) as 'hétéronormativité'.

5 'French feminism' is usually associated with the work of Julia Kristeva, Hélène Cixous and Luce Irigaray, none of whom is French and only the latter of whom calls herself a feminist. For an account of the advent of and problems with this label, see Delphy, 'The Invention of French Feminism'.

6 Butler uses the terms 'sexual practices' and 'sexual minorities', derived from Gayle Rubin ('Traffic in Women' and 'Thinking Sex'), because neither is identity-based. See *GT*: xi and 'CS': 347.

7 Butler, 'Revisiting Bodies and Pleasures', p. 12.

8 Haraway, '"Gender" for a Marxist Dictionary', p. 131.

9 Oakley, *Sex, Gender and Society*, p. 16. Simone de Beauvoir is often credited with prefiguring this division between sex and gender with her claim, 'one is not born, but rather becomes, a woman', *The Second Sex*, p. 295. (The variant on this quote in n. 21 below is due to the way in which Butler translates Beauvoir from the French.)

10 Cranny-Francis et al., *Gender Studies*, pp. 1–4.

11 For a critique of Oakley's failure to deal with the asymmetrical and hierarchical relations between genders, see Delphy, 'Rethinking Sex and Gender'.

12 Rubin with Butler, 'Sexual Traffic', p. 64.

13 Rubin, 'Traffic in Women', p. 534.

14 Ibid., p. 538.

15 Tong, *Feminist Thought*, p. 49.

16 Chodorow, *The Reproduction of Mothering*.

17 Lloyd, *Man of Reason*.

18 Rubin, 'Traffic in Women'; Firestone, *Dialectic of Sex*; and Millett, *Sexual Politics*. All three favour androgyny as the way forward, though they

all conceive this post-gendered androgynous future in different ways.

19 Gatens, 'A Critique of the Sex/Gender Distinction', p. 140. Those who rejected the idea of the sex/gender distinction included certain psychoanalytic feminists who argued that sex, gender (and sexuality) could simply not be distinguished from one another in the way assumed by gender theorists because they were 'causatively intertwined' (Mitchell, 'Introduction – I', p. 2), as well as feminist philosophers such as Gatens who argued against the distinction because of its alleged assumption that both the body and the psyche were passive surfaces awaiting inscription by gender. See also Jackson, *Christine Delphy*, p. 116.

20 Delphy, 'Rethinking Sex and Gender', p. 1, my emphasis. See also Delphy, *Close to Home*. For a discussion of Delphy's work, see Jackson, *Christine Delphy*.

21 The five quotations are: 'One is not born a woman, but becomes one' (Beauvoir); 'Strictly speaking, "women" cannot be said to exist' (Kristeva); 'Woman does not have a sex' (Irigaray); 'The deployment of sexuality . . . established this notion of sex' (Foucault); 'The category of sex is the political category that founds society as heterosexual' (Wittig) (cited in *GT*: 3).

22 The word 'phallogocentric' brings together the idea of 'logocentrism', which in this context refers to the stress that a number of male writers place on the *logos* (or word) as a way of accessing the truth, and 'phallocentrism', which, very simply put, might be seen to capture the idea that the male/masculine represents the norm, or the privileged term. As used by Irigaray, and other feminists, phallogocentrism might be thought of as a masculine style of language that can be contrasted with a feminine style. For further discussion see Wright, ed., *Feminism and Psychoanalysis*, pp. 316–18.

23 Although it is beyond my concerns in this book, the point of the designation 'the sex which is not one' is to show that women do not have one sexual organ (like men – the penis/phallus) but rather have several (vagina, clitoris, labia). A signifying economy that assumes unitary sex cannot, therefore, encompass women.

24 It is important to note, however, that Butler does perceive Irigaray as important in opening up the question of sexual difference, though she continues to question the relationship between sexual difference as a framework of thought and the institutional prospects it unlocks. See 'End'.

25 Jackson, *Christine Delphy*, p. 125.

26 For an example of the difficulties Foucault has with 'gender', see the interview between Mort and Peters and Foucault entitled 'Foucault Recalled'.

27 In her later work, she extends this to the idea of a mournable death.

28 See also *GT*: 194, fn. 6, where Butler makes clear her debt to both Wittig and Rich.
29 Wittig, 'One is Not Born a Woman', p. 53. For Wittig, so extensive is the reach of the idea of dyadic sex that it even structures language for, as she notes, despite differences between French and English (i.e. that all nouns in French are gendered, via *le* and *la*, whereas they are not in English), when it comes to signifying people both languages 'are bearers of gender to the same extent'. Wittig, 'The Mark of Gender', p. 3; see also *GT*: 212, fn. 25.
30 Rich, 'Compulsory Heterosexuality', p. 637.
31 *GT*: 194, fn. 6. Foucault, *History of Sexuality*, p. 93.
32 In the 1999 preface, where the term 'normative violence' originates, Butler illustrates this by talking about her 'uncle incarcerated for his anatomically anomalous body . . . gay cousins forced to leave their homes because of their sexuality, real and imagined; my own tempestuous coming out at the age of 16' (*GT*: xix, xx).
33 Butler is explicitly referring to the work of Wittig and Foucault here as ways of contesting sexual difference. See also the earlier piece on which this essay is based, though from which it takes some critical distance, namely, 'Sex and Gender in Simone de Beauvoir's *Second Sex*'.
34 Wittig, 'One is Not Born a Woman', p. 53. There is some ambiguity in Wittig's work as to whether it is lesbianism *per se* that affords the opportunity for liberation from heteronormativity or whether other non-heterosexual practices (including male homosexuality) also present equivalent possibilities.
35 Fuss, *Essentially Speaking*. For a discussion rejecting Wittig's understanding of lesbianism, see Jackson's remarks in Hird, 'Theorizing the End of Gender', pp. 268–9.
36 See, for instance, her discussion of lesbianism at the start of 'Imitation' (13).
37 It is Derrida's suggestion that anticipating the authority of the law, in effect, produces that authority that inspires Butler. This, she argues, appeared to parallel the performativity of gender (*GT*: xiv). I'll explore her debt to Derrida and Austin further in Chapters 3 and 5.
38 Roden, for instance, suggests that Butler invokes their work in order to differentiate her own account of performativity and performance more forcefully from other prior and/or contemporaneous accounts ('Becoming Butlerian', p. 26), while Allen contends that Butler's turn to Austin and Derrida is designed to address problems of agency bequeathed by her reliance on a (loosely) Foucauldian understanding of power in *Gender Trouble* (see 'Power Trouble', p. 456 and *The Power of Feminist Theory*).
39 The papers in question are: 'Sex and Gender in Simone de Beauvoir's *Second Sex*', 'Variations on Sex and Gender', 'Gendering the Body' and 'Performative Acts and Gender Constitution'.

40 For an explanation of this see Kruks, *Retrieving Experience*, p. 39, n. 13.
41 Heinämaa, 'What is a Woman?', p. 25; see also Heinämaa, *Toward a Phenomenology of Sexual Difference*.
42 Kruks, *Retrieving Experience*, p. 7.
43 Butler's interest in phenomenology goes back, of course, to Hegel, here phenomenology is understood as a philosophy of consciousness rather than embodiment. Butler has also written on Maurice Merleau-Ponty: see her 'Sexual Ideology and Phenomenological Description' (written in 1981, though published in 1989), and 'Merleau-Ponty and the Touch of Malebranche'. See also Vasterling, 'Body and Language'.
44 Butler initially uses this phrase in 'Performative Acts' a propos of Beauvoir, commenting that Beauvoir's understanding of becoming a woman grows out of her 'appropriating and reinterpreting [the] . . . doctrine of constituting acts from the phenomenological tradition. In this sense, gender is in no way a stable identity or locus of agency from which various acts proceed; rather, it is an identity tenuously constituted in time – an identity instituted through a *stylized repetition of acts* ('PA': 519). In *Gender Trouble*, at the conclusion of her discussion of gender performativity, now shorn of reference to Beauvoir, she notes: 'Gender ought not to be construed as a stable identity or locus of agency from which various acts follow; rather, gender is an identity tenuously constituted in time, instituted in an exterior space through the *stylized repetition of acts*' (*GT*: 179).
45 Although I cannot develop this argument here, it is not clear to me that Butler has ever actually been able to expunge all traces of phenomenology from her work.
46 Beauvoir, *Second Sex*, p. 295.
47 See also 'VSG'. This is essentially the same as 'SG' except that it incorporates an assessment of Wittig and Foucault and includes a conclusion in which Butler considers the possible pitfalls of existentialism. At this point, she reads Beauvoir's account of woman as an anti-essentialist thesis.
48 Young, 'Lived Body vs. Gender', p. 16.
49 In 'Gendering the Body', she thus cites the example of the 'man from Maine' who 'walks down the street in a dress, walking the way that women are supposed to walk' and who is found the next day 'dead in a ravine' ('GB': 256).
50 See *GT*: 17. Here Butler also implies that Beauvoir is closer to Sartrean existentialism, which privileges consciousness (mind), than to existential phenomenology, with its emphasis on lived embodiment. One account that challenges Butler's changing readings of Beauvoir is Heinämaa, 'What is a Woman?' One of the observations that Heinämaa rightly makes is that when Butler offers her more critical reappraisal of Beauvoir in *Gender Trouble*, she furnishes no argument

as to why she has jettisoned her own earlier reading of Beauvoir. This is certainly true. On Butler's reading of Beauvoir, see also Kruks, *Retrieving Experience*.

51 Notably, at this point, Butler distances her work from that of Erving Goffman ('PA': 528). I will return to this in the next chapter.

52 Significantly, Butler does note that gender performances in 'non-theatrical contexts' are usually more restricted and more severely punished than in the theatre ('PA': 527).

53 Where, prior to *Gender Trouble*, Butler has read Beauvoir as subscribing to the notion of the body as an historical idea, in this text she now argues that Beauvoir believes in a natural sexed body.

54 Bell, *Feminist Imagination*, p. 88. Or, as Butler puts it: 'interiority is an effect and function of a decidedly public and social discourse', a fabrication 'manufactured and sustained though corporeal signs and other discursive means' (*GT*: 173).

55 It is important to note at this juncture that temporality (repetition, incessant reproduction) is central to Butler's account of gender performativity; see Chapter 3 for a fuller consideration of temporality.

56 I will come back to this in the next chapter.

57 Newton, *Mother Camp*.

58 Butler later applies the same logic to transgender, a topic she does not discuss in *Gender Trouble*. In *Undoing Gender* she notes that because it disrupts the sex/sexuality/desire nexus, it is impossible to determine if the sexuality of the transgendered individual is homosexual or heterosexual. Commenting on the film *Boys Don't Cry*, Butler notes that Brandon Teena (who is anatomically female) 'identifies as a heterosexual boy' not as a lesbian in his desire for a woman; he crosses from being a girl to being a straight boy (*UG*: 142).

59 See also Campbell and Harbord, 'Playing it Again', p. 229.

60 For a similar, albeit brief, discussion, see Deutscher, *Yielding Gender*, p. 29.

61 See also 'CF'.

62 We will evaluate her alternative conception of feminist/gender politics in Chapter 3.

63 Segal, *Straight Sex*, p. 192.

64 Nussbaum, 'Professor of Parody'.

65 Benhabib, 'Feminism and Postmodernism'.

66 See Fraser, 'False Antitheses', p. 70. On the relation between feminism and democracy, see 'End'. I will explore her democratic theory in Chapter 6.

67 A particularly clear treatment of Delphy and Wittig's materialism is given in Jackson, *Christine Delphy*.

68 See, for instance, Braidotti, *Metamorphoses*, pp. 39–58; Tyler, 'Boys will be Girls'.

69 In a couple of essays ('Against Proper Objects' and 'The End of Sexual Difference?'), Butler herself reflects upon the way that feminism and

queer theory have come to be distinguished on the basis that the former is taken to concentrate on theories of gender and the latter on issues of sexuality.

Chapter 3 Towards a Subversive Gender Politics

1 Hennessy, 'Queer Visibility', p. 142.
2 Socialist and Marxist feminists were also committed to an emancipatory politics, but in the latter case it was capitalism rather than the gender order that required overthrowing.
3 Brown, *Edgework*, p. 108.
4 Sargisson, *Contemporary Feminist Utopianism*, p. 1.
5 In Chapter 5, we will examine in more detail the reasons why she is sceptical of a state-based or legalistic politics.
6 Kristeva's favoured example of semiotic disruption is poetry, which with its emphasis on rhythm and sound exposes the subject's link with the semiotic. For a fuller explanation of the terms and ideas contained in this summary of Kristeva, see my 'Julia Kristeva'. I explore the Oedipal stage more fully in the next chapter.
7 Similarly, because of Kristeva's presumption that homosexuality is outside of culture, lesbianism cannot be conceived of as a 'new or unacknowledged cultural form', but only as a psychotic form (*GT*: 111; see also 106–12).
8 Butler's anxieties about Foucault's appeal to some kind of emancipatory ideal are evident in another, more recent, essay, 'Revisiting Bodies and Pleasures'. It should be noted that with regard to Wittig and Foucault, in particular, Butler's readings have been criticized. On Foucault see, for instance, Deutscher, *Yielding Gender*, p. 23 and Ferguson, *Man Question*, pp. 136–44, esp. pp. 139, 140, while on Wittig see Deutscher, *Yielding Gender*, p. 23 and Jackson, *Christine Delphy*, pp. 136–7.
9 See also, Deutscher, *Yielding Gender*, p. 31.
10 Sedgwick, 'Queer Performativity', p. 1.
11 See, for instance, Bordo, 'Postmodern Subjects', pp. 292–3 and 'Bringing Body to Theory'; Ebert 'Ludic Feminism'; Hawkes, 'Dressing-Up'; Hennessey, 'Queer Visibility'; Walters, 'From Here to Queer'; Žižek, 'Class Struggle or Postmodernism?', p. 132, n. 30. Interestingly, Butler claims to have been surprised by readings of this kind: see *BTM*: 125 and 'GP': 33; see also my 'Performativity'.
12 See Deutscher on the former, *Yielding Gender*, p. 29 and Cvetkovich for a discussion of visibility, 'Fierce Pussies', p. 284.
13 Cvetkovich, 'Fierce Pussies', p. 284. See also Bronfen, 'Redressing Grievances' and Spargo, *Foucault and Queer Theory*.
14 Halperin, *Saint Foucault*, p. 29. See also Segal, *Straight Sex*, p. 188.
15 For her retrospective reflections on drag and politics, see the essay 'The Question of Social Transformation' in *UG*: 213–17.

16 Halperin, *Saint Foucault*, p. 29.
17 Ibid., p. 48. This includes drag balls, Queer Nation kiss-ins and ACT UP die-ins; see *BTM*: 233 and 'GP': 38.
18 Walker, 'Why Performance?', p. 162.
19 Brown, *Edgework*, p. 109.
20 Barvosa-Carter, 'Strange Tempest', p. 125.
21 Ibid.
22 Benhabib reflects on her misreading of Butler in 'Subjectivity, Historiography, and Politics', p. 109. For a brief discussion of Butler and Goffman, see, for example, Ashe et al., *Contemporary Social and Political Theory*, pp. 119–23; Bordo, 'Postmodern Subjects', pp. 289–90; and Hood-Williams and Harrison, 'Trouble with Gender', pp. 74, 76.
23 See, for instance, Goffman *Presentation of the Self* and *Asylums*.
24 Benhabib, 'Feminism and the Question of Postmodernism', p. 215; see also her 'Subjectivity, Historiography, and Politics', p. 109. See also Butler's preface to *BTM*: x.
25 Benhabib, 'Feminism and Postmodernism', pp. 22, 21, 20. Benhabib famously misquotes Butler (and Nietzsche) when talking of a 'doer beyond [rather than behind] the deed'. For a fuller consideration of the debate between Butler and Benhabib, see my *Beyond Identity Politics*, Chapter 5 and Webster, 'The Politics of Sex and Gender'.
26 How this squares with Benhabib's Goffmanesque reading of Butler is unclear to me.
27 Weir, *Sacrificial Logics*, p. 113; see especially, pp. 125–8.
28 Ibid., p. 127.
29 Allen, 'Power Trouble', p. 460.
30 Bordo, 'Postmodern Subjects', p. 294. Sara Ahmed offers a variation on the voluntarist theme in her '"She'll Wake Up"'.
31 For a different reading, see Kruks, *Retrieving Experience*, pp. 72, 73.
32 Benhabib, 'Feminism and the Question of Postmodernism', p. 218; see also Allen, 'Power Trouble', p. 461; Barvosa-Carter, 'Strange Tempest', p. 126; Fraser, 'False Antitheses', pp. 66–7; and Nussbaum, 'Professor of Parody'.
33 Austin, *How to Do Things with Words*, p. 22.
34 Derrida, 'Signature Event Context', p. 104; cited, for instance, in *BTM*: 13, 226; *ES*: 51.
35 Derrida, 'Signature Event Context', p. 103.
36 Allen, 'Power Trouble', p. 462. Whether Austin actually sanctions a performer prior to the performative is a matter of some dispute in Butler scholarship: ibid.; Hood-Williams and Harrison, 'Trouble with Gender', pp. 78–81; and Nussbaum, 'Professor of Parody'.
37 The significance of the idea of conventionality for linguistic action will be discussed in more detail in Chapter 5.
38 In treating iteration as a *concept*, Butler may, as Hood-Williams and Harrison suggest, be deviating significantly from Derrida's deconstructive reading of Austin ('Trouble with Gender', pp. 81–2).

39 Foucault, 'An Aesthetics of Existence', p. 50.
40 See, for instance, Allen, 'Power Trouble', p. 463; McNay, 'Subject, Psyche and Agency', p. 177.
41 See also McNay, 'Subject, Psyche and Agency', p. 177.
42 Nealon, 'Between Emergence and Possibility', p. 432.
43 Not all her critics were convinced by these changes, however; see, for instance, Benhabib, 'Subjectivity, Historiography, and Politics', p. 110. In Chapter 5, I will also explore what I perceive to be some of the particular difficulties of relying on Derrida's notion of citationality.
44 In the case of *Some Like it Hot*, however, Butler overlooks the fact that at the end of the film, Jack Lemmon's character is still with 'his man', even though that man knows he is not female.
45 See, for instance, Allen, 'Power Trouble', p. 461; Fraser, 'False Antitheses', p. 68.
46 See also on this point Hekman, 'Material Bodies', p. 68. I return to this example in Chapter 5.
47 Lloyd, *Man of Reason*.
48 White, *Sustaining Affirmation*, p. 4.
49 Nussbaum, 'Professor of Parody'.
50 Bigwood, 'Renaturalizing the Body', pp. 102–3; Bordo, *Unbearable Weight*, p. 38; Pearce, *Rhetorics of Feminism*, p. 144; Segal, *Straight Sex*, p. 192.
51 Bigwood, 'Renaturalizing the Body', p. 103.
52 Stone, 'Towards a Genealogical Feminism', p. 11.
53 Kirkby, 'When All That Is Solid', p. 266.
54 One of her earliest formulations of deconstruction can be found in 'Contingent Foundations'. Here she argues that her political purpose is not to repudiate women as a category for feminism (the position she seemed to adopt in *Gender Trouble*) but to deconstruct that category. In essence, this means setting it free from the political ontologies within which it has been confined in order to allow it to develop in newer ways. See also 'HB': 278.
55 Here Butler discusses the normative violence involved in rape.
56 See Vasterling, 'Butler's Sophisticated Constructivism', for more detailed consideration of the relation between ontological and epistemological claims in Butler's work; see also 'HB': 276; and her reply to her interviewers in '"There is a Person Here"', p. 12.
57 Some commentators remain unconvinced. If the body can only be known through language, they suggest, then Butler does not appear to have shifted very far from the position she is refuting, namely linguistic idealism, since, as one puts it, language continues to function as the 'necessary condition of materiality' (Wilson, 'Butler's Corporeal Politics', p. 112); see also Bray and Colebrook, 'Haunted Flesh'; Kirkby, 'When All That Is Solid'; Olkowski, 'Materiality and Language', p. 39. Indeed, for Kirkby, Butler appears to have reinstated the nature–culture binary that she attempted to problematize through her critique of sex

and gender. For Butler's thoughts on the relation between nature and naturalization, see Butler, '"There is a Person Here"', p. 12; and 'HB': 277.

58 Kirkby, 'When All That Is Solid', p. 268.

59 In *Powers of Horror*, Kristeva thus considers issues from the bodily waste that the individual expels (including tears, saliva, faeces, urine, mucus and vomit), through cultural taboos such as the law against incest and various defilement rights, to the horror of the Nazi death-camps.

60 Grosz, *Sexual Subversions*, p. 71.

61 In fact, as Butler presents it, abjection often appears to be an inevitable aspect of discursive subject production: what needs to be repudiated (denied, foreclosed or disavowed – she uses all these terms) in order for the subject to exist. It could even be seen as evidence of Butler's Hegelianism – her non-synthetic dialectic.

62 Wilson, 'Butler's Corporeal Politics', p. 114.

63 Grosz in Ausch et al., 'Interview'.

Chapter 4 Psychoanalysis and the Gendered Subject

1 Clough, *Feminist Thought*, p. 149.

2 Rubin, 'Traffic in Women', p. 548.

3 Ibid., pp. 542, 546.

4 Rubin with Butler, 'Sexual Traffic', p. 68.

5 Rubin, 'Traffic in Women', p. 543.

6 Ibid., p. 551.

7 See, for instance, Freud, *Interpretation of Dreams*, 'A Special Type of Object-Choice' , and 'The Ego and the Id'; Mitchell, *Psychoanalysis and Feminism*; Sjöholm, 'Family Values'; and Young, *Oedipus Complex*.

8 This is not to say that Freud pays no attention to the origins of the incest taboo. Indeed, *Totem and Taboo* is concerned with that very question.

9 The reason for the different experience is that the girl, like the boy, desires her mother but on discovering that she has no penis – that she has apparently already been castrated – the girl renounces the mother and turns her desires on her father. She then renounces her desire for her father (substituting the desire for a baby instead) and identifies with her mother.

10 Freud, 'Mourning and Melancholia', p. 253.

11 Fuss, *Identification Papers*, p. 1.

12 Freud, 'The Ego and the Id', p. 368.

13 Disch, 'Judith Butler and the Politics of the Performative', p. 548.

14 In arguing such losses are ungrieved, Butler appears to hold onto Freud's original distinction between mourning and melancholia.

15 This is confirmed for Butler in the fact that, unlike incestuous heterosexual desires, where desire for a particular object (the parent of the opposite sex) is repressed but the 'modality of desire' (heterosexuality) is not, with homosexual desire both the object (same-sex parent) and the modality of desire (homosexuality) are denied (*GT*: 75).
16 Butler acknowledges as much both in 'Critically Queer' (p. 24) and in the 1999 preface to *Gender Trouble*, p. xv. See also *GT*: 192, fn. 9.
17 Kruks, *Retrieving Experience*, pp. 19–20.
18 This public prohibition on grief has various effects (*BTM*: 236): it produces anger, it leads to suicide in some cases, and, on occasion, it generates a collective determination to remember. Here Butler cites the example of the NAMES Project Quilt that records homosexual deaths from AIDS.
19 See also Payne, *Reading Theory*.
20 Grosz, *Sexual Subversions*, pp. 19–20.
21 Lacan also draws here on the structural linguistics of Saussure.
22 Butler challenges the 'morphological imaginary' that grounds Lacan's theory in *BTM* in a chapter provocatively titled 'The Lesbian Phallus'.
23 In the Lacanian scheme, the child's desire for its mother results in it endeavouring to understand what the mother desires and to be that thing for her. Submitting to the Law of the Father is a recognition that what the mother desires is determined by the conventions and laws of the symbolic order.
24 Grosz, *Jacques Lacan*, p. 70.
25 Stavrakakis, 'Jacques Lacan', p. 23.
26 Grosz, *Sexual Subversions*, p. 22.
27 Butler notes, however, these two positions should not be taken to exhaust all possible sexed positionalities foreclosed within Lacanian psychoanalysis (*BTM*: 103).
28 Grosz, *Sexual Subversions*, p. xviii.
29 Deleuze and Guattari, *Anti-Oedipus*, p. 51.
30 Butler discusses various of these developments, from changing demographics through various legislative initiatives for same-sex relations, in *Antigone's Claim*; *Contingency, Hegemony, Universality*; and 'Kinship'.
31 I provide a fuller account of the story in 'Butler, Antigone, and the State'. It should be noted that Butler's reading of Antigone is somewhat different from most in that she concentrates primarily on the relation between Creon and Antigone whereas others emphasize what, for Sophocles, was the key theme: the tension between divine law and human law.
32 Deleuze and Guattari, *Anti-Oedipus*, p. 52; see also Wright, *Psychoanalytic Criticism*, p. 101. Butler's critique of the incest taboo also engages with the work of Lévi-Strauss, though I have not discussed it here. For an interesting debate on Lévi-Strauss, see Rubin with Butler in 'Sexual Traffic'.

33 Kirsten Campbell is certainly right that 'the "social", the "cultural", the "symbolic" and the "norm" are not clear and distinct conceptual categories' in Butler's work and thus that there is a certain slipperiness about her attempts to reconceptualize the symbolic ('Politics of Kinship', p. 647). I would suggest, nevertheless, that what *is* clear is that Butler's understanding of the social and cultural is, as Laclau notes, diametrically opposed to the kind of *a priori* universals on which Lacan relies ('Structure, History and the Political', p. 188). As I indicate in the next chapter, I think a bigger problem is that Butler's revised version of the social/symbolic suffers from an inattention to historical and cultural specificity.
34 McRobbie, 'Mothers and Fathers', p. 130.
35 Ibid.
36 See also Campbell, 'Plague of the Subject', pp. 35–6.
37 Disch, 'Judith Butler and the Politics of the Performative', p. 550.
38 Brown, *States of Injury*, pp. 73–4.
39 In *PLP* Butler acknowledges that her own analysis of attachment is indebted to Brown's (202, n. 2).
40 According to Butler, it is not only Althusser who lacks an explanation for submission; so too do Foucault, Nietzsche and Hegel.
41 Salih, ed., *Butler Reader*, p. 7.
42 Disch, 'Judith Butler and the Politics of the Performative', p. 554.
43 Chambers, *Untimely Politics*, p. 146.
44 In *The Psychic Life of Power*, for instance, Butler uses the term 'desire for existence' explicitly to link the preoccupations of Hegel, Freud, Foucault and Nietzsche with desire to Spinoza's *conatus* (62); and in a footnote, she links it to autonomy in terms that could describe her own views on agency (203–4, n. 14). She picks up this theme in *Undoing Gender*, where she links it to the politics of survival, and in *Precarious Life* in her account of ethics. Indeed, the link between the desire for existence and an ethical project is prefigured in *PLP*: 45. See Chapter 6.
45 Chambers, *Untimely Politics*, p. 147.
46 For a fuller treatment of these questions see ibid., Chapter 5.
47 Salih, ed., *Butler Reader*, p. 8; Disch, 'Judith Butler and the Politics of the Performative', p. 550.
48 Copjec, 'Sex and the Euthanasia of Reason', p. 19.
49 Ibid., p. 20.
50 Lacan, she claims, develops the idea of foreclosure from his reading of Freud's discussion of 'disavowal' and 'repudiation'; Campbell, Plague of the Subject', p. 43.
51 Ibid.
52 Ibid., p. 44.
53 Braidotti, 'Feminism by Any Other Name', p. 47.
54 Braidotti, *Metamorphoses*, p. 44.
55 Ibid., pp. 49, 50.

56 Campbell, 'Plague of the Subject', pp. 44–5. Indeed, from this Campbell concludes that Butler's account is Freudian rather than Lacanian – an odd claim to make given that Butler is quite explicit that her account of melancholia derives from Freud!

57 Disch, 'Judith Butler and the Politics of the Performative', p. 554.

Chapter 5 'Talking Back' – Resignification and Politics

1 Walzer, *Spheres of Justice*, p. 304.

2 The political debates surrounding hate-speech have a long history in the US, cutting across ideological positions and social movements. Pro-regulation advocates have included not only feminists and critical race theorists, but also conservative politicians. The anti-regulation camp includes anti-censorship feminists, gays and lesbians, libertarians, pornographers and many liberals. See Smith, 'Words that Matter'.

3 Butler, 'Force of Fantasy', p. 121. The Helms amendment is the amendment proposed by right-wing Republican Senator Jesse Helms in 1989, to prevent the National Endowment for the Arts from offering federal funding to support artistic projects that were perceived to be 'obscene'. Central to Helms's campaign was an attack on the work of Robert Mapplethorpe.

4 Matsuda et al., *Words that Wound*, p. 1

5 MacKinnon, *Only Words*, p. 7.

6 *Chaplinsky* v. *New Hampshire*, 315 U.S. (1942) cited in Matsuda et al., *Words that Wound*, p. 107.

7 Ibid., pp. 67–8.

8 MacKinnon, *Only Words*, p. 15.

9 Matsuda et al., *Words That Wound*, p. 36.

10 MacKinnon, *Only Words*, p. 9. For a related argument see Langton, 'Speech Acts and Unspeakable Acts'.

11 MacKinnon, *Only Words*, p. 17.

12 Lawrence in Matsuda et al., *Words that Wound*, p. 62.

13 MacKinnon, *Only Words*, p. 18.

14 Thomas cited in Matsuda et al., *Words that Wound*, p. 61.

15 It should be noted that Butler's reading of Austin is a highly mediated one: that is, it echoes closely Derrida's engagement with Austin in his 'Signature Event Context'.

16 It is the distinction between locutionary, illocutionary and perlocutionary speech-acts that displaces that between constatation and performativity noted in Chapter 3.

17 Austin, *How to Do Things with Words*, p. 109.

18 Ibid.

19 Ibid., my emphasis.

20 Ibid., pp. 14–15.
21 Ibid., p. 107.
22 It is, of course, important to be aware here that when Butler talks of convention, she is using the term in Derrida's sense to refer to the iterability or citationality of language and not in Austin's as referring to institutions or circumstances.
23 The point is that although it appears that illocution works through a distinct series of acts, drawing on de Man and Nietzsche Butler suggests it, in fact, works through a continuous ritual doing (*ES*: 45).
24 McNay, 'Subject, Psyche and Agency', p. 179.
25 Indeed, the same is true of all names, including proper names (*ES*: 29).
26 McNay, 'Subject, Psyche and Agency', p. 179.
27 MacKinnon, *Only Words*, p. 27.
28 Austin, *How to Do Things with Words*, p. 14. A misfire is an utterance that fails to produce its intended effect, while an abuse is one that produces the effect when it ought not to (ibid., p. 16).
29 Austin lists various forms of infelicities (including misinvocations, misapplications and misexecutions) (ibid., pp. 17–18).
30 Delgado in Matsuda et al., *Words that Wound*, p. 107; cited in *ES*: 100.
31 For instance, in 'Force of Fantasy', Butler argues that Helms's work is itself an exercise in pornography of the very kind he is attempting to prevent (p. 196).
32 Indeed, *Gender Trouble* is consistently read as a piece of Foucauldian feminist writing, even though this occludes Butler's debts to other theorists; see, for example, Monique Deveaux, 'Feminism and Empowerment'. For two accounts that recognize the hybridity of her work, see Schrift, 'Reconfiguring the Subject' and Nealon, 'Between Emergence and Possibility'. For an account that contests an easy alignment between Foucault and Butler, see Mills, 'Contesting the Political'.
33 McNay, *Foucault*, p. 69.
34 Foucault, *History of Sexuality*, pp. 100, 101.
35 Fraser, 'False Antitheses', p. 67.
36 For a fuller discussion of this point see my *Beyond Identity Politics*, Chapter 5. See also the discussion of linguisticism and the body in Chapter 3 above.
37 See Chapter 3 above.
38 She does indicate later in *ES* (101) that it is 'less worrisome' for universities to regulate speech.
39 By institutional, Butler means how racist speech accretes over time; she does not mean that specific economic and political structures sustain racism (as do Matsuda et al.).
40 Mills, 'Contesting the Political', p. 269. Butler explicates a fuller account of responsibility in *GAO*.
41 Ibid.

42 Butler uses the famous example of Rosa Parks's refusal to yield her seat on a bus in Montgomery, Alabama in 1956 as an example of such authorization. For discussions of this example, see Disch, 'Judith Butler and the Politics of the Performative', Lovell, 'Resisting with Authority' and my 'Radical Democratic Activism'.
43 Disch, 'Judith Butler and the Politics of the Performative', p. 555.
44 Bakhtin, *The Dialogic Imagination*, p. 294.
45 For a discussion of her conception of politics in relation to context and contingency see 'OSRM': 166.
46 Mills, 'Contesting the Political', p. 270.
47 I'll expand upon this in the next chapter. For Butler's discussions of gay marriage, see *CHU*: 177, 'Kinship' and *AC*.
48 For Butler's discussion of Bourdieu see *ES*: 134–5, 141–3, 145–7 and 161. For a critique of Butler indebted to Bourdieu, see McNay, *Gender and Agency*, pp. 59–60.
49 This does not, of course, take account of the possibility of citizens' arrests. I think, however, that the point is clear enough.
50 Butler is also critical of other aspects of Bourdieu's thought, namely, his attempt to distinguish the social from the linguistic, which she sees as inseparable, and his idea that interpellation needs to be backed officially in order to be productive socially. She also rethinks his notion of habitus as a mode of performativity.
51 This also applies, according to Butler, to Bourdieu's account of bodily habitus, which stresses the reproduction of dominant (habitual) norms and thus fails to see the transformative potential attaching to bodily resistances or moments of ambiguity (*ES*: 155). See also Butler and Connolly, 'Politics, Power and Ethics'; McNay, 'Subject, Psyche and Agency', 181–3.
52 Butler defends her use of the term 'social' in *Contingency, Hegemony, Universality*, where she notes that she lets it 'assume a status of givenness' (269) in order, first, to recognize its importance and, second, and paradoxically, to contest its very givenness within certain schemes of thought where it operates as 'something of a superseded past' (270).
53 Smith, 'Words that Matter', p. 391.
54 Mills, 'Contesting the Political', p. 267.
55 In *Precarious Life* (51–62), Butler turns to the issue of governmentality.
56 So, for instance the case of 2 Live Crew discussed by Crenshaw in Matsuda et al., *Words that Wound*, pp. 111–36; *ES*: 74.
57 Smith, 'Words that Matter'; see also Disch, 'Judith Butler and the Politics of the Performative'.
58 Matsuda et al., *Words that Wound*, p. 6.
59 Butler's scepticism of censorship extends beyond that sanctioned by the state (see *ES*: 126–63). See also 'No, It's Not Anti-Semitic', which appeared in the *London Review of Books* in August 2003, and the longer version in *PL*.

60 See *BTM*: 21–2.
61 Laclau and Mouffe, *Hegemony and Socialist Strategy*, p. 180.
62 Mills, 'Contesting the Political', p. 266.
63 Passavant and Dean, 'Laws and Societies', p. 381.
64 Ibid.
65 Ibid., p. 386.
66 Kirkby, 'When All That Is Solid', p. 274; see also Mills, 'Contesting the Political', p. 270.
67 See also *ES*: 77 and Jenkins, 'Heeding of Differences', p. 368.
68 Passavant and Dean, 'Laws and Societies', p. 381.
69 Jenkins, 'Heeding of Differences', p. 373.
70 Ibid.

Chapter 6 What Makes for a Liveable Life?

1 Butler uses the term 'undoing' in at least two senses: first, to signal a lack of recognition, and, second, to indicate that there might be occasions when recognition is conferred – or offered – in a mode that is repugnant to the individual, because it asks them to embrace norms they repudiate, and so they are equally undone (*UG*: 2).
2 Predicated as it is on the idea of a normal gender identity, a diagnosis of GID is made, according to Butler, when persons of one gender show characteristics of another gender or, alternatively, wish to live as someone of that gender. It is, however, one of the ironies of being diagnosed with GID that the diagnosis furnishes a 'form of social recognition' (*UG*: 99) in that those who receive a diagnosis of GID are allowed sex-reassignment operations and thus may be able to live the lives they want to, though at a price: the pathologization of transsexualism and the reinforcement of dominant gender norms.
3 Gwen Araujo was a transgendered woman beaten and killed in California in 2002; Mathew Shephard was murdered in Wyoming in 1998 for being an effeminate gay male; and Brandon Teena, the subject of the film *Boys Don't Cry*, was murdered for being transgendered.
4 'Endangered/Endangering'.
5 This statement is made by Butler in response to a question about whether the stress on 'the heterosexual matrix . . . [may] also obscure the performative powers of the sexual divisions *among* women' ('HB': 283). Butler's concern is that if lesbianism is reduced to simply one of several ways in which the distinction between proper and improper forms of female sexuality are produced, then the specific threat posed by lesbianism to gender (in terms of challenging the relation between gender and sexuality constitutive of heterosexuality) will be occluded.
6 Thinkers considered in the study include Theodor Adorno, Adriana Cavarero, Michel Foucault, G. W. F. Hegel, Jean Laplanche, Friedrich

Nietzsche and, in particular, Emmanuel Levinas. Feminists drawing on Levinas include Cavarero and Irigaray. See, for instance, Butler's discussion of Levinas in *GAO*: 84–101 and in *PL*: 128–51.

7 Grosz, *Sexual Subversions*, p. 141. Grosz is discussing Irigaray's relation to Levinas.

8 It might have been assumed that since in *Psychic Life* the idea of exposure to the other was explained in terms of a (pre-discursive) existential desire to exist, such that subjects willingly submitted to the other in order to 'be', Butler might have argued for an egoistic ethics: that is, one where relations with the other are governed essentially by the desire to preserves one's own existence. She does not.

9 Grosz, *Sexual Subversions*, p. 143.

10 Butler also rejects Levinas's assumption that the ethical encounter only involves two persons: the subject and the other. This misses the fact that in politics 'there are always more than two subjects at play in the scene' (*PL*: 139). It may, thus, be violence done against loved ones (rather than against the self) that prompts the ethical question of how best to react.

11 Butler indicates that it was the Bush Administration's failure to grieve – exemplified in George W. Bush's announcement only twelve days after 9/11 that the US had finished grieving and now needed 'resolute action to take the place of grief' – that partially fuelled its militaristic response to 9/11.

12 See Fraser, 'Mapping the Feminist Imagination'. There is a huge literature on the topic: selected examples include Benhabib, 'Redistribution or Recognition?'; Fraser, 'Rethinking Recognition'; Kenny, *Politics of Identity*; Markell, *Bound by Recognition*; Young, *Inclusion and Democracy*.

13 Markell, *Bound by Recognition*, p. 1.

14 Butler accepts that Hegel is undoubtedly aware of certain limitations with trying to understand the whole of social life through the lens of the dyad Lord and Bondsman. This explains why he argues that a set of customs or social norms (*Sittlichkeit*) emerge from the scene of struggle 'by which reciprocal recognition might be sustained in ways that are more stable than either the life and death struggle or the system of bondage would seem to imply' (*GAO*: 29). This, however, is not enough.

15 Butler criticizes Foucault for over-emphasizing the relation of the self to the self in his account of ethics and thus paying insufficient attention to relations with others.

16 This is Chapter 3 of *PL*, entitled 'Indefinite Detention', pp. 50–100.

17 The US government refers to the prisoners as 'detainees' because it sees them as outside the terms of reference of the Geneva Conventions governing the treatment of prisoners of war.

18 Butler cites plenty of examples of such talk by figures in the Administration, including former Secretary of State for Defense Donald

Rumsfeld and Department of Defense General Counsel Haynes, to which could be added the words of President George W. Bush himself.

19 Intriguingly, the distinction between the two forms of derealization is abandoned in the parallel argument in *UG*: 25. Large parts of the first chapter of *UG* reprise arguments made in Chapter 2 of *PL*.

20 This is illustrated by Butler's comparative assessment of the deaths of Daniel Pearl and the case of the *San Francisco Chronicle*'s refusal to publish either an obituary or a memorial for two families of Palestinians (*PL*: 35–7). On the death of Daniel Pearl, see also Bernard-Henri Lévy, *Qui a tué Daniel Pearl?* for further evidence of the many words expended in the telling of his story, and in the recognition of the brutal violence his corpus suffered.

21 Judith Butler, 'What is Critique?', p. 315.

22 The phrase in inverted commas is taken from 'Kinship' (17).

23 I emphasize the critical nature of this debt because Butler does not blindly follow either Laclau and Mouffe or Laclau. A case in point here is her rejection of Laclau's conception of the universal in *Contingency, Hegemony, Universality*, discussed briefly below. There are additional points of disagreement, however, that I have had to leave aside because of the constraints of space. These are explored by Butler in *CHU*.

24 Norval, 'Democratic Decisions', p. 151.

25 Ibid. The three characteristics identified here owe much to Norval's paper, though I have tailored them specifically to Butler. Two writers who do consider Butler's account of radical democracy are Webster ('The Politics of Sex and Gender') and Mills (whose 'Contesting the Political' owes much of its argument on radical democracy to Webster). The problem with both papers, however, is that they use Butler's description of Laclau and Mouffe's project in *Bodies that Matter* as a definition of her own without paying sufficient attention to the very considerable differences between them.

26 For an example of how Butler's ideas play out in relation to feminism as a democratic movements, see 'End'.

27 Vasterling, 'Butler's Sophisticated Constructionism', p. 33.

28 This is discussed, for instance, by Ackerly and Okin in 'Feminist Social Criticism'.

29 Universalism has constituted something of a problem in contemporary political and philosophical thought, subjected to criticism from feminists, post-colonialists, communitarians, poststructuralists and the like, all of whom in their different ways have endeavoured to show the limited and partial nature of what passes for the universal. Two papers that offer informative overviews of these debates are Phillips, 'Universal Pretensions in Political Thought' and Zerilli, 'This Universalism Which Is Not One'.

30 In particular, she rejects what she sees to be a certain formalism in Laclau's understanding of the universal as well as his reliance on an

alleged *a priori* distinction between the particular and the universal. As a point of information, Laclau sees democracy as depending on a contingent connection being produced between universals and particulars. For further discussion of this see my '(Women's) Human Rights'.

31 'Universality in Culture' is the title of an essay she contributed to the collection *For Love of Country?*

32 She draws attention to the fact that Hegel, when considering the universal, examines competing conceptions of universality (abstract versus concrete universals or official versus spectral universals).

33 A good overview of theories of civil society can be found in Schippers, 'Civil Society'.

34 The issue I have here is that by construing the state almost exclusively in terms of normalization and regulation, Butler fails to consider the role it plays in enabling democratic struggles within civil society (for instance, through rights of association and free speech) and the fact that the state is itself, in part, a product of the politics of civil society (the presence of female representatives in state legislatures is a result of feminist political activity in civil society). The state and civil society have, in other words, a much more dynamic and inter-imbricated relation than Butler allows.

35 Butler says little about Bhabha's conceptualization of cultural translation other than to confess that it informs her own understanding.

36 Bhabha, *Location of Culture*, p. 228.

37 Benjamin, *Illuminations*, p. 75; cited in Bhabha, *Location of Culture*, p. 224.

38 Bhabha, *Location of Culture*, p. 224.

39 Ibid., p. 227.

40 Bhabha notes that the purpose of letting the foreign loose is, 'as Rudolf Pannwitz says, not "to turn Hindi, Greek, English into German [but] instead to turn German into Hindi, Greek, English"' (ibid., p. 228).

41 For a more detailed discussion of the issue of lesbian rights, see 'End', where Butler discusses how the Vatican's preference for the word 'sex' (over 'gender') during the United Nations Meeting on the Status of Women in Beijing in 1995 was a way of rendering lesbians less than human.

42 This is a charge Butler levels at feminists such as Susan Moller Okin and Martha Nussbaum (*CHU*: 35).

43 This is evident in the fact that resignification in *Excitable Speech* (the ways in which 'a speech act without authorization nevertheless assumes authorization in the course of its performance' [*ES*: 160]), is apparently identical to translation (where 'one with no authorization to speak within and as the universal nevertheless lays claim to the term' [*ES*: 91]). In both cases, the emphasis is on the performative contradiction that occurs when those disallowed from speech speak. In this way, examples that once appeared as instances of resignification

(the lesbian demanding entry into the category of the human ['End']) come increasingly to be charted as examples illustrating the difficulties of translation ('CS': 339).

44 'Politics, Power and Ethics', p. 5.

45 Examples include Chambers, 'Normative Violence after 9/11'; McRobbie, 'Vulnerability, Violence and (Cosmopolitan) Ethics'; and Rasmussen, '*Play School*'.

46 See McRobbie, 'Vulnerability, Violence and (Cosmopolitan) Ethics', p. 84.

Bibliography

Works by Butler

A full list of Butler's books is provided. With regard to articles, chapters and interviews, only those referred to in this study are included below. Works by Butler are ordered chronologically in their sections, with books according to date of first publication and articles and interviews according to either date of first publication or date of the edited collection in which they appear. Other works are arranged alphabetically by author. A more complete bibliography of Butler's writings between 1982 and 2001 as well as secondary literature on Butler can be found at: *http://sun3.lib.uci.edu/~scctr/Wellek/butler*.

Books

Subjects of Desire: Hegelian Reflections in Twentieth-Century France (New York: Columbia University Press, 1987). [Paperback 1999.]

Gender Trouble: Feminism and the Subversion of Identity (London: Routledge, 1990).

Feminists Theorize the Political, eds Judith Butler and Joan W. Scott (London: Routledge, 1992).

Bodies that Matter: On the Discursive Limits of 'Sex' (London: Routledge, 1993).

Feminist Contentions: A Philosophical Exchange with Seyla Benhabib, Drucilla Cornell and Nancy Fraser, and with an introduction by Linda Nicholson (New York and London: Routledge, 1995).

Excitable Speech: A Politics of the Performative (New York and London: Routledge, 1997).

The Psychic Life of Power: Theories in Subjection (Stanford: Stanford University Press, 1997).

Gender Trouble: Feminism and the Subversion of Identity, 10th Anniversary Edition (London: Routledge, 1999).

Antigone's Claim: Kinship between Life and Death (New York: Columbia University Press, 2000).

Contingency, Hegemony, Universality: Contemporary Dialogues on the Left, with Ernesto Laclau and Slavoj Žižek (London: Verso, 2000).

What's Left of Theory? New Work on the Politics of Literary Theory, eds Judith Butler, John Guillory and Kendal Thomas (New York and London: Routledge, 2000).

Prejudicial Appearances: The Logic of American Antidiscrimination Law, with Robert Post and Anthony Appiah (Durham, NC: Duke University Press, 2002).

Precarious Life: The Powers of Mourning and Violence (London: Verso, 2004).

Undoing Gender (New York and London: Routledge, 2004).

Giving an Account of Oneself (New York: Fordham University Press, 2005)

Trouble dans le genre. Pour un féminisme de la subversion, preface by Éric Fassin, translation by Cynthia Kraus (Paris: Éditions La Découverte: 2005). [This is a translation of the second edition of *Gender Trouble.*]

Articles and book chapters

'Sex and Gender in Simone de Beauvoir's *Second Sex*', *Yale French Studies*, 72 (1986), pp. 35–49.

'Variations on Sex and Gender: Beauvoir, Wittig and Foucault', in *Feminism as Critique*, eds Seyla Benhabib and Drucilla Cornell (Minneapolis: University of Minnesota Press, 1987), pp. 128–42. Reprinted in *The Judith Butler Reader*, ed. Sarah Salih (with Judith Butler) (Oxford: Blackwell, 2004), pp. 23–38.

'Performative Acts and Gender Constitution: An Essay in Phenomenology and Feminist Theory', *Theatre Journal*, 40, 4 (1988), pp. 519–31. Reprinted in *Performing Feminisms: Feminist Critical Theory and Theatre*, ed. Sue-Ellen Case (Baltimore and London: Johns Hopkins University Press, 1990), pp. 270–82.

'Gendering the Body: Beauvoir's Philosophical Contribution', in *Women, Knowledge, and Reality: Explorations in Feminist Philosophy*, eds Ann Garry and Marilyn Pearsall (Boston: Unwin Hyman, 1989), pp. 252–62.

'Sexual Ideology and Phenomenological Description: A Feminist Critique of Merleau-Ponty's Phenomenology of Perception', in *The Thinking Muse: Feminism and Modern French Philosophy*, eds Jeffner Allen and Marion Young (Bloomington: Indiana University Press, 1989). [Originally written in 1981.]

'The Force of Fantasy: Feminism, Mapplethorpe, and Discursive Excess', *differences: A Journal of Feminist Cultural Studies*, 2, 2 (1990), pp. 105–25. Reprinted in *The Judith Butler Reader*, ed. Sarah Salih (with Judith Butler) (Oxford: Blackwell, 2004), pp. 184–211.

'Gender Trouble, Feminist Theory, and Psychoanalytic Discourse', in *Feminism and Postmodernism*, ed. Linda Nicholson (London: Routledge, 1990), pp. 324–40.

'Imitation and Gender Insubordination', in *Inside/Out: Lesbian Theories, Gay Theories*, ed. Diana Fuss (London: Routledge, 1991), pp. 13–31.

'Contingent Foundations: Feminism and the Question of "Postmodernism"', in *Feminists Theorize the Political* (1992), pp. 3–21; also reprinted in *Feminist Contentions* (1995), pp. 35–57.

'Critically Queer', *GLQ: A Journal of Lesbian and Gay Studies*, 1 (1993), pp. 17–32.

'Endangered/Endangering: Schematic Racism and White Paranoia', in Reading Rodney King/Reading Urban Uprising, ed. Robert Gooding-Williams (New York and London: Routledge, 1993), pp. 15–22. Reprinted in *The Judith Butler Reader*, ed. Sarah Salih (with Judith Butler) (Oxford: Blackwell, 2004), pp. 205–11.

'Against Proper Objects', in *differences: A Journal of Feminist Cultural Studies*, special issue: *More Gender Trouble: Feminism Meets Queer Theory*, 6, 2–3 (1994), pp. 1–26.

'For a Careful Reading', in *Feminist Contentions* (1995), pp. 127–43.

'Universality in Culture', in *For Love of Country? Debating the Limits of Patriotism. Martha C. Nussbaum with Respondents*, ed. Joshua Cohen (Boston: Beacon Press: 1996), pp. 45–52.

'A "Bad Writer" Bites Back', *New York Times*, 20 March 1999.

'Revisiting Bodies and Pleasures', *Theory, Culture, Society*, 16, 2 (1999), pp. 11–20. Reprinted in *Performativity and Belonging*, ed. Vikki Bell (London: Sage, 1999), pp. 11–20.

'The End of Sexual Difference?', in *Feminist Consequences: Theory for the New Century*, eds Elisabeth Bronfen and Misha Kavka (New York: Columbia University Press, 2001), pp. 414–34. Reprinted in a slightly different version in *Undoing Gender* (2004), pp. 174–203.

'Is Kinship Always Already Heterosexual?', *differences: A Journal of Feminist Cultural Studies*, 13, 1 (2002), pp. 14–44. Reprinted in *Undoing Gender* (2004), pp. 102–30.

''No, It's Not Anti-Semitic. Judith Butler Defends the Right to Criticise Israel', *London Review of Books*, 21 August 2003, pp. 19–21. An extended version appears as 'The Charge of Anti-Semitism: Jews, Israel, and the Risks of Public Critique', in *Precarious Life* (2004), pp. 101–27.

'Jacques Derrida', *London Review of Books*, 4 November 2004 (available online at: *www.lrb.co.uk/v26/n21/butl02_.html*, accessed 8 January 2007).

'What Is Critique? An Essay on Foucault's Virtue', in *The Judith Butler Reader*, ed. Sarah Salih (with Judith Butler) (Oxford: Blackwell, 2004), pp. 304–22. It was originally given as the Raymond Williams Lecture at Cambridge University in May 2000 and published in *The Political: Readings in Continental Philosophy*, ed. David Ingram (Oxford: Blackwell, 2001), pp. 212–26.

'Merleau-Ponty and the Touch of Malebranche', in *The Cambridge Companion to Merleau-Ponty*, eds Taylor Carman and Mark B. N. Hansen (Cambridge: Cambridge University Press, 2005), pp. 181–205.

Interviews

'Gender as Performance: An Interview with Judith Butler', *Radical Philosophy*, 67 (1994), pp. 32–9.

'How Bodies Come to Matter: An Interview with Judith Butler', *Signs: Journal of Women in Culture and Society*, 23, 2 (1998), pp. 275–86.

'On Speech, Race and Melancholia: An Interview with Judith Butler', *Theory, Culture and Society*, 16, 2 (1999), pp. 163–74. Reprinted in *Performativity and Belonging*, ed. Vikki Bell (London: Sage, 1999), pp. 163–74.

'Politics, Power and Ethics: A Discussion between Judith Butler and William Connolly', *Theory and Event*, 4, 2 (2000), pp. 24–36.

"There Is a Person Here": An Interview with Judith Butler', *International Journal of Sexuality and Gender Studies*, 6, 1–2 (2001), pp. 7–23.

'Changing the Subject: Judith Butler's Politics of Radical Resignification', in *The Judith Butler Reader*, ed. Sarah Salih (with Judith Butler) (Oxford: Blackwell, 2004), pp. 326–56. Originally published in *jac*, 20, 4 (2000), pp. 731–65.

Other Works

Ackerly, Brooke A. and Okin, Susan Moller, 'Feminist Social Criticism and the International Movement for Women's Rights as Human Rights', in *Democracy's Edges*, eds Ian Shapiro and Casiano Hacker-Cordón (Cambridge: Cambridge University Press, 1999), pp. 134–62.

Ahmed, Sara, '"She'll Wake Up One of These Days and Find She's Turned into a Nigger": Passing through Hybridity', *Theory, Culture, and Society*, 16, 2 (1999), pp. 87–106.

Alcoff, Linda, 'Cultural Feminism versus Post-structuralism: The Identity Crisis in Feminist Theory', *Signs: Journal of Women in Culture and Society*, 13, 3 (1988), pp. 405–36.

Allen, Amy, 'Power Trouble: Performativity as Critical Theory', *Constellations: An International Journal of Critical and Democratic Theory*, 5, 4 (1998), pp. 456–71.

Allen, Amy, *The Power of Feminist Theory: Domination, Resistance, Solidarity* (Boulder, CO: Westview Press, 1999).

Ashe, Fidelma, Finlayson, Alan, Lloyd, Moya, MacKenzie, Iain, Martin, James and O'Neill, Shane, *Contemporary Social and Political Theory: An Introduction* (Milton Keynes: Open University Press, 1998).

Ausch, Robert, Doane, Randal and Perez, Laura, 'Interview with Elizabeth Grosz', *http://web.gc.cuny.edu/csctw/found%5Fobject/text/grosz.htm* (accessed 23 January 2007).

Austin, J. L., *How to Do Things with Words*, 2nd Edition (Oxford: Oxford University Press, 1962).

Bakhtin, Mikhail, *The Dialogic Imagination: Four Essays*, ed. Michael Holquist, trans. Caryl Emerson and Michael Holquist (Austin: University of Texas Press, 1981).

Barvosa-Carter, Edwina, 'Strange Tempest: Agency, Poststructuralism, and the Shape of Feminist Politics to Come', *International Journal of Sexuality and Gender Studies*, 6, 1–2 (2001), pp. 123–37.

Beauvoir, Simone de, *The Second Sex*, trans. H. M. Parshley (Harmondsworth: Penguin, 1983).

Bell, Vikki, *Feminist Imagination: Genealogies in Feminist Theory* (London: Sage, 1999).

Benhabib, Seyla, 'Feminism and the Question of Postmodernism' in *Situating the Self: Gender, Community and Postmodernism in Contemporary Ethics* (Cambridge: Polity, 1992), pp. 203–41.

Benhabib, Seyla, 'Feminism and Postmodernism: An Uneasy Alliance', in *Feminist Contentions* (1995), pp. 17–34.

Benhabib, Seyla, 'Subjectivity, Historiography, and Politics: Reflections on the "Feminism/Postmodernism Exchange"', in *Feminist Contentions* (1995), pp. 107–25.

Benhabib, Seyla, 'Redistribution or Recognition? The Paradigm Change of Contemporary Politics', in *The Claims of Culture: Equality and Diversity in the Global Era* (Princeton, NJ: Princeton University Press, 2002), pp. 49–81.

Benjamin, Walter, *Illuminations*, ed. Hannah Arendt, trans. Harry Zohn (London: Fontana/Collins: 1972).

Bhabha, Homi K., *The Location of Culture* (London: Routledge, 1994).

Bigwood, Carol, 'Renaturalizing the Body (with the Help of Merleau-Ponty', in *Body and Flesh: A Philosophical Reader*, ed. Donn Welton (Oxford: Blackwell, 1998), pp. 99–114.

Bordo, Susan, *Unbearable Weight: Feminism, Western Culture, and the Body* (Berkeley: University of California Press, 1993).

Bordo, Susan, 'Postmodern Subjects, Postmodern Bodies, Postmodern Resistance', in *Unbearable Weight: Feminism, Western Culture, and the Body* (Berkeley: University of California Press, 1993), pp. 277–300.

Bordo, Susan, 'Bringing Body to Theory', in *Body and Flesh: A Philosophical Reader*, ed. Donn Welton (Oxford: Blackwell, 1998), pp. 84–97.

Boyne, Roy and Rattansi, Ali, 'The Theory and Politics of Postmodernism: By Way of an Introduction', in Roy Boyne and Ali Rattansi, eds, *Postmodernism and Society* (Basingstoke: Macmillan, 1990), pp. 1–45.

Braidotti, Rosi, *Metamorphoses: Towards a Materialist Theory of Becoming* (Cambridge: Polity, 2002).

Braidotti, Rosi, with Butler Judith, 'Feminism by Any Other Name', *differences: A Journal of Feminist Cultural Studies*, special issue *More Gender Trouble: Feminism Meets Queer Theory*, 6, 2–3 (1994), pp. 27–61.

Bray, Abigail and Colebrook, Claire, 'The Haunted Flesh: Corporeal Feminism and the Politics of (Dis)Embodiment', *Signs: Journal of Women in Culture and Society*, 24, 1 (1998), pp. 35–67.

Bronfen, Elisabeth, 'Redressing Grievances: Cross-Dressing Pleasure with the Law', in *Feminist Consequences: Theory for a New Century*, eds Elisabeth Bronfen and Misha Kavka (New York: Columbia University Press, 2000), pp. 213–53.

Brown, Wendy, *States of Injury: Power and Freedom in Late Modernity* (Princeton, NJ: Princeton University Press, 1995).

Brown, Wendy, *Edgework: Critical Essays on Knowledge and Politics* (Princeton, NJ: Princeton University Press, 2005).

Campbell, Jan and Harbord, Janet, 'Playing it Again: Citation, Reiteration or Circularity', *Theory, Culture and Society*, 16, 2 (1999), pp. 229–39.

Campbell, Kirsten, 'The Plague of the Subject: Psychoanalysis and Judith Butler's *Psychic Life of Power*', *International Journal of Sexuality and Gender Studies*, 6, 1–2 (2001), pp. 35–48.

Campbell, Kirsten, 'Politics of Kinship: Review Article', *Economy and Society*, 31, 4 (2002), pp. 642–50.

Chambers, Samuel A., *Untimely Politics* (Edinburgh: Edinburgh University Press, 2003).

Chambers, Samuel A., 'Normative Violence after 9/11: Rereading the Politics of *Gender Trouble*', *New Political Science*, 29, 1 (2007), pp. 43–60.

Chodorow, Nancy, *The Reproduction of Mothering: Psychoanalysis and the Sociology of Gender*, 2nd Edition (Berkeley: University of California Press, 1999).

Christian, Barbara, 'The Race for Theory', *Feminist Studies*, 14, 1 (1988), pp. 67–79.

Clough, Patricia Ticento, *Feminist Thought: Desire, Power and Academic Discourse* (Cambridge, MA: Blackwell, 1994).

Collins, Patricia Hill, *Black Feminist Thought: Knowledge, Consciousness, and the Politics of Empowerment* (London: HarperCollins, 1990).

Combahee River Collective, 'A Black Feminist Statement', in *All the Women are White, All the Blacks are Men, but Some of Us are Brave: Black Women's Studies*, eds Gloria T. Hull, Patricia Bell Scott and Barbara Smith (New York: Feminist Press, 1982), pp. 13–22.

Coole, Diana, *Women in Political Theory: From Ancient Misogyny to Contemporary Feminism*, 2nd Edition (Hemel Hempstead: Harvester Wheatsheaf, 1993).

Coole, Diana, *Negativity and Politics: Dionysus and Dialectics from Kant to Poststructuralism* (London: Routledge, 2000).

Copjec, Joan, 'Sex and the Euthanasia of Reason', in *Supposing the Subject*, ed. Joan Copjec (London: Verso, 1994), pp. 16–44.

Cranny-Francis, Anne, Waring, Wendy, Stavropoulos, Pam and Kirkby, Joan, *Gender Studies: Terms and Debates* (Basingstoke: Palgrave Macmillan, 2003).

Crenshaw, Kimberlé, 'Demarginalizing the Intersection of Race and Sex: A Black Feminist Critique of Antidiscrimination Doctrine, Feminist Theory, and Antiracist Politics', *University of Chicago Legal Forum* (1989), pp. 139–67.

Cvetkovich, Ann, 'Fierce Pussies and Lesbian Avengers: Dyke Activism Meets Celebrity Culture', in *Feminist Consequences: Theory for a New Century*, eds Elisabeth Bronfen and Misha Kavka (New York: Columbia University Press, 2000), pp. 283–318.

De Lauretis, Teresa, 'Eccentric Subjects: Feminist Theory and Historical Consciousness', *Feminist Studies*, 16, 1 (1990), pp. 115–50.

Deleuze, Gilles and Guattari, Félix, *Anti-Oedipus: Capitalism and Schizophrenia*, preface by Michel Foucault, trans. Robert Hurley, Mark Seem and Helen R. Lane (London: Athlone Press, 1984).

Delphy, Christine, *Close to Home: A Materialist Analysis of Women's Oppression,* trans. and ed. Diana Leonard (London: Hutchinson, 1984).

Delphy, Christine, 'Rethinking Sex and Gender', trans. Diana Leonard, *Women's Studies International Forum,* 16, 1 (1993), pp. 1–9.

Delphy, Christine, 'The Invention of French Feminism: An Essential Move', *Yale French Studies,* special issue *Another Look, Another Woman: Retranslations of French Feminism*, 87 (1995), pp. 190–221.

Derrida, Jacques, 'The Pit and the Pyramid: Introduction to Hegel's Semiology', in *Margins of Philosophy,* trans. Alan Bass (Chicago: University of Chicago Press, 1982), pp. 69–108.

Derrida, Jacques, 'Signature Event Context', in *A Derrida Reader: Between the Blinds,* ed. Peggy Kamuf (New York and London: Harvester Wheatsheaf, 1991), pp. 80–111.

Deutscher, Penelope, *Yielding Gender: Feminism, Deconstruction and the History of Philosophy* (London: Routledge, 1997).

Deveaux, Monique, 'Feminism and Empowerment', *Feminist Studies,* 20, 2 (1994), pp. 223–47.

Dietz, Mary G., 'Current Controversies in Feminist Theory', *Annual Review of Political Science,* 6 (2003), pp. 399–431.

Disch, Lisa, 'Judith Butler and the Politics of the Performative', *Political Theory*, 27, 4 (1999), pp. 545–59.

Di Stefano, Christine, 'Dilemmas of Difference: Feminism, Modernity, and Postmodernism' in *Feminism and Postmodernism,* ed. Linda Nicholson (London: Routledge, 1990), pp. 63–82.

Duberman, Martin, *Stonewall* (New York: Plume Books, 1994).

Ebert, Teresa, 'Ludic Feminism, the Body, Performance, and Labor: Bringing *Materialism* Back into Feminist Cultural Studies', *Cultural Critique* (Winter 1992–3), pp. 5–50.

Elam, Diane, *Feminism and Deconstruction: Ms. en Abyme* (London: Routledge, 1994).

Ferguson, Kathy E., *The Man Question: Visions of Subjectivity in Feminist Theory* (Berkeley: University of California Press, 1993).

Firestone, Shulamith, *The Dialectic of Sex: The Case for Feminist Revolution* (New York: Morrow, 1970).
Foucault, Michel, *The Order of Things*, trans. Alan Sheridan (London: Routledge, 1970).
Foucault, Michel, *The Archaeology of Knowledge*, trans. Alan Sheridan (London: Routledge, 1972).
Foucault, Michel, *The History of Sexuality, Volume 1: An Introduction*. trans. R. Hurley (Harmondsworth: Penguin, 1978).
Foucault, Michel, 'The Discourse on Language', in *The Archaeology of Knowledge and the Discourse on Language*, trans. Rupert Swyer (New York: Pantheon, 1982), pp. 215–38.
Foucault, Michel, 'An Aesthetics of Existence', trans. Alan Sheridan, in *Michel Foucault: Politics, Philosophy, Culture: Interviews and Other Writings 1977–1984*, ed. Lawrence D. Kritzman (London: Routledge, 1988), pp. 47–53.
Fraser, Nancy, 'False Antitheses', in *Feminist Contentions* (1995), pp. 59–74.
Fraser, Nancy, 'Rethinking Recognition', *New Left Review*, 3 (2000), pp. 107–21.
Fraser, Nancy, 'Mapping the Feminist Imagination: From Redistribution to Recognition to Representation', *Constellations: An International Journal of Critical and Democratic Theory*, 12, 3 (2005), pp. 295–307.
Freud, Sigmund, *The Interpretation of Dreams*, trans. James Strachey (Harmondsworth: Penguin, 1976).
Freud, Sigmund, 'The Ego and the Id', in *On Metapsychology*, trans. James Strachey (Harmondsworth: Penguin, 1984), pp. 350–407.
Freud, Sigmund, 'Mourning and Melancholia', in *On Metapsychology*, trans. James Strachey (Harmondsworth: Penguin, 1984), pp. 251–68.
Freud, Sigmund, 'A Special Type of Object-Choice Made by Men', in *On Metapsychology*, trans. James Strachey (Harmondsworth: Penguin, 1984), pp. 163–76.
Freud, Sigmund, *Totem and Taboo*, in *The Origins of Religion*, trans. James Strachey (Harmondsworth: Penguin, 1985), pp. 43–224.
Fuss, Diana, *Essentially Speaking: Feminism, Nature and Difference* (London: Routledge, 1989).
Fuss, Diana, ed., *Inside/Out: Lesbian Theories, Gay Theories* (London: Routledge, 1991).
Fuss, Diana, *Identification Papers* (London: Routledge, 1995).
Gatens, Moira, 'A Critique of the Sex/Gender Distinction', in *Imaginary Bodies: Ethics, Power and Corporeality* (London: Routledge, 1996), pp. 3–20.
Goffman, Erving, *Presentation of the Self in Everyday Life* (London: Penguin, 1959).
Goffman, Erving, *Asylums* (London: Penguin, 1968).
Grant, Judith, *Fundamental Feminism: Contesting the Core Concepts of Feminist Theory* (London: Routledge, 1993).

Griffin, Gabriele and Braidotti, Rosi, eds, *Thinking Differently: A Reader in European Women's Studies* (London and New York: Zed Books, 2002).

Grosz, Elizabeth, *Sexual Subversions: The Three French Feminists* (St Leonards, NSW: Allen and Unwin, 1989).

Grosz, Elizabeth, *Jacques Lacan: A Feminist Introduction* (London: Routledge, 1990).

Halperin, David, *Saint Foucault: Towards a Gay Hagiography* (Oxford: Oxford University Press, 1995).

Haraway, Donna, 'Manifesto for Cyborgs: Science, Technology, and Socialist Feminism in the 1980s', *Socialist Review*, 80 (1985), pp. 65–108.

Haraway, Donna, '"Gender" for a Marxist Dictionary: The Sexual Politics of a Word', in *Simians, Cyborgs, and Women: The Reinvention of Nature* (London: Free Association Books, 1991), pp. 127–48.

Hawkes, Gail, 'Dressing-Up – Cross-Dressing and Sexual Dissonance', *Journal of Gender Studies*, 4, 3 (1995), pp. 261–70.

Hegel, G. W. F., *Phenomenology of Spirit*, trans. A. V. Miller (Oxford: Oxford University Press, 1977).

Heinämaa, Sara, 'What is a Woman? Butler and Beauvoir on the Foundations of Sexual Difference', *Hypatia*, 12, 1 (1997), pp. 20–39.

Heinämaa, Sara, *Toward a Phenomenology of Sexual Difference: Husserl, Merleau-Ponty, Beauvoir* (Boulder, CO: Westview Press, 2003).

Hekman, Susan, 'Material Bodies', in *Body and Flesh: A Philosophical Reader*, ed. Donn Welton (Oxford: Blackwell, 1998), pp. 61–70.

Hekman, Susan, 'Beyond Identity: Feminism, Identity and Identity Politics', *Feminist Theory*, 1, 3 (2000), pp. 289–308.

Hennessy, Rosemary, 'Queer Visibility in Commodity Culture', in *Social Postmodernism: Beyond Identity Politics*, eds Linda Nicholson and Steven Seidman (Cambridge: Cambridge University Press, 1995), pp. 142–83.

Hird, Myra, 'Theorizing the End of Gender: A Conversation with Stevi Jackson', *International Feminist Journal of Politics*, 3, 2 (2001), pp. 263–74.

Hood-Williams, John and Harrison, Wendy Cealey, 'Trouble with Gender', *Sociological Review*, 46, 1 (1998), pp. 73–94.

hooks, bell, *Ain't I a Woman: Black Women and Feminism* (Boston: South End Press, 1982).

hooks, bell, *Feminist Theory: From Margin to Center* (Boston: South End Press, 1984).

Hurtado, Aída, 'Relating to Privilege: Seduction and Rejection in the Subordination of White Women and Women of Color', *Signs: Journal of Women in Culture and Society*, 14, 4 (1989), pp. 833–55.

Hutchings, Kimberly, *Hegel and Feminist Philosophy* (Cambridge: Polity, 2003).

Irigaray, Luce, *This Sex Which Is Not One*, trans. Catherine Porter (New York: Cornell University Press, 1985).

Jackson, Stevi, *Christine Delphy* (London: Sage, 1996).

Jameson, Frederic, *Postmodernism: Or, the Cultural Logic of Late Capitalism* (London: Verso, 1991).

Jenkins, Fiona, 'The Heeding of Differences: On Foreclosure and Openness in a Politics of the Performative', *Constellations: An International Journal of Critical and Democratic Theory*, 8, 3 (2001), pp. 364–75.

Kenny, Michael, *The Politics of Identity* (Cambridge: Polity, 2004).

King, Deborah K., 'Multiple Jeopardy, Multiple Consciousness: The Context of Black Feminist Ideology', *Signs: Journal of Women in Culture and Society*, 14, 1 (1988), pp. 42–72.

Kirkby, Vicky, 'When All That Is Solid Melts Into Language: Judith Butler and the Question of Matter', *International Journal of Sexuality and Gender Studies*, 7, 4 (2002), pp. 265–80.

Kristeva, Julia, *Powers of Horror: An Essay on Abjection*, trans. Leon S. Roudiez (New York: Columbia University Press, 1982).

Kruks, Sonia, *Retrieving Experience: Subjectivity and Recognition in Feminist Politics* (New York: Cornell University Press, 2001).

Laclau, Ernesto, 'Structure, History and the Political', in *Contingency, Hegemony, Universality* (2000), pp. 182–212.

Laclau, Ernesto and Mouffe, Chantal, *Hegemony and Socialist Strategy: Towards a Radical Democratic Politics* (London: Verso, 1985).

Langton, Rae, 'Speech Acts and Unspeakable Acts', *Philosophy and Public Affairs*, 22, 4 (1993), pp. 293–330.

Lévy, Bernard-Henry, *Qui a tué Daniel Pearl?* (Paris: Grasset, 2003).

Lloyd, Genevieve, *The Man of Reason: 'Male' and 'Female' in Western Philosophy* (London: Methuen, 1984).

Lloyd, Moya, 'Performativity, Parody and Politics', *Theory, Culture and Society*, 16, 2 (1999), pp. 195–213.

Lloyd, Moya, 'Julia Kristeva (1941–)', in *Contemporary Critical Theorists: From Lacan to Said*, ed. Jon Simons (Edinburgh: Edinburgh University Press, 2004), pp. 135–51.

Lloyd, Moya, *Beyond Identity Politics: Feminism, Power and Politics* (London: Sage, 2005).

Lloyd, Moya, 'Butler, Antigone, and the State', *Contemporary Political Theory*, 4 (2005), pp. 451–68.

Lloyd, Moya, 'Radical Democratic Activism and the Politics of Resignification', *Constellations: An International Journal of Critical and Democratic Theory*, 14, 1 (2007), pp. 129–46.

Lloyd, Moya, '(Women's) Human Rights: Paradoxes and Possibilities', *Review of International Studies*, 33, 1 (2007), pp. 91–103.

Lorde, Audre, *Sister Outsider: Essays and Speeches by Audre Lorde* (Freedom, CA: The Crossing Press, 1984).

Lovell, Terri, 'Resisting with Authority: Historical Specificity, Agency and the Performative Self', *Theory, Culture and Society* 20, 1 (2003), pp. 1–17.

Lyotard, Jean François, *The Postmodern Condition: A Report on Knowledge*, trans. Geoff Bennington and Brian Massumi (Manchester: Manchester University Press, 1984).

MacKinnon, Catharine A., *Feminism Unmodified: Discourse on Life and Law* (Cambridge, MA: Harvard University Press, 1987).

MacKinnon, Catharine A., *Only Words* (London: HarperCollins, 1994).

McNay, Lois, *Foucault: A Critical Introduction* (Cambridge: Polity, 1994).

McNay, Lois, 'Subject, Psyche and Agency: The Work of Judith Butler', *Theory, Culture and Society*, 16, 2 (1999), pp. 175–93.

McNay, Lois, *Gender and Agency: Reconfiguring the Subject in Feminist and Social Theory* (Cambridge: Polity, 2000).

McNay, Lois, 'Out of the Orrery? Situating Language', *Journal of Political Ideologies*, 8, 2 (2003), pp. 139–56.

McRobbie, Angela, 'Mothers and Fathers: Who Needs Them?', *Feminist Review*, 75 (2003), pp. 129–36.

McRobbie, Angela, 'Vulnerability, Violence and (Cosmopolitan) Ethics: Butler's *Precarious Life*', *British Journal of Sociology*, 57, 1 (2006), pp. 69–86.

Markell, Patchen, *Bound by Recognition* (Princeton, NJ: Princeton University Press, 2003).

Matsuda, Mari J., Lawrence, Charles R., III, Delgado, Richard and Crenshaw, Kimberlé Williams, *Words that Wound: Critical Race Theory, Assaultive Speech and the First Amendment* (Boulder, CO: Westview Press, 1993).

Megill, Allan, '*Subjects of Desire: Hegelian Reflections in Twentieth-Century France; Knowing and History: Appropriations of Hegel in Twentieth-Century France*: Review Essay', *Journal of Modern History*, 63, 1 (1991), pp. 124–8.

Millett, Kate, *Sexual Politics* (London: Virago, 1977).

Mills, Catherine, 'Contesting the Political: Butler and Foucault on Power and Resistance', *Journal of Political Philosophy*, 11, 3 (2003), pp. 253–72.

Mitchell, Juliet, *Psychoanalysis and Feminism: A Radical Reassessment of Freudian Psychoanalysis* (London: Penguin, 1975).

Mitchell, Juliet, 'Introduction - I', in *Feminine Sexuality: Jacques Lacan and the École Freudienne*, eds Juliet Mitchell and Jacqueline Rose (Basingstoke: Macmillan, 1982), pp. 1–26.

Mort, Frank and Peters, Roy, 'Foucault Recalled: Interview with Michel Foucault', *New Formations*, 55 (2005), pp. 9–22.

Nealon, Jeffery, 'Between Emergence and Possibility: Foucault, Derrida and Judith Butler on Performative Identity', *Philosophy Today*, 40, 3–4 (1996), pp. 430–9.

Newton, Esther, *Mother Camp: Female Impersonators on America* (Chicago: University of Chicago Press, 1972).

Nietzsche, Friedrich, *On the Genealogy of Morality*, trans. Carol Diethe (Cambridge: Cambridge University Press, 1994).

Norval, Aletta, 'Democratic Decisions and the Question of Universality: Rethinking Recent Approaches', in *Laclau: A Critical Reader*, eds Simon Critchley and Oliver Marchart (London: Routledge, 2004), pp. 140–66.

Nussbaum, Martha, 'Professor of Parody', *http://www.md.ucl.ac.be/ebim/scientif/Recherche/GenreBioethique/Nussbaum_NRO.htm* (accessed 23 January 2007).

Oakley, Ann, *Sex, Gender and Society* (London: Temple Smith, 1972).

Olkowski, Dorothea, 'Materiality and Language: Butler's Interrogation of the History of Philosophy', *Philosophy and Social Criticism*, 23, 3 (1997), pp. 37–53.

Passavant, Paul and Dean, Jodi, 'Laws and Societies', *Constellations: An International Journal of Critical and Democractic Theory*, 8, 3 (2001), pp. 376–89.

Payne, Michael, *Reading Theory: An Introduction to Lacan, Derrida, and Kristeva* (Oxford: Blackwell, 1993).

Pearce, Lynne, *The Rhetorics of Feminism: Readings in Contemporary Cultural Theory and the Popular Press* (London: Routledge, 2004).

Phelan, Shane, *Identity Politics: Lesbian Feminism and the Limits of Community* (Philadelphia: Temple University Press, 1989).

Phelan, Shane, *Getting Specific: Postmodern Lesbian Politics* (Minneapolis: University of Minnesota Press, 1994).

Phillips, Anne, 'Universal Pretensions in Political Thought', in *Destabilizing Theory: Contemporary Feminist Debates*, eds Michèle Barrett and Anne Phillips (Cambridge: Polity: 1992), pp. 10–30.

Pippin, Robert B., '*Subjects of Desire: Hegelian Reflections in Twentieth-Century France*: Review Essay', *Philosophical Review*, XCIX, 1 (1990), pp. 129–31.

Radicalesbians, 'The Woman-Identified Woman', in *Radical Feminism*, eds Anne Koedt, Ellen Levine and Anita Rapone (New York: Times Books, 1973), pp. 240–1.

Rasmussen, Mary Lou, '*Play School*, Melancholia, and the Politics of Recognition', *British Journal of Sociology of Education*, 27, 4 (2006), pp. 473–87.

Rich, Adrienne, 'Compulsory Heterosexuality and Lesbian Existence', *Signs: Journal of Women in Culture and Society*, 5, 4 (1980), pp. 531–60.

Rich, Adrienne, *On Lies, Secrets, and Silence: Selected Prose 1966–78* (London: Virago, 1980).

Riley, Denise, *Am I That Name? Feminism and the Category of Women in History* (Basingstoke: Macmillan, 1988).

Roden, Frederick, 'Becoming Butlerian: On the Discursive Limits (and Potentials) of *Gender Trouble* at Ten Years of Age', *International Journal of Sexuality and Gender Studies*, 6, 1–2 (2001), pp. 25–33.

Rowland, Robyn and Klein, Renate Duelli, 'Radical Feminism: Critique and Construct', in *Feminist Knowledge: Critique and Construct*, ed. Sneja Gunew (London: Routledge, 1990), pp. 271–303.

Rubin, Gayle, 'Thinking Sex: Notes for a Radical Theory of the Politics of Sexuality', in *Pleasure and Danger: Exploring Female Sexuality*, ed. Carole S. Vance (London: Pandora Press, 1987), pp. 267–319.

Rubin, Gayle, 'The Traffic in Women: Notes on the "Political Economy" of Sex', reprinted in *Literary Theory: An Anthology*, eds Julie Rivkin and Michael Ryan (Oxford: Blackwell, 1998), pp. 533–60.

Rubin, Gayle with Butler, Judith, 'Sexual Traffic: An Interview', *differences: A Journal of Feminist Cultural Studies*, 6, 2–3 (1994), pp. 62–99.
Salih, Sara, 'Judith Butler and the Ethics of Difficulty', *Critical Quarterly*, 45, 3 (2003), pp. 42–51.
Salih, Sara, ed. (with Judith Butler), *The Judith Butler Reader* (Oxford: Blackwell: 2004).
Sargisson, Lucy, *Contemporary Feminist Utopianism* (London: Routledge, 1996).
Sarup, Madan, *An Introductory Guide to Post-structuralism and Postmodernism* (Hemel Hempstead: Harvester Wheatsheaf, 1988).
Schippers, Birgit, 'Civil Society', in *Political Concepts: A Reader and Guide*, ed. Iain MacKenzie (Edinburgh: Edinburgh University Press, 2005), pp. 343–54.
Schrift, Alan D., 'Reconfiguring the Subject as a Process of the Self: Following Foucault's Nietzschean Trajectory to Butler, Laclau and Mouffe, and Beyond', *New Formations*, 25 (1995), pp. 28–39.
Sedgwick, Eve Kosofsky, 'Queer Performativity: Henry James's *The Art of the Novel*', *GLQ*, 1 (1993), pp. 1–16.
Segal, Lynn, *Straight Sex: The Politics of Pleasure* (London: Virago, 1994).
Segal, Lynn, *Why Feminism? Gender, Psychology, Politics* (Cambridge: Polity, 1999).
Seidman, Steven, 'Deconstructing Queer Theory or the Under-Theorization of the Social and the Ethical', in *Social Postmodernism: Beyond Identity Politics*, eds Linda Nicholson and Steven Seidman (Cambridge: Cambridge University Press, 1995), pp. 116–41.
Silverman, Kaja, *The Subject of Semiotics* (Oxford: Oxford University Press, 1982).
Sjöholm, Cecilia, 'Family Values: Butler, Lacan and the Rise of Antigone', *Radical Philosophy*, 111 (2002), pp. 24–32.
Smith, Anna Marie, 'Words that Matter: Butler's *Excitable Speech*', *Constellations: An International Journal of Critical and Democractic Theory*, 8, 3 (2001), pp. 390–9.
Spargo, Tamsin, *Foucault and Queer Theory* (Cambridge: Icon, 1999).
Spelman, Elizabeth V., *Inessential Woman: Problems of Exclusion in Feminist Thought* (London: The Women's Press, 1990).
Stavrakakis, Yannis, *Lacan and the Political* (London: Routledge, 1999).
Stavrakakis, Yannis, 'Jacques Lacan (1901–81)', in *Contemporary Critical Theorists: From Lacan to Said*, ed. Jon Simons (Edinburgh: Edinburgh University Press, 2004), pp. 18–33.
Stone, Alison, 'Towards a Genealogical Feminism: A Reading of Judith Butler's Political Thought,' *Contemporary Political Theory*, 4, 1 (2005), pp. 4–24.
Taylor, Charles, 'The Politics of Recognition', in *Multiculturalism: Examining the Politics of Recognition*, ed. Amy Gutmann (Princeton, NJ: Princeton University Press, 1994), pp. 25–73.

Thacker, Andrew, 'Foucault and the Writing of History', in *The Impact of Michel Foucault on the Social Sciences and Humanities*, eds Moya Lloyd and Andrew Thacker (Basingstoke: Macmillan, 1997), pp. 29–53.

Tong, Rosemarie Putnam, *Feminist Thought: A More Comprehensive Introduction* (Boulder, CO: Westview Press, 1998).

Tyler, Carole-Anne, 'Boys will be Girls: The Politics of Gay Drag', in *Inside/Out: Lesbian Theories, Gay Theories*, ed. Diana Fuss (London: Routledge, 1991), pp. 32–70.

Vasterling, Veronica, 'Butler's Sophisticated Constructionism: A Critical Assessment', *Hypatia*, 14, 3 (1999), pp. 17–38.

Vasterling, Veronica, 'Body and Language: Butler, Merleau-Ponty and Lyotard on the Speaking Embodied Subject', *International Journal of Philosophical Studies*, 11, 2 (2003), pp. 205–23.

Walker, Julia, 'Why Performance? Why Now? Textuality and the Rearticulation of Human Presence', *Yale Journal of Criticism*, 16, 1 (2003), pp. 149–75.

Walters, Suzanna, 'From Here to Queer: Radical Feminism, Postmodernism, and the Lesbian Menace (Or, Why Can't Woman Be More Like a Fag?)', *Signs: Journal of Women in Culture and Society*, 21, 4 (1996), pp. 830–69.

Walzer, Michael, *Spheres of Justice: A Defence of Pluralism and Equality* (New York: Basic Books, 1983).

Warner, Michael, 'Introduction: Fear of a Queer Planet', *Social Text*, 29 (1991), pp. 3–17.

Webster, Fiona, 'The Politics of Sex and Gender: Benhabib and Butler Debate Subjectivity', *Hypatia*, 15, 1 (2000), pp. 1–22.

Weeks, Jeffery, *Sexuality and Its Discontents: Meanings, Myths and Modern Sexualities* (London: Routledge, 1985).

Weir, Allison, *Sacrificial Logics: Feminist Theory and the Critique of Identity* (London: Routledge, 1996).

White, Stephen K., *Sustaining Affirmation: The Strengths of Weak Ontology in Political Theory* (Princeton, NJ: Princeton University Press, 2000).

Wilson, Natalie, 'Butler's Corporeal Politics: Matters of Politicized Abjection', *International Journal of Sexuality and Gender Studies*, 6, 1–2 (2001), pp. 109–21.

Wittig, Monique, 'One is Not Born a Woman', *Feminist Issues*, 1, 2 (1981), pp. 47–54.

Wittig, Monique, 'The Mark of Gender', *Feminist Issues*, 5, 2 (1985), pp. 3–12.

Wright, Elizabeth, ed., *Feminism and Psychoanalysis: A Critical Dictionary* (Oxford: Blackwell, 1992).

Wright, Elizabeth, *Psychoanalytic Criticism: A Reappraisal*, 2nd Edition (New York: Routledge, 1998).

Young, Iris Marion, *Inclusion and Democracy* (Oxford: Oxford University Press, 2000).

Young, Iris Marion, 'Lived Body vs. Gender: Reflections on Social Structure and Subjectivity', in *On Female Body Experience: "Throwing Like a Girl" and Other Essays* (Oxford: Oxford University Press, 2005), pp. 12–26.
Young, Robert M., *Oedipus Complex* (Cambridge: Icon Books, 2001).
Zerilli, Linda, 'This Universalism Which Is Not One', *Diacritics*, 28, 2 (1998), pp. 3–20.
Žižek , Slavoj, 'Class Struggle or Postmodernism? Yes, Please!', in *Contingency, Hegemony, Universality* (2000), pp. 90–135.

Index